RISE OF THE RUDDBOT

RISE OF THE RUDDBOT

OBSERVATIONS from the GALLERY

Annabel CRABB

Published by Black Inc.,
an imprint of Schwartz Media Pty Ltd
Level 5, 289 Flinders Lane
Melbourne Victoria 3000 Australia
email: enquiries@blackincbooks.com
http://www.blackincbooks.com

National Library of Australia Cataloguing-in-Publication entry:

Crabb, Annabel.

Rise of the Ruddbot : observations from the gallery / Annabel Crabb.

ISBN: 9781863954839 (pbk.)

Political parties--Australia.
Politicians--Australia.
Australia--Politics and government--2001-

324.29407

Book design by Thomas Deverall
Typeset by Duncan Blachford

Printed in Australia by Griffin Press

CONTENTS

INTRODUCTION

Australians treat governments like university students treat bed linen. We usually wait a tiny bit too long to do it, and even then we do it only when the matter has become seriously unavoidable.

When, in 2007, the Australian electorate exchanged John Howard for Kevin Rudd, you could feel it coming. The antics of the longstanding Howard government took on a horrible garishness. I don't know about you, but for my money the Sydney APEC conference in September 2007 – where by day Kevin Rudd spouted Mandarin uncontrollably and George W. Bush thanked 'Austria' for having him, and by night the Howard cabinet ministers gathered to smoke cigars and come up with cack-handed plans to assassinate their leader – was the richest example of this idiocy-in-decline.

People started to heckle the prime minister in the street. Previously, John Howard's morning walk had been an event of some dignity – a sign of a vigorous, thrusting leader, *mens sana* and all that. As the election approached, the scales seemed to fall from the eyes of the nation, and the prime minister started to look like an elderly gent, dressed in a rather silly tracksuit, striding intently from nowhere to nowhere pursued by a pack of puffing press secretaries.

Nothing seemed to work any more, and everything Mr Howard and his troops did to try and fix it seemed to make matters worse. Desperate to project an image of calm unity, the prime minister and his perpetually denied deputy, Peter Costello, granted a joint interview to *Today Tonight*, in which they came across like an ageing gay couple reviewing the terms of their civil union.

It all seemed hopeless. And then there was Kevin to consider.

The best thing about Australian politics is the agility with which the electorate regularly wrong-foots the practitioners of politics and its ranks of attendant commentators. The rise of Kevin Rudd was like that; all along, it has been a two-speed affair.

By December 2006, when he became the leader of the Australian Labor Party, he was well known in Canberra.

Well known? Scratch that. He was notorious. He was everywhere in Canberra and had been for ages, a dynamo of ambition and persistence, showing up everywhere from foreign policy forums to cheese nights with go-nowhere senators in East Bum-Crack. There could not have been a junior press-gallery journo who had not felt the insistent vibrato of Kevin Rudd's late-night text messages. Editors who put their papers to bed and then wearily followed were periodically awoken by Labor's shadow foreign-affairs spokesman, mercilessly alert in some unidentifiable airport hotel.

'Hi, it's Kevin.'

One former staffer told me, her shoulders shaking with laughter, of the day Kevin bounded into the office of her backbench senator, which was located so deep in suburbia that even peripatetic Kevin could not make his visit appear accidental.

'Hey!' beamed Rudd, addressing the staff in their open-plan office. 'You look like a groovy bunch of funsters!'

That's what Kevin was like. Everywhere. Relentless. Sort of daggy. A man who still said 'groovy' without donning the forgiving cloak of retro-irony. You always had the feeling that he took himself more seriously than anyone else possibly could.

But if, by late 2006, Canberra insiders were exhaustedly familiar with ambitious Mr Rudd, the rest of Australia was just getting to know him. Everyone seemed keen to know more about Kevin (no one more so than the candidate himself, whose relentless self-interrogation quickly became a hallmark). And Kevin made sure that they liked what they found.

Kevin Rudd took every trouble to form himself into the leader for which Australians could most easily swap John Howard.

Someone younger.

Someone industrious.

Someone capable, but not dangerously interesting.

Like a determined gardener tackling an ancient stand of bamboo, he brought his fondness for diplomatic jargon under control. All of that irrepressible energy and persistence, which hitherto had rather got on the nerves of his Labor colleagues (no one likes a smarty pants, and this goes double for Caucus), now served the Labor leader well as he wooed the electorate. With a struggling Howard pitching out inducements by the billions, Rudd opted to speak in favour of fiscal prudence, and it worked.

Watching him at the 2007 Labor campaign launch, as the Labor faithful adoringly cheered his promises not to spend any money on any of their pet projects, I thought: He's like a robot. A Ruddbot. A political Terminator, forming himself into whichever guise most befits the situation.

And so he has continued. In office, the Ruddbot's shapeshifting ways distinguish him clearly from John Howard, a man whose style and demeanour remained rigidly, almost comically recognisable irrespective of whether he was addressing the Millennium Forum or Mardi Gras. In any given week, as he pings around between industry forums and hospital wards, you can see Kevin Rudd morphing effortlessly – now TechnoBot, now ScrubsBot, always moulding his pitch to suit his audience.

For most of his first term, Kevin Rudd was a rich political conundrum – beloved by a multitude, but viewed by many of his closest professional associates with something much more like cool tolerance at best. 'Everybody loves Kevin, so long as they haven't actually met him,' growled one colleague to me once – a comment I remember often.

As this collection goes to print, a change is taking place; the Ruddbot has purged his systems mercilessly and has shelved the emissions trading scheme, his planned internet filter and a promise to build more childcare centres, amid sundry other detritus of the Kevin 07 campaign. His popularity in the published polls – always the best defence against internal criticism – has taken a sickening dive.

It's been a successful first term, in some respects, and of course incumbency always changes leaders. But Kevin 07's unswerving, Joan of Arc-like commitment to budget surpluses and carbon emissions reduction is increasingly difficult for memory to conjure, given the tumbling zeroes of our present deficit and the confirmed dormancy of the PM's solution to climate change, 'the greatest moral challenge of our time'.

This collection charts much more, of course, than the rise of the Ruddbot and the messy, largely self-inflicted political fate of his predecessor. It covers the Liberal Party's subsequent attempts to replace John Howard – a series of one-act plays veering wildly between tragicomedy (Brendan Nelson), epic soliloquy (Malcolm Turnbull) and physical theatre (Tony Abbott).

Reading back over these columns, which appeared originally either in the pages of the *Sydney Morning Herald* or on *The Drum*, the ABC's commentary and analysis website where I now work, it's hard to believe that all of the action has taken place over such a short period of time. There were fears, when Kevin Rudd replaced John Howard, that Australia had resigned itself permanently to the Revenge of the Nerds, and that politics would never be interesting again. Cartoonists mourned the departure of Peter Costello's jug ears and Alexander Downer's hosiery, and the Australian tracksuit industry quietly farewelled its salad days.

But boring the Ruddbot has not been.

Beware the suggestion of mundanity, carefully fostered by those chinos (how *does* he get them so high?) and the dad jokes. This is a rare flower of a man, full of secret rages and unknowable hungers, leavened by surprising turns of kindness. His pitch to the Australian public – 'I'm Kevin, and I'm here to help' – was so simple, and yet after a term in government sometimes I think we understand him less than ever.

It's been fun trying, though.

I would like to thank my colleagues at the *Sydney Morning Herald* and the ABC for their company, and for the ideas and wisecracks I may have pilfered over the years. I apologise additionally for any stray pilferage from the sketch writers I most admire, including the *Times*' Matthew Parris, the *Guardian*'s Simon Hoggart and the late, lamented Matt Price. Thanks are due to a succession of tolerant editors, Alan Oakley in particular, for letting me have such a ridiculous and fun job.

And most importantly, I am very much obliged to the creatures of Parliament themselves – the great and terrible Ruddbot, People Skills, the irrepressible Malcolm Turnbull, La Gillardine, and all their kind – for so good-humouredly enduring the nonsense that follows.

Annabel Crabb

ART OF THE POISONED PEN

In 1995, I was working in a fruit and vegetable shop in the Glasgow suburb of Pollokshields. Having taken a year out from my law degree to travel, I had found a job there, among the chatty Glaswegian locals and the old ladies from the housing projects across the road who, upon discovering I was Australian, dialled up their accents from 'Thick' to 'Unintelligible', just to watch me gape with incomprehension as they bought their half-a-turnip or single potato.

The *Times* had embarked on a cover-price discounting war. It only cost twenty pence a copy, so I bought one every day to read in my lunch break and after a while found myself hunting for the daily articles by political sketch writer Matthew Parris.

Parris was a former Conservative MP, a rather diffident recruit to Margaret Thatcher's army who won preselection for the seat of West Derbyshire after a series of modest achievements including the RSPCA medal, which he won for rescuing a dog from the Thames. He didn't last very long. In 1986, Parris resigned from Parliament to present the television program *Weekend World*. When that foundered, he began writing daily sketches for the *Times*, an occupation in which he thrived.

I loved reading his articles. They beckoned me into a lifelong interest in politics, with their affectionate and mischievous portrayals of Westminster's principal cast. The rest of the paper told me what happened; Parris gave me the rich lunacy of politics and a whiff of what it must be like to be John Major, whose promise to bring British politics 'back to basics' had rather unluckily coincided with an unprecedented outbreak of conspicuous debauchery among his colleagues.

Parris combined a good knowledge of political history and sympathy for his subject with an elegantly whimsical style. 'This may not be Mrs Thatcher's Waterloo', I am sure I can remember reading about the resignation of Thatcher's deputy, Geoffrey Howe, in 1990. 'But it may well be her Clapham Junction.'

Parliamentary sketch writing is something of a British tradition. Its roots are, funnily enough, in fiction. The Westminster system has only been open to direct public scrutiny for about 200 years. Before that, journalists were not allowed to witness parliamentary debates. As the Commons itself put it, it would be a 'high indignity to and a notorious breach of privilege of this House for any news writer to give any account of the debates or other proceedings of the House'. Samuel Johnson, Britain's most distinguished early sketch writer, had to rely on second-hand accounts and gossip to fashion his 'Parliamentary Debates' column for the *Gentleman's Magazine*. Equipped with scraps of information, Johnson simply recorded what he thought politicians might have said; so sensitive was the chamber to scrutiny that he was obliged to disguise his accounts as pure fiction, attributing them to the 'Senate of Lilliput', an imaginary legislature whose occupants bore striking resemblance to those of Westminster. Johnson's work was, quite literally, a 'sketch' or artist's impression of political events, and established the tradition that persists to this day.

Reporters were finally allowed to take seats in the chamber in 1803, relieving them of the need to make everything up. But a delicious confusion between the literary and political cultures continued. Some of England's greatest writers – Dr Johnson, Charles Dickens, Bernard Levin and Frank Johnson – also worked as political sketch writers. And some of its most memorable politicians have themselves been writers of note. The disgraced Jeffrey Archer is the only rolled-gold fiction blockbuster among them, but British politics generates more political diaries and memoirs than any other jurisdiction. Some of them (such as Alan Clark's ribald diaries and the work of Henry 'Chips' Channon) constitute significant historical as well as literary achievements.

Sketch writers are still, however, notorious for making things up. In the early days of my addiction to Parris, John Major was enmeshed in leadership difficulties and faced a direct challenge from John Redwood, his former minister for Wales. Parris was convinced that the angular, calculating, cold-eyed Redwood was not human at all but 'a new creature, half human, half Vulcan, brother of the brilliant, cold-blooded Spock'. He returned again and again to the theme; he consulted imaginary Vulcanologists about Redwood's behaviour and attributed Redwood's rash parliamentary tactics to changes in lunar alignments or instructions from the Vulcan intergalactic high command. Such mockery both reflected and perpetuated perceptions about Redwood among his colleagues and the public; like good political cartooning, good political sketch writing tends to find a thread of truth and spin it into an edifice. The more sharply observed it is, the longer lived, and Redwood, who never became leader but is still the Conservative member for Wokingham, never quite escaped the Vulcan tag.

American political reporting has never quite picked up the sketch-writing tradition, perhaps because its Congress does not provide the daily theatre of question time. In Australia, there have been a handful of practitioners, including in recent years the *Sydney Morning Herald*'s Mike Seccombe, the *Australian*'s late Matt Price and the *Age*'s Tony Wright, among others.

A celebrated sketch writer, Price died the day after one of his most regular targets, Kevin Rudd, finally won the 2007 election. Having written extensively about the cult of 'Kevinism', Price was deprived by cancer of the chance to see it made flesh in the government of Australia. Price was an equal-opportunity tormentor; while he lampooned Rudd as a man who could 'sniff microphone foam from one end of Parliament House to another', he dubbed John Howard the 'Evil Genius' and – as Howard's popularity rating plummeted towards the end of his reign – 'The Unpreferred Prime Minister'.

The odd thing about politics is the extent to which the targets of such lampooning are unperturbed by the attention. Rudd, launching a collection of Price's columns in 2008, wryly recalled some of Price's cruellest lines about his hand gestures, his passion for self-interrogation and, of course, his hair ('With the greatest respect, Kevin, it's a shocker'). Howard himself was known to enjoy a quiet smirk about the 'Evil Genius' tag.

In the schadenfreude-racked world of politics, it is not unusual for the sketch writer who has sent up a particular MP to receive delighted telephone calls both from the target and from his or her enemies. When I first arrived in Canberra as a political reporter in 1999, I went to a party in the suite of Bronwyn Bishop, then the minister for aged care, and was stunned to see her private office: it was a shrine to the political cartoonist's art. Even the most savage cartoons were there, proudly framed and hung.

She's still a good sport. In late 2008, when a brocade-clad Bishop sat gloweringly behind her new leader, Malcolm Turnbull, in question time, having just been dumped from the front bench, I described her as looking like a 'small, malevolent armchair'. Of course, I ran into her the following day in a corridor. Resisting the urge to flee, I was rewarded with a brilliant and diamond-hard Bronny smile. Phew.

Tony Abbott is another hardy soul; not only has he remained unfailingly polite in the face of my insistence on calling him 'People Skills' or – in moments of religious controversy – 'Papal Skills', but he also one day graciously received a prank call from my infant daughter and made no mention of the fact I had called him a 'suicide bomber' in the *Herald* that day.

The beauty of the sketch writer's job is that the peculiarities can emerge, allowing the reader to enjoy some of the farce and folly that make politics so fascinating. Take Andrew Thomson, who served John Howard briefly as minister for sport and was ultimately hunted out of the seat of Wentworth by Peter King, who was duly hunted out by Malcolm Turnbull. Thomson was a magnificently eccentric MP. One day, I noticed him reading a glossy magazine during question time; subsequent inquiries revealed it was *Bacon Busters*, the premier journal of the recreational Australian pig shooter. *Bacon Busters* is not a publication for the faint-hearted. It features a section called 'Babes 'n' Boars', to which readers are invited to submit pictures of themselves (if female) or their girlfriends, seated triumphantly athwart a freshly shot pig.

Thomson was also something of a writer and kept the Liberal back bench entertained with daily instalments of a serialised drama. Set far into the future, it described a world in which a defeated Liberal Party, reduced to a defiant rump by Labor, was led in brave resistance by Brendan Nelson and Julie Bishop. It seemed pretty crazy at the time but clearly he was onto something. Every now and again, Thomson was kind enough to conceal one of his daily instalments somewhere around Parliament House and tip me off as to its whereabouts – perhaps taped under the cafeteria billiards table or hidden in a pot plant.

Such oddities do not have a place in orthodox political reporting, of course; sketch writing is not designed to stand alone; it provides an accompaniment to straight news reporting.

Sketch writers have the great luxury of being permitted impossible latitude in our coverage of a day in politics. I once read a Parris column in which his entire account of question time was taken up with his chance sighting of Peter Mandelson checking that his sock had not fallen down. 'To do so, the Minister Without Portfolio pulled his left trouser halfway up the leg. We were afforded a full view of the leg. The sock extended all the way up to the knee. No flesh was visible, just sleek, discreetly bulging, thin grey cotton, elegantly sheathing ankle and calf', he wrote. 'There was something pre-war Berlin about the hosiery.'

To write such a column was, of course, a fabulous indulgence. But somehow it conveyed more about Mandelson's slightly sinister, fastidious clinicism than might a whole page of news coverage devoted to what he actually said.

A common criticism of sketch writing is that it is essentially insulting; that in poking fun at politicians and concentrating on their quirks, the sketch writer reduces the noble cause of politics to low comedy. By concentrating on personalities, this argument goes, the sketch writer perverts Parliament into a kind of slapstick beauty pageant. As you might expect, I disagree. Most people will tell you politics is boring. It isn't, and one of the reasons it isn't is because it is a terrifyingly unpredictable science. Personalities matter because sometimes – no, regularly – the difference between the success or failure of a policy will come down to the relationship between two ministers or two factions, or to what sort of a week the prime minister is having.

And if political sketch writing can induce readers who otherwise couldn't be bothered to take an interest in politics, as it did me – well, isn't that a good thing?

2007: THE TRIUMPH OF MACHINE OVER MAN

SCALABLE AND AVAILABLE

June 2007 found Prime Minister John Howard stalked by Kevin Rudd – a younger, nerdier version of himself, who knew how to turn on a computer and who set about harnessing the rage of any Australian tortured by slow internet speeds. Striking back, Mr Howard announced his own $958 million broadband plan. In his haste, he omitted to rehearse some of this field's treacherous vocabulary.

A new leader is born.

Gone is the old prime minister, who, one always suspected, had a Beta video recorder stashed away somewhere in Kirribilli House, and a clutter of outdated remote controls at which he might ritually yell imprecations while trying in vain to tape *The Bill.*

That prime minister was getting on the nose, if you believe the polls. However, John Howard is fibre-to-the-node. He is scalable and available. He is the Nine Hundred and Fifty-Eight Million Dollar Man – built at speed and in secret using bleeding-edge technology, bits of old Senate reports and the body parts of several decommissioned Telstra executives. Universal connectivity is the landscape through which the new, upgraded prime minister will stride unchallenged, with new policy, new spending, and – most importantly – a new vocabulary.

Yesterday he took the new gear for a spin. Predictably, there were some glitches.

While the Nine Hundred and Fifty-Eight Million Dollar Man was able to clear some of the technical terms with a mighty bound – 'WiMAX is a scalable technology', he smoothly assured the House at one point – he clipped a few others. ADSL (asymmetric digital subscriber line, to the non-bionically enhanced) – became 'ADLS' yesterday morning as he announced the policy in Goulburn. By the time question time arrived, the proposed ADSL2+ technology had morphed into 'ADSL Two Slush', only to become 'ADSL Plus Two' in another prime ministerial variation.

Ever the stoic, the PM continued manfully, jargon spilling from his lips like marginal seat funding from a pre-election budget paper. 'Megabits' became 'migabits' (although to be fair, a man of Howard's family sensibilities could be forgiven for unfamiliarity with a word that is, after all, but a consonant away from being a pornographic magazine title).

The evolution of the Nine Hundred and Fifty-Eight Million Dollar Man, like all projects involving hair-trigger precision and scientific leaps of faith, has not been without its setbacks. Even the great Lee Majors had difficulties with his bionic eye from time to time, and Howard will doubtless ease into his new persona, given further practice. But political leaders in general should always be cautious about speaking publicly in a foreign language, as John F. Kennedy discovered all those years ago with '*Ich bin ein Berliner*'.

In November 2000, when Howard visited Brunei (in human form) for an Asia-Pacific Economic Co-operation summit, he made an experimental incursion into technical jargon during a now notorious news conference and reduced a room full of grubby journalists to fits of giggles with his heartily expressed enthusiasm for 'digital penetration'. Sensibly, he sought extensive advice and assistance before re-entering the fray in a serious way yesterday.

It is no surprise that people and things become redundant, and that analog will inevitably give way to digital with the passage of time. The trick is to evolve rather than face replacement, as any good cyborg knows.

19 June 2007

A BLUE-FOOTED BOOBY

John Howard was not the only political figure behaving oddly. Imminent democratic events do strange things to most politicians.

In the bird world the onset of the mating season triggers an extraordinary parade of aberrant behaviour. The great frigatebird inflates a red pouch on its neck to barely feasible proportions, the blue-footed booby prances around with its beak and tail held in the air, while the Australian lyrebird impersonates anything from car alarms to Barry White.

A change in the behaviour of the Australian politician is similarly noticeable once every three years as the time draws near for another act of democratic intercourse. Visibility is considerably increased. Repetitive, flamboyant gestures are observed, and a range of 'theatres' visited for ritual, stylised displays. Primary schools, for instance, where the political suitor might read to children, or feign the taking of tea from a plastic tea set. Or factories, where the candidate admires widgets while posing for photographs in a hard hat.

Yesterday the treasurer – Peter Costello – performed a classic of the genre, 'Politician Visits Vibey Radio Show and Talks Hip to the Kids'. The scene was 2Day FM, its presenters Jackie O and Kyle Sandilands.

These intersections with the popular media are humiliating affairs for politicians, but Costello's gift for goof puts him among the most successful of his peers at this perilous game. Yesterday he was called upon to rate a selection of seven grocery items by price, a task he cheerfully bungled before conceding that he was not regularly charged with the Costello family's weekly shop.

On being asked whether he ever cried, however, the treasurer's form returned.

'I get moved by movies from time to time', he said. 'I get moved by talent shows, you know, things like *Australian Idol* – sometimes when the singers get put down and cry. My family … watched it all the way through the series and I thought it was a good series.'

To appreciate the treasurer's craft here, you have to ignore the infeasibility of the central image – that of the treasurer bursting into tears every time some wannabe is told he has a terrible voice. Admire instead the man's ability to fulfil the two key goals of these slots: ingratiate yourself with the hosts, and pretend to like reality TV. Sandilands, of course, is a judge on *Australian Idol*.

The Labor leader, Kevin Rudd, was a guest of 2Day FM in April. His name appears in its archives between those of the former *Australian Idol* contestant Dean Geyer and the Black Eyed Peas singer Fergie ('Find out the real reason the sultry pop princess wet herself on stage!'

Fergie's interview promo gasps). In that interview, Mr Rudd aced the hosts' pop quiz, showing enviable knowledge of popular music and the home life of Britney Spears, and rounded off by nominating *The Simpsons* as his favourite show.

Looks like mating season will be especially colourful this year.

11 July 2007

A LOVELY OLD BLOKE, AND SAY NO MORE

As July drew to a close, Opposition leader Kevin Rudd convened a summit on the question of housing affordability. This sort of caper is very popular with Opposition leaders. Mr Rudd, meanwhile, was careful to remind voters at every turn that his 68-year-old opponent was out of touch, befuddled, rickety, ramshackle, and everything else that means 'old', without actually ever saying so.

Hello, Australia. Kevin here. Good to be with you. Can I just say this? The last thing I want is for this housing summit to be seen as an opportunity to attack the prime minister on housing prices.

I'm not that kind of Opposition leader – you know, nasty and carping and personal.

And I've got nothing negative to say about the prime minister, or any other elderly person, for that matter, can I say? I mean, I'm not prejudiced, I'm just here to help.

In terms of housing affordability, can I say that, when I was born in Nambour, just forty-nine short years ago (Good Lord! The prime minister would already have been able to vote by then! Don't know why that popped into my head, sorry), yes, when I was a young, fiscally conservative, struggling baby in Nambour, houses cost next to nothing?

And that was only forty-nine years ago! Which isn't even a long time – nowhere near as long, for instance as sixty-eight years, which is a fair old age, I mean, time.

I was thinking about all this the other day as I was filling up our car with petrol, which is a job that Thérèse and I take turns at doing, because we are a modern and contemporary family, not that I would want that to be turned in any way into a criticism of the prime minister and his surprisingly well-preserved wife.

Anyway, it's only a small car but it cost sixty-eight dollars to fill up! Can you believe these petrol prices? Sixty-eight! And that's a lot of money! Sixty-eight is a big number, if you think about it. I mean, if you had sixty-eight cats, that would be a lot of cats to feed, especially with grocery prices the way they are, as I'm sure I don't need to tell you.

And if you were sixty-eight years old, I guess you would be feeling pretty old, not that I mean that in any way as a comment on the prime minister, who one of my staffers has just mentioned was actually, coincidentally, sixty-eight yesterday although that of course bears no relevance to my remarks.

Sorry, so back to 'arrogant and out of touch', I mean, housing. Those of us who grew up doing it tough – you know, living in cars, kicking bricks for footies – we know what a struggle it is to get a roof over your kids' heads. John Howard and I are actually in lockstep on this one.

And can I say, just because he operates two taxpayer-funded mansions (total cost to you, $20 million in the past ten years) doesn't mean in any way that he can't empathise with those who struggle to keep a mortgage going?

I'd be the last person to suggest otherwise. After all, I was raised to respect my elders.

27 July 2007

BUCKLE UP, LADIES AND GENTLEMEN

Migrant doctor Mohamed Haneef was detained under Australia's spanking new anti-terrorism laws and questioned at length about his supposed involvement in a bombing in the UK. The whole affair degenerated into an unholy farce, with Haneef proving perfectly innocent.

Do you know how to fly a plane? Nope, neither do I. But when I fly, I do so in confidence, or at the very least hope, that there is somebody – generally several somebodies – somewhere near the front of the machine who does know how to fly a plane. It's a matter of trust.

It's exactly the same with the operation of these anti-terrorism laws. We don't know what's going on and we accept that we don't know. We just have to trust that somebody sitting in the appropriate seat does know and is doing the right thing.

This whole Mohamed Haneef adventure started reasonably sedately with those of us in cattle class all strapped in and snug and secure, our tray tables in the upright position, gnawing happily at our unopenable foil sachets of in-flight beer nuts.

When the captain's announcement came that an issue had arisen, we were alert but not alarmed. Obviously, if this chap had had his collar felt, there was probably something up. Probably best to look into it. And if his phone card ended up in the jeep that was torched in Scotland, well, that certainly sounded a bit fishy. Good on the federal fuzz for keeping an eye on all this terrorism malarkey; it can't be an easy job.

Another drink, madam? Well, I don't mind if I do. No need to panic.

But as irregularities emerged, it was difficult to restrain a nagging sense of doubt about the stewardship of the operation.

When the Australian Federal Police commissioner, Mick Keelty, confirmed this week that a vital piece of evidence – the presence of Haneef's SIM card in the burning Glasgow jeep – did not exist, it was as if the aircraft's captain had reeled back into the economy cabin brandishing a half-empty bottle of scotch and bellowing show tunes.

By the time co-pilot Damian Bugg revealed his intention to revisit the charges, Keelty was blaming the whole thing on Bugg, while flight-steward Kevin Andrews maintained his firm intention to boot Haneef out of the country, notwithstanding the apparent wreckage of the Commonwealth's entire case.

Most of the flight crew, in other words, appeared to be milling around in the galley throwing punches.

Nobody likes to be the first person on board to panic. But the question can now be asked quite urgently: who the hell is flying this thing?

The underlying story of the anti-terrorism laws is not just that they do away with settled legal concepts such as habeas corpus, or the right not to be held without charge. It's that they create enormous responsibilities for a few select people.

People like Bugg and Keelty and Andrews, who now find themselves responsible for maintaining a balance between fairness and public order, based not on a routine system of legal convention but on their own discretion. This must put an extraordinary amount of pressure on these individuals – particularly on Keelty, who has looked as sick as a parrot all week, and no wonder.

Accidents happen. Mistakes are made by even the most capable officials. But when those people carry such significant responsibility and trust on behalf of the entire Australian population, blunders can assume disastrous proportions.

Andrews, the immigration minister, has been looking rather less troubled by the whole thing, but managed to come up with this truly magnificent exchange yesterday with an ABC interviewer, Chris Uhlmann.

Andrews: Ultimately, this can all be tested because there can be reviews in the courts and the courts have the ability to test the information.

Uhlmann: Well, minister, I understand under the act, section 503 of the Migration Act means that no court, no Parliament, no parliamentary committee and no person can actually ask you to reveal what you were told by police. Isn't that correct?

Andrews: Well, that's true, subject to being advised that it's safe to release some of that information. And obviously where national security is of paramount interest, it's important, it's crucial that we don't reveal things which could lead to a situation potentially that someone who has been acting contrary to the interests of Australia and Australians could be involved in some criminal behaviour which we would then be precluded from actually investigating and even charging someone with.

Good on Uhlmann for knowing his stuff.

Most people would probably assume that Andrews's first comment was accurate, that appeals would be possible or that in some way the minister's claim to be in possession of secret knowledge could be tested or reviewed. But that assumption is no longer available; what we have instead is a finely balanced network of trust – and a forlorn hope that somebody remains at the controls.

28 July 2007

A SMILE ON THE PM'S DIAL

Meanwhile, the PM's love affair with talkback radio continued.

You can keep your new-fangled interweb thingy and MyTube and YouSpace – the prime minister's a wireless man and always will be. At a lunch celebrating forty years of talkback radio yesterday, John Howard broke bread with a host of his current and past interlocutors and confessed shyly that radio was his favourite format.

'Radio is the best means of communication because it is only through radio that you can even come close to having a personal conversation with the Australian people', he said. 'It is an immediacy, it is a directness that is totally missing from the other mediums.'

Nodding sagely at the prime minister's words over lunch were a collection of people who over the years have had him for breakfast: the retiring radio behemoth John Laws, Steve Price, Melbourne's Derryn Hinch and John Burns, Perth's Howard Sattler and the retired greats Gary O'Callaghan and Ron Casey among them.

'I do feel part of the fraternity, if I can put it that way', Howard ventured.

Towards the end of lunch, as was probably inevitable, Lawsie took to the lectern to accept a tribute from the industry and to let spill a few drops of what is now a finite supply of honey from those magnificent lips. Among them were his summary of what appealed to him about radio back when he began his career in Bendigo in 1953: 'Money, and girls.'

Tempting as it is, we must dismiss the idea that the prime minister is also in it for money and girls. What he has been seeking over his thirty-three years in politics, he explained yesterday, was unprotected intercourse with the Australian public.

Howard has made his career on the airwaves, where he can speak directly to the great unwashed without fear of being edited, interrupted or misinterpreted by irritating journalists or editors. But yesterday he took things a step further.

'I am, as you know, a strident opponent of the view that this country should have a bill of rights … I think that when you start writing rights down you probably end up circumscribing people's rights', he said. He explained that there were three things in Australia that obviated the need for a bill of rights: a vigorous parliamentary system, an incorruptible judiciary and a free media. 'And there is nothing quite so free', he concluded, 'when it comes to the media in this country, as talkback radio.'

Who needs a bill of rights when you've got Lawsie?

31 July 2007

THE SQUIRE RIDES AGAIN

The APEC conference, planned as a pre-election triumph for Mr Howard, instead became a perfectly ridiculous platform for Kevin Rudd to speak Mandarin in public and for the prime minister's colleagues to bumble about in an inexpert attempt to induce their leader to abdicate in favour of Peter Costello – only to be effortlessly outfoxed. At the end of the conference, after George W. Bush thanked 'Austria' for hosting the event, the global leaders lined up to be photographed in Drizabones. I borrowed from Banjo Paterson to salute the PM's heroic final stand.

There was fear and speculation,
As the word was passed around,
That the Squire was poised to give it all away,
And hand the station – all of it, both rich and rocky ground –
To the Kid (himself grown old along the way).
The Squire had diced with Death before, had more lives than a cat;
Been laughed at, mocked, derided – and survived.

But with the dusk approaching, he was none the cheered for that,
And wouldn't be, till cavalry arrived.
But the riders who had made their names a-thunder by his side
Fell silent as the shadows grew and leapt.
And Howard checked his tack, and steed, and planned his final ride,
And thought again, and thought, while others slept.
Only Piers (a blunderbuss athwart his shapely knee)
Remained inside the bunker till the end;
Uncorking first an '86, and then a '63
To help, libate, and succour his old friend.
For none's more lonely
Than a man of unrelenting stuff
Who comes across a chasm at full tilt
And must decide in seconds: draw the rein, and call 'Enough'?
Or leap? Of such grand feats are legends built.
There's little doubt the Squire had the stomach for the ride;
The steep, uncertain thrill of the descent.
But tell that to his musterers, who twitched Australia-wide
On primaries of thirty-nine per cent.
The Kid, too, seemed to falter as the long-sought prize drew near
His yearning features turning strangely blank.
The crumbling of the kingdom served to stoke his central fear:
'I'd do much better working for a bank.'

10 September 2007

ART OF THE LEADERSHIP SPILL

Parliament resumed, with Mr Howard still in charge.

The past few days of leadership destabilisation in the Liberal Party have exposed an obvious complication: none of the Libs is any good at it. They are deeply, vastly and irredeemably out of practice, in fact, and it shows.

Every time a tiny public jab is made against the prime minister, a great squeal goes up and everybody dashes for cover and shooshes each other until the next poke of the stick occurs. Honestly, it's like watching a pack of seven-year-old girls going at a brown snake.

By the time Mr Howard arrived in question time yesterday, most of his ministers were deeply involved in studying their papers. It's quite incredible, in a sitting week distinguished by so little actual legislation, that everybody would suddenly need quite so many folders, notebooks and pamphlets. Mal Brough alone, who is understood to be one of the prime cabinet agitators against Mr Howard's continued tenure, had about eight folders, to which he devoted himself assiduously.

When the PM turned in his seat, as he does from time to time, barely anyone on the front bench would meet his eye. The unprecedented turnout in the press galleries, which Kim Beazley later likened to 'three rows of crows, waiting for the sheep to die, yum yum', was unwarranted; it was an uneventful hour.

After question time, ministers scurried away lest they be approached for a comment. All, that is, but Peter Costello, who remained for a few words with Malcolm Turnbull, while delighted Labor MPs shrieked at the pair to 'take it outside'. If this were the Labor Party, someone's head would be on a stick by now, and the victors would be on their second round of duck pancakes.

The problem is that the Liberal Party has forgotten how to do leadership spills – nasty ones, that is, where the incumbent has to be dynamited out like a badger from its burrow. Unfortunately for the anti-Howard camp, the one person with some knowledge of leadership destabilisation is the prime minister himself – which makes things quite ticklish, as you can imagine.

So who is running this thing? Well, nobody, really. It doesn't seem to be much more than a flustered telephone tree of people who are terribly anxious but don't want to say anything. As a rule of thumb, though, it seems at this point that the PM would be best advised to beware anybody called Malcolm. Mal Washer from Western Australia (Petit Mal) has been reasonably vocal; Malcolm Turnbull and Mal Brough (currently battling it out for the title of Grand Mal) are two more senior folk who have been fingered as flirters with the idea of change.

But the only person who is happy to discuss the covert leadership coup against the PM is its target, who seemingly cannot be kept off the airwaves. And the putative challenger, the treasurer? In doing nothing, he has come closer than most to doing something. Strange days.

12 September 2007

TURNBULL STRUGGLES FOR A LOYAL WORD

With Mr Howard under siege, who could possibly replace him? Conventional wisdom was that the treasurer, Peter Costello, was the man for the job. Malcolm Turnbull, then the environment minister, is anything but conventional.

Being Malcolm Turnbull must be quite pleasant most of the time; the pay is good, the accommodation first-class, and the views unparalleled. But for four minutes yesterday, from 2.25 p.m. until 2.29, being Malcolm Turnbull was uncomfortable.

It began when Labor's Anthony Albanese asked Mr Turnbull about his attendance at a meeting in the foreign minister's hotel room last week, at which the prime minister's shortcomings reportedly underwent genteel discussion.

Now, it would be impolite to describe Mr Albanese as a muckraker, exactly, but you do hear the barely perceptible sound, when he rises to ask a question, of latex gloves being snapped on. And this was a curly one for the environment minister, whose recent efforts to redesign the Liberal leadership environment were crushed finally and expertly yesterday under the prime ministerial boot.

Mr Turnbull rose to his feet and edged towards the dispatch box, then paused halfway as he heard the speaker, David Hawker, voice the opinion that the question was very nearly out of order.

Off the hook.

Mr Turnbull beetled back towards his seat with relief, until an explosion of laughter stopped him in his tracks. He stopped, swivelled; a rich indecision overcame his handsome features.

'I will answer it. I will take the question', he muttered as he ploughed back to the dispatch box to announce: 'I attended that meeting. That is the answer to your question.'

On the way back to his seat, however, the environment minister realised the import of what he had just said. To confirm attendance at the meeting, without indicating a full retraction of sentiments expressed at it? Suicidal. To return and add to the answer? Embarrassing.

Once again, Mr Turnbull wheeled about, then hovered in agony. Frozen between inclination and humiliation, his body language looked very much like that of a man trying to buy a pornographic magazine in a busy service station.

Finally, he noticed the prime minister's lowered brow, and the slight incline of the prime ministerial head that indicated, in the politest possible way: 'Get back here and clear that up, would you?'

Eventually Mr Turnbull rushed the counter and babbled out his repentance: 'I attended that meeting. The prime minister has the support of everybody at that meeting. The discussions at the meeting are not part of my portfolio responsibilities, but I have answered the question. The prime minister has the support, as prime minister, of everybody in the cabinet. That is the answer.'

Yesterday was that sort of day. Much stout talk of loyalty, and support for the prime minister, and 'going forward as a team' and 'winning the election seat by seat' (is there any other way?) and a magnanimous guarantee from the PM that there would be no recriminations against anybody. Apart from losing their seats, one or two sourpusses observed.

Wilson Tuckey, the bow-legged warrior from the west, came the closest to public insurrection. Asked on his way into the party meeting whether the prime minister enjoyed his support, Mr Tuckey answered, magnificently: 'That is a matter of the circumstances of the moment.'

Once inside, he apparently held forth at length on the topic of wheat, which tells you just about all you need to know about the state of the anti-Howard camp yesterday.

13 September 2007

INTRODUCING THE WE GENERATION

Mr Howard's leadership was finally safe, nailed into place with a clunky succession plan which promised a Costello handover sometime during the next term. All of a sudden, Mr Howard was obliged to talk in more inclusive terms about his deputy.

Have you heard about the new DIY show that's taking Parliament House by storm? It's called *Changing Pronouns.*

Here's the challenge: before a national TV audience, the *Changing Pronouns* team has a matter of days to remove every instance of the word 'I' in the federal government's campaign literature and replace it with 'we'. Work began overnight on Wednesday, right after John Howard's announcement that he would 'probably … certainly' retire some time well into his next term of government, and that in the meantime a vote for the Coalition would be supersized to include a complimentary Costello.

The 'we' pronoun was unveiled within hours. Liberal web monkeys removed the picture of the prime minister from the Liberal Party website and replaced it with a chummy shot of him gazing at the treasurer. And yesterday the ministerial wing was like a construction site: dust sheets and scaffolding everywhere, and taciturn blokes in overalls trudging from office to office unbolting 'I's and hammering up 'we's instead.

'We've got a huge program for the future of Australia', trumpeted Peter Costello, an early and enthusiastic user of the new pronoun.

In question time, Mr Howard took it for a test drive. There were a few stumbles, naturally. At first the PM kept slipping back into the old format by accident. 'It's a policy that I intro— that we introduced', he said, reminiscing about a particular point of health policy.

All in all, the pilot program went very well. The next phase, however, is far more ambitious. The foreign minister, Alexander Downer, it is understood, is finalising plans to edit all mentions of Australia's involvement in the Middle East; Iraq will now be known as 'Weraq'. Similarly, Joe Hockey has in recent days combed Australia for a couple of non-unionised metalworkers to angle-grind the 'I's out of his own portfolio. Industrial relations will still be a cornerstone election issue for the Coalition's team, but it will henceforth be known as WeR, instead of IR. Mr Costello, who now more than ever warrants his title of subprime minister, is expected to present the quarterly Consumer Price Index figures next month, except of course they will be the CPWe figures.

Not everybody is going to find the new style easy, particularly the Coalition backbench, which has been subjected to much trauma of late and now displays a certain whimpering intolerance for sudden change. For this reason, a new information pack will be issued jointly by the offices of the prime minister and the subprime minister. Coalition MPs will be able to download the info as a podcast onto their WePods. Or they can read about it by logging into the prime minister's OurSpace page. Or download the video version on WeTube.

Several extreme applications of the new policy were rejected. Janette Howard, for instance, will not be known as 'our wife'. But otherwise, the new rule is absolute. After all, as the subprime minister might privately reflect, there's no 'I' in team, even if there is a 'you' in 'Thanks for strangling my career, you stubborn old bugger.'

14 September 2007

NEVER MIND THE PM, IT'S ALL ABOUT ME

The new emphasis on togetherness did not extend to Malcolm Turnbull, the Parliament's most celebrated solo artist.

Brandishing one of Malcolm Turnbull's glossy pamphlets, Tanya Plibersek was the latest Labor figure yesterday to goad the environment minister on the subject of his own ambition.

'Can the minister explain why this newsletter does not once mention the prime minister by name nor make any reference to the Howard government?' Ms Plibersek enquired.

'Point of order!' shrieked Bronwyn Bishop, struggling to make herself heard over her jacket (a masterpiece in deafening yellow of which any Tour de France leader would be justifiably covetous).

Mrs Bishop, who aspires to the speaker's chair, is a regular taker of points of order. She likes to stay limber, in case there is ever a World Parliamentary Standing Orders Games, at which she would certainly 'podium' for Australia. Her case yesterday was that the question to Mr Turnbull was out of order, seeing as it did not relate to his portfolio (standing order 98c). The speaker, David Hawker, who is well aware of Mrs Bishop's aspirations and loathes her accordingly, nixed her argument and Mr Turnbull took the floor.

'It's a newsletter for me as the local member and naturally it focuses on me', he declared. 'So there you go.'

A lesser man might – in view of the past week's events – have added some craven line about his undying respect for the prime minister, but the environment minister offered nothing of the kind.

Has Ms Plibersek ever met Mr Turnbull? Her intervention does rather beg this question, given that anyone with any familiarity at all with the work of Mr Turnbull would find it deeply unsurprising that a newsletter put out by him in his electorate would contain mentions of no one else at all.

The front page of the newsletter, which documents Mr Turnbull's visit to St Vincent's Hospital to pat its new MRI machine, gives us a rough idea of the news values inherent in the Turnbull publishing arm. The picture shows a tiny magnetic resonance imaging machine in the background, flanked by an equally tiny nun. Both are dwarfed by the billion-megawatt smile of the environment minister, whose form takes up about half the photo.

What do you have to do to appear in Mr Turnbull's campaign literature? 'Be Malcolm Turnbull' may be the most obvious answer, but it is not the only one. Given that Mr Turnbull's three dogs – Mellie, Jojo and Rusty – have their own blogs on Mr Turnbull's official website, 'Be prepared to fetch sticks for the minister at Rose Bay Park' might be another.

'Mellie has an orthodontic problem, known as an underbite', readers are informed in one of the dog entries. 'This makes it difficult for her to eat bones.' Mr Turnbull also has something of an orthodontic problem, which might best be termed a strategic overbite, or tendency to bite off slightly more than he can chew. This makes it difficult for him to eat humble pie.

18 September 2007

THE FINE AND LESSER ARTS OF LEADERSHIP

Question time started slowly yesterday.

Government ministers and MPs still seemed to be feeling the effects of their specially designated 'vision and ideas' party meeting, which of course turned out to be a two-and-a-half-hour barkfest from which refugees were sporadically witnessed escaping to the cafeteria, bleeding from the ears.

Coalition party-room spokesman Andrew Southcott, asked to summarise the session, could only report limply that there had been more than fifty contributors on the subjects of housing, water policy and drought; out of respect for his ordeal, we did not press him too keenly.

Kevin Rudd's troops, meanwhile, had just emerged from their own meeting during which Mr Rudd admonished them not to engage in 'hubris, arrogance or cockiness'. Without a sniff of irony, Mr Rudd then distributed what appeared to be beer mats featuring his own image and the legend: 'I Have a Plan for Australia's Future'.

Journalists had our own psychological cross to bear. We had just endured a press conference with Mark Vaile, twenty minutes of whose oratory on the subject of the Brisbane Airport runway is just about enough to make you feel like going out and lying on it.

Thank goodness question time turned its attention, eventually, to art. The subprime minister, Peter Costello, had overnight disinterred a copy of Labor's arts policy, announced by Peter Garrett, and was immediately captured by one of its elements, a promise to 'introduce initiatives that enable artists currently on welfare greater opportunity to produce work and generate employment'.

'Well, blow me down!' exclaimed the treasurer, who may not know much about art, but knows a slow-moving tax policy target when he sees one. 'What are the responsibilities of someone who is on welfare? Do they have to turn up at the office at 8 a.m. and take themselves away from their easel? What exactly is keeping them from producing their art? Here are your obligations: you have to keep a job diary, which would ask you to record ten job search efforts every fortnight. I do not think that would get in the way of the next Mona Lisa.'

Peter Garrett himself, of course, used to be a pace-setting artist of the pop art school, where he worked mainly in Oils. But nowadays, like most of his frontbench colleagues, he no longer works under his own name, having apprenticed himself to the demanding studio of the modern master Kevin Rudd. The Rudd studio tends to attribute all major works to the master himself, but frontbenchers are occasionally allowed to try their hands at daubing minor pieces; the announcement of lesser inquiries, summits and working groups, for example, or the odd low-level task force. This explains why Mr Garrett – whose principal responsibility is the environment – was allowed to announce the arts policy, but not the forestry policy.

Critics are still trying to define the master's ever-changing style. On tax policy, he is minimalist; his industrial work tends towards classic revisionism, while on federal–state relations he strays boldly into neo-absurdism.

And like many young artists convinced of their own imminent greatness, he is already selling T-shirts.

19 September 2007

KEV'S AFFAIR TO REMEMBER

In a rare lapse, Kevin Rudd botched an interviewer's pop quiz about tax rates. Such questions are the nightmare that stalks every politician.

Cramming season is upon us.

Wild-eyed frontbenchers roamed Parliament's corridors last night in search of the last remaining back issues of Budget Paper One, 2007, lest they be asked to recite tax rates as Kevin Rudd was asked to do yesterday with such tragic results.

The more nervous among them – both government and Opposition – stayed up till late, tearfully rote-learning tables of company tax rates, diesel fuel excise rebates, eligibility for Family Tax Benefit Part B, as well as Australia's GDP, CPI, and current account deficit – not to mention the price (seasonally adjusted) of a Golden Gaytime. As panic spread, supermarkets within Comcar range were looted by gangs of MPs, desperately price-checking loaves of bread, cartons of milk, boxes of tampons (what if *Women's Weekly* asks?) and denture paste.

Appearing in front of an audience is tempting fate for this sort of stuff – and few MPs have escaped that sinking feeling when, miked-up, viscid-palmed, they hear their interlocutor turning the subject innocently around to the specific question of grain subsidies, or the eminently forgettable name of a beloved local mayor.

Peter Costello was overjoyed to see Mr Rudd in such straits yesterday, and immediately mounted a parliamentary attack that had to be viewed through one's fingers, such was its brutality. The Opposition was in no mood to continue question time, and promptly moved a motion of dissent to the speaker. The government did not have, therefore, the opportunity to discuss some important new information that had emerged the night before in *Today Tonight*'s profile of the Opposition leader.

'Kevin's journey started as a teenager ...', the misty account commenced. But as viewers wrenched themselves away from the image of young Kevin, emerging from the womb bespectacled, fourteen and already trilingual, they were rewarded with a nugget of genuine insight as Mr Rudd commented on his political influences.

Earlier in his career, these were drawn from a deep and wide pool, ranging from the Lutheran theologian Dietrich Bonhoeffer to Robert Menzies. Now, it seems, the list of role models has been winnowed down to one – and the good news is that Mr Rudd can seek guidance from his muse, face to face, every time he shaves.

'Someone asked me the other day, "Who do you model yourself on?"' Mr Rudd told the *Today Tonight* reporter, Anna Coren. 'And I said, "Ah ... Kevin." I'm just me.'

So there you have it, in case you were wondering. The Opposition leader has built himself in his own image. One can only imagine the years of crushing doubts about whether he could live up to his exacting standards and the crucial teenage years, when young Kevin's dreams of himself took on an innocently erotic blush. And the thrill of meeting and working with himself, first in the Department of Foreign Affairs, where a relationship of mutual faith and trust was forged that would ultimately take him, along with himself, all the way to the leadership of the party that he loved.

20 September 2007

PULSES RACE IN MATTERS OF HEART

Press reports revealed that the Opposition leader, many years ago, had undergone an aortic valve transplant, in which he accepted a donor heart valve. No suggestion was made that Mr Rudd was anything but fighting fit these days, but Labor MPs sniffed dirty tricks.

It started as a light dispute about a two-centimetre piece of gristle deep within the thoracic cavity of the Opposition leader.

It ended in parliamentary Pompeii: an eruption of bile and spite which blanketed the Parliament on what will probably prove its last day of togetherness before the election.

Like a domestic dispute that starts with 'Why do we always have to have chicken on Thursdays?' and ends with 'You bastard! I hate you, and the kids aren't yours!' the fracas yesterday escalated with blistering speed until everybody was saying all the things they'd been dying to say all year.

The central question, if we retrieve it from the bloody fray and wipe it down, is this: Was the government responsible for telling Channel

Nine about Kevin Rudd's heart operation, in which, fourteen years ago, he had a new aortic valve fitted to his heart?

But in a two-hour ecstasy of abuse, the following questions were also given vigorous consideration: Is the Opposition leader a weak-chinned, snivelling sooky-boy who can't stand up for himself? Is the prime minister a nasty old schemer who digs dirt on Labor MPs? And is the treasurer a pea-hearted chump who is destined to fail?

Normally, Mr Rudd's demeanour in question time is one of dignified transcendence. He frowns, he scribbles, he sucks his pen and gazes at the ceiling as if seeking divine inspiration; he looks much more like a composer struggling to finish a particularly knotty concerto than a politician grubbing his way through yet another question time. Most of the time, he ignores the government's ministers entirely – even when they're answering his questions.

And yesterday there was an absurd feel to the early parts of the Labor attack; while Jenny Macklin and Anthony Albanese demanded shrilly to know whether the government had been snooping around Mr Rudd's medical records, the owner of the controversial aorta himself buried his head in his papers and looked as if he couldn't be less interested.

Peter Costello put an end to this lunacy by calling off question time and introducing instead a procedural motion directing Mr Rudd to outline personally his allegations against the government. This had the very precise effect of freaking the Opposition leader out; the scribbling intensified, and there was a bit of 'Why won't the government use this time to talk about the future of this country', which was a tiny bit rich coming from the bloke whose mates had picked the fight in the first place.

But eventually his charges emerged; his face reddened, his features contorted, and the saintly Mr Rudd found himself – concerto abandoned – baying and howling and pointing like everybody else. Points of order flew like spitballs.

Labor screamed 'Smear!'

The government screamed that the above-listed scream in itself constituted a smear.

For two scintillating hours, we got a very clear view of what the Australian Union of Students must have looked like in its heyday.

Why did this fight happen yesterday? And was it really about aortas – is it, indeed, a smear to circulate the fact that a man had a new aorta installed in 1993? Nobody seems to be able to identify anything especially politically portentous in that fact itself. Cursory research indicates that Anthony Burgess, Frank Zappa and Pablo Escobar all died that same year. Perhaps if Mr Rudd had received their aortas, it might have been a hotter story.

No – yesterday was about bigger things.

On the Labor side, it was about an attempt to gain sympathy from a public already nicely receptive to the idea that politicians dig dirt. And on the government's account, it was about terminal annoyance at Mr Rudd for being such a smarty-pants.

21 September 2007

BEAZLEY'S FAREWELL

Meanwhile, the man deposed by the heart valve's adoptive owner – former Labor leader Kim Beazley – bowed out of politics.

The walls of the House of Representatives chamber are still being sponged down after Thursday afternoon's gore-fest, so it's easy to forget that Thursday morning brought one of the nicest half-hours the room has ever seen. I'm referring to the last parliamentary speech of Kim Christian Beazley.

A speech from the former Labor leader is always a wandering affair. And Thursday's oration was like nothing so much as one last ramble with a beloved old dog: full of joyous detours and fun, and long periods of fond indulgence on the part of the listeners while the speaker galumphed off to snuff deeply at some fragrant irrelevance just over the rise.

Beazley did appear to be speaking from notes, but they proved an extremely weak leash for a hound of – even in retirement – such bounding narrative exuberance.

'I had not intended talking about that', he mused aloud, after casually revealing by way of digression that Gough Whitlam had actually required a great deal of convincing (from the late Mick Young) to visit China in 1972. This nugget in itself is a significant revision to the orthodoxy that Whitlam's eagerness to engage with China at that time was a masterful piece of prescience on his part.

But enough! The old dog was straining at the leash again; time to move on. 'The thing I will miss most, having lost the leadership of the party and in leaving it, is the opportunity to get around the place', he reflected. 'I do like branch meetings. I do like those occasions when you get in behind candidates, when you sit there and hear one conspiracy theory after another to deflect this or that and when you get one great suggestion after another about what will be decisive that will win the election, and then – when you go back, not having won the election – to be informed by the person, "If you'd taken some notice of me, comrade, we would be in office." I love that remonstrance of the average party member; it is terrific.'

When Beazley says he loves this stuff, he is not joking, or dog-whistling, or raising an oratorical eyebrow at his party's tiresomest people for the enjoyment of those who continue to have to deal with them. He means it – just as he meant the generous words that followed for Kevin Rudd, the man who stripped him of his leadership.

'It is something I know my current leader will never experience, because I am sure he will go around the party after the next election to utter adulation. He will not experience the vicissitudes and horrors of what your party members do to you when they think you have failed them.'

Onwards, via the union movement, Zimbabwe, the collapse of the Soviet Union, corporate salaries and a brief cock of the leg over economic policy. ('Let me tell you a thing or two about the IMF …')

From a brief subsequent romp on the topic of the US alliance, Beazley returned with a juicy bone: the revelation that as defence minister he authorised espionage against the Americans to extract vital radar codes for our Hornets. 'That is not to say that I do not love the Americans and think that they are our most important ally, but they are a bunch of people you have got to have a fight with every now and then to get what you need out of them!' – this directed genially to the current defence minister, Brendan Nelson.

The prime minister was prevented from looking in on his old foe's speech on Thursday, being engaged in a pep rally with Coalition staff concerning his approaching battle. The men have always maintained a courtly respect for each other, notably exhibited last year when Howard offered his plane so the devastated Beazley, who had just been deposed, could fly home in peace to bury his brother.

So goodbye, Kim – we may never again have to hover exasperatedly over your viscous prose, looking for a way to hack it to size for an ordinary news paragraph. We won't see you in the Parliament House courtyard any more, puffing on a cigar, or blink through another of your enthusiastic comparisons between cabinet minister X and some long-forgotten American general. We won't have any more hour-long press conferences, where journos up the back sometimes stole away at the three-quarter mark like naughty children while you chugged on, giving even the most junior of us the courtesy of a full answer. Thank you for that courtesy.

Let's hope the collective brain of the parliamentary community can recover from the loss of about 80 per cent of its vocabulary. And that the path ahead is full of buried treasure.

22 September 2007

LABOR'S NO-UNDIES TRICK GRANTS IMMUNITY FROM THE WEDGE

After all sorts of heartache, much of it emitting from his own electorate, environment minister Malcolm Turnbull approved the controversial proposed pulp mill, to be built in Tasmania's Tamar Valley.

What an odd week. Malcolm Turnbull approves the Tamar Valley pulp mill, and no doubt will spend the weekend being pelted with cubes of Gruyère by angry pinot noir drinkers in his Sydney electorate. Peter Garrett concurs with Mr Turnbull and an eerie silence reigns among his Labor colleagues. The Labor Party of four years ago would not have stood by while its environment spokesman condemned a stretch of Tasmanian landscape to pulpery.

Four years ago, there would have been sit-ins, Labor 4 the Tamar and an orchestrated campaign of Brisbane wholefood purveyors baking plaintive bran muffins in the shape of Tassie devils and delivering them to Kevin Rudd's electorate office.

What's happened? Well obviously, there are many Labor supporters who hear the victory bells in the distance and who feel they can stand almost anything in order to hear them draw closer. But the other thing that's different is the Senate. When the government won control of the Senate in the 2004 election, it was like a final kick to the head of a party that had again fallen over in the street. The sale of Telstra, workplace relations reform; each of the government's longed-for reforms, now made gloriously possible by a Coalition-ruled Senate, seemed like further blows raining down on the ALP's prostrate form.

Labor – until that point – had always been tremendously busy in the Senate. The compulsion to amend, debate and redraft legislation – to fiddle – often proved irresistible for Labor, who took very seriously their mandate to ameliorate what they saw as the worst excesses of the government's program.

Of course, given that all of them had different ideas about how this should be done, public bickering was common. And the government, aware of this, used to bait them mercilessly. Why was the Tampa legislation so divisive when it plopped onto the Senate table in late August 2001? Because it was awful, sloppy legislation – legislation that nobody could in all conscience support. It was an invitation to division, in fact, which the ALP gobbled up exactly as it was meant to do, tearing itself apart publicly in its attempts to fix things up.

The dominance of John Howard over his first three terms had a lot to do with his ability to scatter ideological cherry-bombs, while his earnest Labor opponents – first Kim Beazley, then Simon Crean and then Mark Latham – cursed and dodged in his explosive wake.

But this has changed since the government won control of the Senate. To be blunt, the arse has dropped out of the amendments industry. In the last parliament Labor drafted and passed 540 Senate amendments, amid much horse-trading and haggling with the Democrats.

Since the Senate changed hands, however, their success rate on amendments has dived – to six. Just six successful amendments. Which means that all the time the Labor back bench used to spend agonising, brawling, scribbling, ripping up, scribbling again and sobbing into midnight beers, they now spend doing other things – who knows? Possibly hanging out with constituents. Because it no longer matters a tinker's cuss what they think about the government's latest legislative onslaught.

As a result, the flipside of Labor's electoral humiliation in 2004 is a strange new cultural phenomenon within the party itself; it's now immune to the wedge. If you need a demonstration, just have a look at the Northern Territory intervention the government staged mid-year. It had everything that would normally make for an ALP super-wedge: federal interference, paternalism, the bullying of a territory Labor government – and strong public support. And yet the Labor back bench absorbed it with the blank stare of the heavily sedated. Labor presented a couple of amendments in the Senate, but didn't insist on them; what would have been the point? As any wise nine-year-old in a schoolyard will tell you, you don't live in fear of a wedgie if someone's already nicked your underwear.

The government, too, has learned the hard way that you must always be careful what you wish for. For a decade, the prime minister struggled with Labor and the Democrats in the Senate to inch through diluted versions of his wildest-dreams model of industrial reform. Given the run of the Senate, he got his wish – and it's turned out to be an electoral loser whose ill effects he is now trying to reverse. The government was forced to embrace its inner Democrat in May and amend Work Choices to introduce a fairness test. When once this sort of softening would have been done in the Senate, it ended up being a slightly ungainly manoeuvre performed solely by the government.

Much as it must be fun to have your own Senate, the PM must yearn sometimes for the long nights when Parliament's northern wing was lit only by the comforting glow of Labor senators setting themselves on fire.

6 October 2007

GENERAL HOWARD GOES OVER THE TOP

Mr Howard announced a new history syllabus. Culture warriors salivated.

A brief frisson ran around the trenches of the culture warriors yesterday morning with the confirmation that General Howard was planning to go over the top.

A new history syllabus? A federally mandated version of Australian history, personally approved by Mr Howard himself? Would this be like Michael Jackson's *HIStory*, or Robin Morgan's 'herstory' – were we about to see the formal emergence of Howardstory?

You could almost hear the metallic scrape of pins being eased from grenades, and bayonets being lowered as the members of the glorious cultural resistance prepared for a final stand.

What no one will ever admit about culture warfare is that the combatants just love it. The culture wars impart dash and glamour to our public intellectuals in a way that reasoned, proportionate thought never could. Who could bear the thought of mouldering away in the faculty tearoom when you could be at the front, blasting away magnificently with the smell of cordite in the nostrils?

Culture wars also work (like real wars) as job-creation schemes; there are whole magazines that owe their existence to the hostilities and if culture peace were suddenly to strike, one suspects legions of brainiacs would never work again. So news of a fresh skirmish was bracing for everyone.

There was a tang of irony, too – yesterday marked the one-month anniversary of the PM's address to his own restive troops, when he told them voters wanted to hear the government talk about the future, not the past. Does talking about history count as talking about the past? If you're talking about the future teaching of past events, does that count as talking about the future? (What if you do it in txt-speak? Discuss in 500 words or less.)

But what a strange day it became. The syllabus itself turned out to be a model of cultural bipartisanship; for every cricket milestone mentioned, there was a nod to multiculturalism or a reference to Patrick White. Mr Howard modestly omitted the election of his own government from the digest of 'interesting things that happened between 1976 and 2000', but included the inception of the multicultural broadcaster SBS.

If all that were not enough, the prime minister bobbed up last night with the casual revelation that he was planning a national referendum to include a new acknowledgment of Aboriginal Australia in the constitution. On hearing this, Mr Howard's culture warriors might well be forgiven for surreptitiously arranging an assessment by the platoon's medical officer.

In terms of reversals, it's quite a doozy – imagine Shane Warne confessing a sudden fondness for sushi, or Elton John a distaste for sequins. What next? An honorary Howard chair in surfing at Griffith University? An Order of Australia for John Pilger? Vegetarians in the Lodge?

Today, the cultural battlefield will stand silent with genuine, bipartisan bafflement.

12 October 2007

CAPTAIN WACKY AT THE HELM

With the polls the way they are, much attention has been focused of late on the question of what everybody will do if – or when – the government is tipped out.

Will the prime minister stay on in Bennelong? Will Janette tape a few prawn heads under the desk drawers of the prime ministerial den in Kirribilli on her way out?

In many ways, however, it's more interesting to look at what will happen if the government wins, and the prime minister is forced to inhabit the lumpy federal landscape he has spent the past few months building for himself. Think about it – at last count he has: his own personal hospital in Tasmania; several thousand new health administrators on local hospital boards, according to a recently announced proposal whose documentation amounts very precisely to one press release; a large stretch of the Northern Territory to administer; a referendum in eighteen months; a handover of power to his treasurer some time quite soon after that. (Why not just have an election then and there, and let the voters choose Costello if they want him?)

Every week, it seems, there's a new idea, bearing no critical relevance to its predecessor. It's a bit like watching a three-year-old building a pizza – 'ham AND cheese AND Smarties AND apple AND toothpaste AND olives AND ...' The result is, of course, interesting. But is it workable? And, to ask the crucial question that hovers invariably on the lips of campaign veterans: is it saleable?

In the world of campaign strategy, if we may step into it for a moment (and a weird, crepuscular little world it is too, lonely and littered with Styrofoam coffee-cups – hi, fellers!) the most important priority is what they call 'message'. Choosing a message, that is; making sure it's simple, making sure it's relevant, and making sure it's said over and over and over again by anybody who is allowed near a camera, until everyone is sick to death of it, and then saying it a couple of million times more.

This has always been a particular strength of the prime minister's. You'll easily remember some of his past triumphs; the way, for instance, during the 2004 election campaign, he demonstrated that there were very few questions on earth that could not be answered with the words, 'That brings me to the matter of interest rates.'

What is the big message this time? It's sort of about the economy and sort of about federalism, and sort of about being thankful for good fortune and not putting it at risk.

As of Wednesday night, it's sort of about reconciliation, too. Interestingly, the 'manifesto' Mr Howard handed out yesterday – a document he said was a summary of the government's achievements and aspirations – had no mention of the planned referendum, suggesting that the referendum itself was an extremely recent idea.

There are several ways of describing this kind of decision-making. If you were being optimistic, you'd call it front-foot, if you were being polite, you might call it ad hoc, and if you were being brutally honest, you'd call it panic. After all, Wednesday had been a relatively good day for the government, with historically low rates of unemployment announced; why distract from what should be a reminder of the government's successes?

Late in his prime ministerial term, Paul Keating is reported to have toyed – under pressure from advisers Don Watson and Don Russell – with the idea of a sharp lurch to the right to recapture the imagination of the Australian people. The plan was to have involved an announcement of stringent new measures to punish dole cheats; it was abandoned in the end, on the grounds that it was just too late to change tack.

But the 1996 campaign subsequently run by Keating and Labor remains as one of the great political parables about loss of touch, panic and division between a party leader and his campaign apparatus. It was during this time that Keating gained the nickname Captain Wacky, courtesy of the then Labor national secretary, Gary Gray.

There is more than a touch of the Captain Wackies about our prime minister at the moment. And there is little doubt that if Captain Wacky is indeed riding again, he is riding alone; the prime minister's principal teammate, Peter Costello, was nowhere near the decision about the government's new direction on reconciliation. When asked at his news conference yesterday why he had not included Costello in his formulation of the new referendum policy, Howard was silent for several seconds before venturing: 'Well, I had no reason to believe that he wouldn't agree with what I had to say.'

Perhaps the treasurer is better off out of it.

13 October 2007

IT'S A LOVE TRIANGLE, IF A LITTLE OBLIQUE

Finally – the tension unbearable – Mr Howard called the election.

Dressed neatly in dark suits, hair brushed and glasses polished, John Howard and Kevin Rudd went a-courting yesterday.

Both sought the hand of the Australian electorate in democratic union.

Both wore blue ties.

The similarities ended there, pretty much.

Mr Howard, who went first, seemed nervous initially and plagued by the fluffy birch pollen floating through the brilliant Canberra day. He choked up suddenly on mention of the Australian health system, sounding temporarily as if he were in quite urgent need of it. But on recovering, he made his suit a startlingly unambitious one. Never was an aspiring bridegroom quite so relaxed about the possibility of inspiring revulsion in the breast of his intended.

'Love me or loathe me, the Australian people know where I stand on all the major issues', he declared.

Fair enough. When the *Herald*/Nielsen poll has your disapproval rate at 44 per cent, you probably do need to start addressing the loathers directly.

Mr Howard's pitch was all about comfort and predictability, a classic marriage of convenience; everyone would have a job, and not much would change. Paraphrased, it would sound something like this: 'You know me, and I know you. We're neither of us spring chickens. Let's settle for each other and get the house paid off, shall we?'

In Brisbane, meanwhile, Kevin Rudd was offering something quite different. Life with Mr Rudd would be a whirl of activity, we were invited to conclude; every day there would be a new adventure, what with Kyoto protocols to sign, industrial relations changes to reverse, education revolutions to have, and broadband infrastructure to build together.

It would be a marriage of passion – passion about education, passion about Australia's future, even passion about Queensland, to which a slightly carried-away Mr Rudd confessed at one point as he warmed to his theme.

The road ahead would be full of laughter and tears, shared together. Kevin would come home every night with a big bunch of fresh ideas for the vase in the hallway. As for the mortgage? Well, we'd get by somehow.

Mr Rudd had taken the step of preparing a special backdrop for his proposal, with 'New Leadership' printed all over it. In case anyone missed the reference, he also mentioned 'new leadership' seventeen times during his remarks.

Mr Howard, having no doubt got wind of Mr Rudd's campaign slogan, offered a dry dismissal of it. '[Australia] does not need new leadership. It does not need old leadership. It needs the right leadership', he said.

Mr Howard spent some time canvassing the shortcomings of his rival. His inexperience and lack of prospects, for example, not to mention his questionable friends in the union movement.

Youth and vision and 'fresh ideas' might be well and good, he all but sniffed, but they don't pay the bills.

15 October 2007

ANSWERS? THAT'S OUT OF THE QUESTION

The Opposition leader's penchant for interrogating himself quickly became a nationally recognised phenomenon.

Kevin Rudd went to south-western Sydney yesterday, to visit Ingleburn Gardens Estate in the federal electorate of Werriwa. Or at least, the patch of earth where Ingleburn Gardens Estate will one day be.

The estate, at this stage, consists of a roundabout, a hole, two lamp-posts and a Bobcat, perched on a bare and sun-blasted rise overlooking the M5. As we disembarked from our bus and watched it drive away, it became clear just how exposed Ingleburn Gardens Estate is from a military point of view; any sharpshooter, concealed in the shrubs at the foot of the rise, would have little difficulty in picking off a pack of blundering fools like us. Already half-crazed by the relentless sun, reporters peered nervously about.

However, the moment passed; Rudd arrived, in his white car, and strode briskly across the baking earth to marvel at the roundabout, the hole, and ultimately the Bobcat.

A lush green paper plan of the Ingleburn Gardens Estate was unfurled for Rudd to admire; your reporter briefly considered, then decided against, diving headlong into the foot-square patch of blessed shade it provided. It was a relief when the whole shebang moved into a stand of low gums, for what sentimentalists within the Rudd camp still term a 'press conference'.

A Rudd press conference is generally an event at which the Opposition leader avoids everybody's questions apart from his own. It starts off sensibly enough, with journalists asking the questions and Rudd – talentedly, articulately and at considerable length – failing to answer them. But after a while he starts dealing a few light self-interrogatories into the mix.

'Am I an economic conservative? Yes. Do I support tax cuts wherever it's fiscally responsible to deliver them? You bet.' Et cetera.

Part of me wants to hang back and see if Rudd is just softening himself up with these questions. Maybe he is lulling himself into a false sense of security – the old rope-a-dope. Maybe if we just leave him to it, his line of self-questioning will get tougher.

'So where do I get off announcing that a Labor government might release more Commonwealth land to ease the housing affordability crisis, seeing as when Peter Costello said the same thing three months ago I accused him of missing the point?

'What do I mean, I don't have an opinion on the government's tax cuts yet? In what universe does it take a bilingual man of above average intelligence with dozens of staff more than twenty-four hours to peruse a Treasury document of 275 pages, most of which is padding? Who cut my hair, anyway – the council?'

At this, perhaps, he would finally snap.

'Right, Rudd – now you've gone too far. You can bloody well leave this press conference, and you can take your smart-arse line of questioning with you.'

If he succeeds it is fair to assume that Rudd will ultimately do all journalists out of a job. We should probably call the union.

17 October 2007

TAXING TIMES FOR POOR RUDD

Imminent political Armageddon can inspire substantial recklessness in otherwise cautious politicians, and Mr Howard wasted no time in announcing $34 billion in tax cuts. Mr Rudd kept his powder dry.

Policy nudity is not a comfortable state for any politician.

So imagine what it must be costing Kevin Rudd in sheer willpower to head out every day, tax-wise, with barely a stitch on.

Day after day, he's asked in a dozen different ways – politely, brusquely, by journalists, by talkback callers, by hecklers in the street – about his lack of a tax policy.

The prime minister, thanks to the early blowing of his entire $34 billion wardrobe allowance, is far from naked. He is clothed, and gorgeously so. A five-cent cut to the top two tax rates over five years – in tax policy terms, Howard is kitted out like Marie Antoinette. His rich brocades are the talk of the financial district; the extravagant cut of his train and the height of his pompadour alone are enough to send the Reserve Bank governor to bed for a week with palpitations.

And what does shivering Rudd have by way of a fig leaf? A $15 million policy to halve the withholding tax on distributions from Australian managed funds to non-residents.

Barely enough to cover the knackers, the poor poltroon. Especially when you consider the policy's beneficiaries, being offshore, cannot even express their gratitude in an electorally useful fashion.

So how does he do it, day after day?

Rudd's penchant for uncomfortable closeness to the PM (shoulder to shoulder and in lock-step – ouch!) must be a hellishly hard habit to kick. Every fibre of his being, every nerve and sinew, must surely be shrieking 'ME TOO! ME TOO! ME TOO!'

How he must yearn for Howard's policy robes; to clothe his goose-pimpled form in a few spare folds of velvet and snuffle about companionably in the reassuring costliness of it all.

But today's *Herald*/Nielsen poll tends to suggest he is right to hold out. As long as the 85 per cent of voters who say they're unswayed by the PM's tax cuts are telling the truth, it suggests Rudd has done himself no harm by going bare.

As a matter of fact, Rudd has a long way to go before he becomes the most egregious tax policy nudist in the past fifteen years of federal politics. In 2001 Kim Beazley waited until day fourteen to release his GST 'rollback' package; Mark Latham delivered his tax goodies on day nine in 2004.

But line honours in this department belong to John Howard himself, who streaked bare-arsed for a magnificent twenty-two full days of the 1996 campaign in the face of a constant shellacking from the prime minister, Paul Keating.

'What he's wanted me to do is run my campaign to suit him, and because I won't, it really is getting under his skin', sniffed Howard in response, way back then.

In the intervening eleven years, Howard has had an opportunity to think again, and he now tends rather to see Keating's point.

But Rudd will simply continue to do the best a naked man can in such circumstances: act nonchalant, avoid thorny shrubs, and try to change the subject.

19 October 2007

ALL IN THE FAMILY

When the Labor policy came, it was a cheeky affair which kept all of the Coalition's tax cuts except those for the very rich, which were hived off for tax breaks on books, computers and broadband for school kids. The treasurer, Mr Costello, was incredibly cross about it all.

It is never difficult to picture what Kevin Rudd must have been like as a schoolboy, but yesterday it was especially easy.

As he took his tax plan to the blackboard, with deputy milk monitor Swan at his side, we marvelled at the crispness of his shorts, the neatness of his parting and the smear-free state of his glasses, and realised anew that the Labor leader has in all likelihood been in rolling campaign mode ever since the age of five.

Good news! Money was to be ripped off the rich kids, and spent on stuff for the rest of the class.

It turned out that there is something for everyone in Kevin's tax plan.

Publicly funded books, computers and high-speed internet for the kids.

Tax cuts for Mum.

Granny, quite inexplicably, comes out of it with a new hip.

And just like a Hi-5 DVD, there is a secret appeal to red-blooded dads; after the kids are in bed, Jack and Briony's educational online superhighway becomes a high-speed porn pipe, subsidised to the tune of 50 per cent by the taxpayer. Hooray!

The talk was all impeccably modern; of futures, and bridging the digital divide (at one point, Kevin rashly pledged to 'wire' 2.3 million children, which must have made their parents flinch a little).

Kevin and Wayne had even prepared a little display to go with their presentation. Beside them was a table, piled high with illustrative educational tools. Perhaps they were rushed; the computer looked as though it had been rescued from a Parliament House skip, and the copy of *To Kill a Mockingbird* seemed to have had a few owners.

'This is the toolbox of the twenty-first century!' cried Kevin with passion, as he scooped up a laptop that looked – frankly – more like an artificial reef from the twentieth.

But he was so excited as he waved it and did his little laptop dance (where did he learn that?) that you could easily forgive him.

Indeed, everything was going incredibly well until the original owner of the policy turned up – Big Pete Costello, from Grade 7.

Jug-eared Pete, who holds down a part-time job as the school bully, pointed out with some asperity at his subsequent press conference that the Kevin and Wayne plan was in fact 91.5 per cent the same as his, only with Liquid Paper over the tax cuts for the rich, and a few extra bits pencilled in.

'Mr Rudd talks about education – if he'd have brought his exam paper in after copying 91.5 per cent of the answers from the student sitting next to him, he would have got an F for fail', said Pete, in the low, considered, menacing tone he keeps for occasions of special brutality.

Kevin and Wayne remain unbowed. They believe that there is authority in numbers, and if they can get more than 50 per cent of the class onside, they're going to go around to Big Pete's place and flatten his tax scales.

20 October 2007

THE WORM TURNS

The televised debate between the two leaders – an event traditionally preceded by much chest-beating and horse-trading about lectern height, choice of moderator and sundry other details – was hijacked by the Nine Network's unauthorised use of an audience response mechanism known affectionately as 'The Worm'.

In defiance of John Howard the Worm made a startling return to political discourse last night.

In the process the controversial creature survived two serious attempts on its life: the Nine Network's live coverage was cut twice when it became clear the network was planning to 'Worm' the entire debate live, in defiance of instructions. Nine foiled both attacks, eventually taking its signal from Sky News.

And viewers who chose Nine's coverage over that of the ABC or the debate's official host, Sky News, witnessed clearly why the prime minister wanted the Worm to stay buried. As the debate wore on, Worm-operating voters generally registered either neutral reactions to Mr Howard, or strayed into clearly negative territory. Kevin Rudd's Worm line, in contrast, was at home above the neutral line and often soared to the top of the satisfaction chart.

Nine's decision to use the Worm on its live broadcast was made without warning to either party, but it was twenty-five minutes into the debate before action was taken. Nine's direct feed was cut at about 7.55 p.m., but it switched to a back-up feed from the ABC. Viewers barely noticed. The Worm still turned.

Ten minutes later the back-up feed was cut. Nine did not blink. It instantly rebroadcast the Sky coverage, adding the Worm once more. It was a breach of conditions laid down by the Coalition, but the network was unrepentant.

'So much for free speech in Australia', the program's host, Ray Martin, said on air.

It appeared it was the National Press Club, as debate organiser, that tried to pull the coverage, because Nine was in breach of an agreement. Nine's director of news and current affairs, John Westacott, said, 'I think it's an editorial decision for the Nine Network, not for the leader of the Liberal Party, what we put to air. I can only agree with [News Limited chairman] John Hartigan in his excellent Andrew Olle lecture where he said that political interference in journalism is increasing, not diminishing ... this is a perfect example – the leader of the Liberal Party trying to dictate one of the key events in the election campaign.'

Nine enlisted ninety uncommitted voters to rate the debate from the network's Willoughby studios. Asked for a final verdict, 65 per cent said the debate had been won by Mr Rudd, 29 per cent by Mr Howard and 6 per cent were undecided.

The Worm appeared to be particularly critical of Mr Howard when industrial relations was discussed and did not take kindly to the reminder of Mr Howard's succession plan for his next term in government. But Mr Howard appeared to make some ground in a surprising area, enjoying a surge of approval from the Worm when he spoke in positive terms about the government's plans to take action on climate change. Mr Rudd also enjoyed strong approval on climate change.

In general, audience response was strongest when either combatant spoke positively. A lengthy period of inertia during a discussion of macroeconomic policy suggested that the Worm found practical, domestic matters more interesting.

The Worm – a controversial beast generated by undecided voters twiddling dials – made its first appearance in 1993, when Paul Keating debated John Hewson. That was the only other time it has been broadcast live while the debate proceeded.

Both sides of politics have criticised the live broadcast of the Worm in the past on the grounds that it distracts viewers from what is being said. When the Worm expresses a clear opinion it sticks in the public mind. Its plunge during the 2001 debate when Mr Howard mentioned the GST is one of the most famous moments in Worm history.

But the Worm has a poor record for picking elections. It awarded the debates of 1998 and 2001 to Kim Beazley by big margins, and the 2004 debate to Mark Latham. In each case the Worm thrived in the campaign but ate dirt on election day.

22 October 2007

WARNING: FOCUS GROUPS ARE ADDICTIVE

All politicians rely to some extent on focus groups. Why not? It's the simplest and most effective way to gauge popular opinion; you get your pollster to pay a bunch of folk fifty bucks each to sit in a room with some limp sandwiches and say what they think of you. You never have to meet them and they never know it's you who's asking.

At first it's an experimental thing; you might convene a series of focus groups to help sharpen your plans for transport reform, or healthcare. After a while, though, focus groups can get addictive. When things are going well they're like an organised series of overheard compliments, and who doesn't like to hear that stuff?

When tough times come, the urge gets worse; it becomes a nasty, scratching compulsion as you comb through them over and over, desperately scanning the transcripts for the seeds of salvation.

The prime minister had some strong words to say about focus groups on Tuesday, during an interview with 2GB's Ray Hadley.

'There's one thing I will not do is, I'm not going to sit down with a focus group and work out what I've got to say', John Howard said. 'I've always said what I believe. Sometimes your listeners have agreed with me, sometimes they've violently disagreed with me. But they know what I stand for, they know what I believe in, they know what kind of Australia I want and I'm not going to muck around with focus groups and body-language experts and gurus and all these other things ...'

Now there are many nice things that can be said about the prime minister. He is courteous, in the main. He is an excellent father, by all accounts. He knows how to hug.

But his above statement is not true. In fact, 'not true' is far too pedestrian a descriptor. It is gloriously, demonstrably, hilariously, chest-beatingly, somersault-turningly, sky-writingly, floor-rollingly, operatically untrue.

Imagine Kevin Rudd saying, 'Do you know what? If there's one thing I can't stand, it's a rhetorical question', and you'll get an idea of just how risible such a claim is, coming from John Howard.

The prime minister, bless him, is a focus-group junkie. And, like many junkies, he denies that he has a problem. But evidence of the habit is everywhere; like residue-clogged teaspoons, his own words are strewn all around in eloquent self-accusation.

Let's look at the very first words of that self-same interview, for example, with fond Ray Hadley. Hadley asks him if the Worm-infested leaders' debate served any purpose.

Howard replies: 'Yes, I think it enabled ... speaking for myself, it enabled me to get across the point that, if you elect a Labor government, 70 per cent of the ministry will be former trade union officials.'

Righto.

At his press conference on Monday he was asked four different questions about the debate, and his reply to each was to recite the same stagy answer. To those of you who do not have the privilege of regular attendance at prime ministerial press conferences, this manic repetition would sound like evidence of an entry-level mental disorder. But for those in the trade, it's routine; the prime minister has been advised to hammer home the message that Labor equals Union Thuggery, and he is doing just that.

Mark Textor is Howard's pollster, his focus group operator, his guru – hell, let's just be straight and call him Howard's dealer. In August one of his reports was leaked. It contained a frank warning of impending doom, with some urgent pieces of advice for the Liberal Party on how to avert it.

First, Textor said, the party needed to 'refocus on comparing team strengths, and on highlighting Rudd's inexperience and influences (unions, left factions and state parliaments)'. Hence the PM's mantra about Labor's front bench.

The second directive was to 'stress absolute and issue-linked importance of economic management, international relations and defence (Coalition strengths) and risks posed by Labor'. This would explain the campaign slogan 'Strong, prosperous and secure'.

The third? 'Emphasise that Commonwealth is "bailing out" ineffective and inefficient states.'

Ladies and gentlemen, I give you in response: the invasion of the Northern Territory, the take-over of the Mersey Hospital, the plebiscites on Queensland local government amalgamations, and a giant wodge of road funding, the latest being $400 million for the impoverished souls of Western Australia.

Not going to muck around with focus groups? Pull the other one.

27 October 2007

WHO GIVES A TOSS? WE'RE ALL HOOKED ON THE WORM

The two wannabe treasurers, Peter Costello and Wayne Swan, met at the National Press Club for their own debate.

We knew the Great Treasurers' Debate was in trouble when the coin-toss went awry.

The host, Ken Randall, lobbed the coin competently skyward, but bungled the re-entry as Peter Costello and Wayne Swan looked on, bemused, and the coin skittered away under a table.

'Terrific', voters may well have thought to themselves as all three men scouted earnestly about for the rogue goldie. Two potential treasurers in the forty-second Parliament of Australia, and they've already lost the only piece of actual money in the immediate vicinity.

Order was swiftly restored, however. The coin was recovered, and Swan opened the batting.

The Worm was back by multilateral invitation, in a powerful demonstration of the maxim that there is nothing quite so restorative for one's political image as an assassination attempt.

Tony Abbott's long-term political suspicions about the Worm seemed about to be justified when the wily nematode swarmed immediately up the thigh of the shadow treasurer as he discussed the importance of training. But five minutes later, it was equally enthusiastic about Mr Costello's thoughts on climate change.

We learned a lot about the Worm's personal tastes yesterday. It vaguely fancies, for instance, a full review of appointments to the Reserve Bank board. It likes to hear about automotive manufacturing from Mr Swan, but not from Mr Costello. It maintains a stern lack of interest in pure macroeconomic policy debate.

About twenty-five minutes in, the Worm dozed off during a discussion about the real causes of inflation and a rumour whipped around the *Herald* newsroom that Channel Nine was about to cut its own feed.

Love, fortuitously, intervened and brought everything back to life. Mr Costello had evidently received some pre-debate coaching from Marcia Hines in the art of finding something nice to say about everybody. Gone was his ordinarily combative demeanour. The treasurer is normally very cruel indeed to Mr Swan whenever he gets the chance, but yesterday he was all sweetness and light, suggesting that late conversions to the symbolism of reconciliation are not just for the owner-driver of Kirribilli's most famous eyebrows.

'I'll give credit to the Keating government for the things it got right', Mr Costello offered, silkily.

In an ideal world, the next question would have been: 'Who are you, sir? And what on earth have you done with the treasurer?' But the Worm, that sentimental fool, sensed the love in the air and arched like a stroked cat.

Mr Swan responded awkwardly that he was 'happy to give you credit for your medium-term fiscal strategy'. The Worm arched once more, then reclined – presumably to enjoy a languid cigarette.

Love was the winner.

31 October 2007

SUDDENLY SQUEAKY-CLEAN KEVIN IS A BIT ON THE NOSE

A hideous piece of footage from the Opposition leader's past became a cult destination on YouTube.

We need to talk about Kevin.

Specifically, that incident six years ago that barely anyone noticed at the time, but has since become something of a YouTube phenomenon.

Ladies and gentlemen, there is no way to discuss this comfortably; most of us were hoping to avoid it, I imagine.

But the US talk-show host Jay Leno has aired the footage.

The *Washington Post* has canvassed it in print.

And upwards of 400,000 people have caught it, fascinatedly, on YouTube.

I speak, of course, of ear wax; of Mr Rudd's quest for nourishment from his own left aural canal during a speech, all those years ago, by Labor colleague Anthony Albanese, the grainy footage of which is now so widely viewed that it is probably in the running for a Logie.

Many have snickeringly circulated it; at Mr Rudd's media conference yesterday one journalist made so bold as to ask him about it.

Mr Rudd, when caught out in an act of shamelessness, has quite an endearing automatic response – he grins. And it now seems that the grin also works in situations of irretrievable social agony.

'That's great!' he exclaimed gaily at the news that his exploits had reached the attention of Leno in America. 'I'm really pleased about that – how did I go?' After several further seconds of bravado, however, he conceded: 'All of us in public and private life would wish our behaviour to be more ideal.'

Well, yes.

But the horrifying and sudden implication of the YouTube phenomenon is that this observation is no longer a comfortably academic one for politicians, or indeed public figures of any kind. Thirty seconds of footage – shot years ago when you were tired or bored or overcome by the disorienting effects of an Albanese oration – now has the power to leap out and crash-tackle you without warning. In very precise terms, Mr Rudd has been upstaged by himself – younger, more owlish, and definitely a more adventurous eater.

No wonder viewers of the footage in question invariably crumple in dismay. Part of the brain thinks: 'Ear wax! Gross!' The other part thinks, horrified: 'Imagine if that happened to me.'

It's not much comfort, probably, but Mr Rudd is in reasonable company. The British prime minister, Gordon Brown, features in a popular YouTube video in which he is caught excavating his nose quite determinedly throughout a question time performance by Tony Blair. Much joy has also been had from a video purportedly of the former Italian prime minister Silvio Berlusconi doing the same thing, then washing down the proceeds with a short black coffee in the Continental style.

The video actually features a Berlusconi impersonator, a defence unfortunately not available to Mr Rudd who, from this day on, will carry a hanky.

1 November 2007

THIS ME-TOOISM IS GETTING OUT OF HAND

The two leaders circled and weaved, often nicking each other's policies in an attempt not to miss out on crucial votes. The net effect was often highly confusing, especially for innocent toddlers caught in the middle of it all.

Meet Austin.

At just fourteen months, he is the innocent victim of this 'me-too' election campaign.

Little tackers like Austin, even when they are adorable and live in marginal seats, generally go into federal elections with at least a fighting chance of escaping political embrace. This, however, is 'me-too' year, so yesterday poor Austin was cuddled twice – first by John Howard at 1.21 p.m, then by Kevin Rudd at 3.29 p.m.

Austin's only crime was to venture into Erina for a spot of shopping in the care of his mother, Brooke Byrnes. Little did the pair know that Erina Fair shopping centre was shortly to be the scene of a political walk-off between the prime minister and his challenger, Kevin Rudd, both of whom chose to campaign in the Central Coast seat of Robertson.

'Yeah, it was a bit of a surprise to see the prime minister', Byrnes acknowledged. 'And when the other one turned up, I thought it was John back again with all the cameras around, but it was Kevin Rudd!'

Byrnes reported that both leaders were 'quite nice', but that Rudd was 'more personable in his manner'.

And who would win her vote?

'Probably Kevin'.

It should be noted that Rudd pork-barrelled the pair personally with the gift of three juicy mangoes, while Howard offered nothing more than a quick cuddle and ongoing responsible economic management.

The presence of both leaders in Robertson gives a strong indication of what both parties are learning through private polling. Robertson is held by the Liberals' Jim Lloyd on a margin of 6.9 per cent, but is now viewed as in peril from the advancing Labor hordes.

Howard visited Erina Fair with Lloyd and Lloyd's electoral neighbour Ken Ticehurst, the member for Dobell. The prime minister in a shopping centre is a fearsome sight. Like a shark, he is fast, relentless and perpetually in motion. Lloyd and Ticehurst, despite being on home ground, were no match for him; they bobbed in his wake like fishing lures from an accidentally swallowed angler as the PM shook hands, hugged youths, patted the elderly, signed plaster casts and waved brightly into shops.

'Don't forget Jimmy on the twenty-fourth!' Howard repeated like a mantra, and was so enthusiastic that he at one point demanded of an innocent lady: 'Do you know Tine Keshurst?' The matter was quickly cleared up, with no damage done to Ticehurst, who on 4.8 per cent has other things to worry about in any event.

Janette Howard, looking very trim in a pink jacket and trousers, demonstrated her own proficiency in this field, sometimes driving prey directly into the path of her husband, sometimes diplomatically consoling those who did not catch the prime ministerial eye.

When Rudd arrived at Erina Fair he was also accompanied by his spouse and his candidates for Robertson and Dobell, Belinda Neal and Craig Thomson. The two leaders did not cross paths, but a Labor campaign bus featuring eight-foot mugshots of Neal (a former senator) and Rudd did menace the prime ministerial motorcade as it gunned away.

Rudd's shopping-centre style is quite different from that of his rival. If Howard is a shark, the Labor leader may well be a grouper – rather than moving constantly, Rudd will stop and deforest an entire head of coral before cruising off again. On meeting Howard, a member of the public might expect a handshake, a quick 'How are you?', then a cordial and more or less immediate goodbye. Rudd is more likely to subject shoppers to an extensive discussion of Labor policy.

As a result, he covers less ground, but he has made up for this by visiting more shopping centres so far in this campaign. The Labor leader's right hand tells an epic story; it is grazed between the thumb and forefinger from the friction of a thousand and one shopping-centre handshakes.

It is an impressive injury. Perhaps the prime minister will get one, too.

6 November 2007

THEIR OWN BIG HEFFALUMP TRAP

John Howard and Peter Costello won the 2004 election campaign decisively with their terrifying talk of higher interest rates under Labor. Sod's Law, assisted by the Reserve Bank, ensured that the 2007 campaign found interest rates at uncomfortably high levels, with a rate hike announced just weeks from polling day.

It was reckless talk from Christopher Robin about Heffalumps – those terrifying, shambling creatures – that first planted the idea for Pooh and Piglet.

They would build a Heffalump trap!

You may be familiar with the story; the intrepid pair dig a Very Deep Pit in the woods, in the hope of ensnaring the fabled beast through sheer cunning.

'Pooh rubbed his nose with his paw, and said that the Heffalump might be walking along, humming a little song, and looking up at the sky, wondering if it would rain, and so he wouldn't see the Very Deep Pit until he was halfway down, when it would be too late.'

Pooh and Piglet's Heffalump trap was baited with honey, which was a very clever choice of bait. And it was cunningly disguised, so as to take the fearsome Heffalump completely unawares. In fact, it was such a brilliant trap that after a while Pooh and Piglet forgot they had even built it, which was around about the point at which they both fell into it.

Three years ago in Australia, another pair of adventurers came up with a similar sort of trap. One of the adventurers was shortish, with eyebrows of a beetling type, and the other tallish and loudish and sort of pleasingly treasurer-shaped. Unlike poor Pooh, both of them had quite big brains. And they spent quite a bit of time building their Heffalump trap.

The pit they built was deep and terrifying, with steep, scrabbly sides and a bottom that was so deep you could yell 'Who do you trust?' into it and all you would hear back, after a few minutes, was '… rust?' It was so big, in fact, that people worried their whole houses might fall into it.

In 2004, it even worked. It caught a Large Shambling Latham, who was walking along, swearing a little bit under his breath and thinking mean thoughts about the president of the United States when he fell into the Heffalump trap with a crash, and was barely heard from again.

But the thing about Heffalump traps is that they don't go away.

And if you've been especially clever, and your Heffalump trap is especially cunning and well disguised and temptingly baited, then there might come a day when you are wandering through the woods, humming a little tune and thinking about honey, when suddenly you step on a piece of the Forest which has been left out by mistake, and you find yourself … in the bottom of your own Heffalump trap.

Which is where our two adventurers found themselves yesterday.

With apologies to A.A. Milne and the *Spectator.*

8 November 2007

SORRY'S STILL THE HARDEST WORD

Asked to apologise to the nation for interest-rate rises, Mr Howard employed a familiar formula.

Once again the nation has found itself in the middle of a prime ministerially led semiotics tutorial about the concept of remorse.

Mr Howard is sorry that interest rates have risen. That is, he regrets it as one would regret the rain that falls on a birthday picnic, or an ice-cream that drops on the ground before anyone's had the chance of a lick.

That is not to say the prime minister is apologising, he is swift to point out. He did not cause the rates to rise, just as he does not cause rain to fall, and nor did he author the laws of physics that occasionally cause unexpected things to happen to newly purchased ice-creams.

And in his national case for the defence, Mr Howard is not just relying on lawyerly fancy footwork; he has concrete items of evidence for the jury. He is not guilty of the rates offence for the following reasons. Exhibit A: the drought. Exhibit B: oil prices. Exhibit C: the strong economy.

It's an impassioned case he makes. But is he defending himself against the right charge? I mean, idly, one could readily be convinced that the prime minister is not personally responsible for the movements of interest rates. There seem to be quite a lot of factors that have a far greater influence than anything the prime minister could achieve by dint of garden variety competence or incompetence.

But all of these lend weight to the proposition that the prime minister should never have held himself out as being able to keep rates down. And isn't that the offence for which he is really being tried?

Let's go to another perspective on remorse, expressed yesterday by another news figure of the moment: Britney Spears's mother, Lynne. 'I blame myself – what mother wouldn't?' she says of her hard-living daughter's travails.

This sounds dangerously like an admission of culpability, on the Howard analysis. But Spears demonstrates quite niftily with her next breath that even overt self-blame does not necessarily imply guilt, as long as the excuse is good enough. 'I wish I'd been there more while she was touring', she told *Life & Style*. 'But I couldn't be. I had the other kids to look after.'

One is reminded of E.M. Forster's fussy Charlotte Bartlett, who is constantly declaring 'I shall never forgive myself!' until tartly reminded by Lucy Honeychurch: 'You always say that, Charlotte. And then you always do forgive yourself.'

For the closest Australian political analogy to the Spears/Bartlett approach, we really need to head north, to the work of former Queensland premier Peter Beattie, the successful parts of whose career were spent in an ecstasy of cheerful self-criticism. Mr Beattie's approach, in times of rottenness in the party structure or dreadful failings in the Queensland health system, was always: 'Blame me. Blame me, but love me anyway!' Perhaps the prime minister should try it.

9 November 2007

FOR GRANDMA READ INTEREST RATES, THEN SPIN

The question of responsibility for interest-rate rises continued to dog the campaign. This column required dozens of pages of amateurish algebraic doodling, and several telephone conferences with the Sydney Morning Herald*'s endlessly patient and mathematically literate sub-editors. My apologies to them, and to actual mathematicians. I didn't make up the bit about the Mike Adams study, though, bless him.*

The American biology academic Mike Adams, in his seminal 1990 study of what is now widely known as Dead Grandmother Syndrome, identified a chilling trend among Connecticut families.

Using data gathered from his students over two decades, he discovered that the mortality rate for grandmothers went through extraordinary peaks that coincided freakishly with the exam periods of their grandchildren. In fact, he concluded that, regardless of age and physical condition, a grandmother was never in graver danger than when her college-age grandchild had a big examination or assignment drawing near.

Some grandmothers, he sensationally concluded, were so cripplingly afflicted by this syndrome that they died several times over the course of their descendants' academic careers.

This is why we have science, to draw order from chaos.

For some days now, I have been attempting to draw similar order from the chaotic state of the debate about interest rates. To what extent, exactly, are Australian governments responsible for interest-rate fluctuations?

I have listened faithfully to the words of the prime minister, who is, according to the polls, still the go-to man on economic management, and thus presumably more reliable on these matters than the young pup from Queensland. What the prime minister identifies is a fascinating phenomenon.

Let's express governmental responsibility for interest rates as a percentage; call it *n*. As we look back at the past few decades, we find that *n* increases proportionately with interest rates when Labor is in office. But when the Coalition is in office, the exact opposite occurs; in fact, the lower rates fall under a Coalition government, the stronger the government's central role becomes, and as they start to rise, the level of responsibility drops away.

It really is quite puzzling.

In the interest of structured thought, I have devised a rough formula which, I think, makes the whole thing very clear.

It is: $100 - [(a/b)/r \times 1000] = n$, where a is the number of seats held by the Coalition, b is the number of seats in the House of Representatives at the time, and r is the standard variable mortgage interest rate.

If you take my little formula for a spin, you will find, for example, that in 1982, when John Howard was treasurer and the Coalition held 74 of the 125 Reps seats, mortgage rates peaked at 13.5 per cent but the government's responsibility for this surge was quite low, at just 56 per cent.

Seven years later, however, it was quite a different story. The Coalition, then in Opposition, held 62 seats out of 148, so when rates hit a high of 17 per cent, the government responsibility rating was appreciably higher, at 75 per cent.

The formula is imperfect, I suspect, but it's the best I could do in the limited period for which I could remain conscious while considering these matters.

Order from chaos. That's the ticket.

10 November 2007

DID THE KISS WAKE HIM, OR THE SMELL OF PORK?

Just before the 2007 election campaign began, John Howard became a grandfather. It was a joyful event for Mr Howard, who gained a grandson, Angus. And it was a joyful event for Mr Rudd, who gained a whole new way of reminding voters that Mr Howard wasn't getting any younger.

Of the 1700 people who piled into the Queensland Performing Arts Centre yesterday, we know of only one who had definitely never seen a John Howard campaign launch before. That young man was Angus Benjamin Howard McDonald, who is only eleven weeks old but already enjoys some considerable advantages of birth.

It is not just that he is the prime minister's only grandchild; he is also, by virtue of his age, the beneficiary of most of the new policies his granddad announced yesterday. Angus arrived at 12.25 p.m. in a blue bunny rug, and was able to catch the big-screen video presentation in which messages of calm authority from various cabinet ministers (remember the Coalition's strong team!) were interspersed with shy observations from miners, farmers and other such horny-handed sons of toil (definitely not out of touch or anything like that).

Nestled sweetly in the arms of his mother, Melanie, Angus remained calm as the lord mayor of Brisbane, Campbell Newman, bounded out on stage to give the Queensland Labor government a brief savaging. Perhaps Angus was reflecting on the fact that Newman may be only twelve days away from greatness; after all, if Granddad is defeated on 24 November, Newman would become the country's highest Liberal office-holder.

Signs of distress from within the folds of the bunny rug only became apparent after Peter Costello took the microphone and began enumerating the dire threats that lay in wait for the unsuspecting public. The oil crisis, the drought, the collapse of the US subprime lending market; Angus began to squeak audibly, and by the time the treasurer had got around to speculating on what might happen to this economic powder-keg should Rudd, Swan and Gillard ever get near it with a match, no amount of jiggling on Melanie's part could quell the boy's cries.

Fortunately, the next speaker was Mark Vaile. It is virtually impossible to remain awake during a Vaile speech even if you are an adult who has just drunk two cups of coffee (as your correspondent did, knowing the deputy PM was on the bill). Angus, therefore, never stood a chance; he was immediately subdued by Vaile's powers and appeared to slumber peacefully through the rest of the deputy PM's oration, through the tumult of applause that accompanied the arrival of the prime minister, through the spectacle of Janette Howard kissing both the treasurer and Tanya Costello, and through the first twenty minutes of Howard's speech.

Angus has clearly inherited some of his grandfather's innate cunning. Some people can go to two or three Coalition campaign launches before they work out that they are much more fun if you nap through the National Party leader's speech and the first half of the prime minister's.

Like a hardened marginal-seat voter, the child was only revived in the end by the whiff of pork. And luckily, almost all of the pork was for Angus and his fellow young Australians.

Sounds of excitement were detected as Granddad announced simplified childcare payments and more childcare places; when he got on to tax-free savings accounts, Angus was briefly overcome and had to be removed from the front row by Melanie until he calmed down sufficiently to return and hear about the $6 billion Granddad was planning to spend on school uniforms, fees, school camps and musical instruments (should Angus turn out to be that way inclined).

What die will be cast for Angus on 24 November, when voters go to the polls to pronounce their verdict on his grandfather? Costello, during a moment of abandon in his speech, declared that 'millions of Australians' lives depend upon that choice!' This may have been something of an exaggeration, but it must feel that way to the Howards, whose lives have been defined by politics for so long.

The good news for Angus is that if Granddad wins, he'll get extra cash for education expenses, a tax-free savings account and a marginally enhanced chance of a childcare spot. If Granddad loses, he'll get a full-time granddad.

13 November 2007

ADDICTION OUT OF THE QUESTION

Something very odd is going on with Kevin Rudd. Through an almighty act of will power, he has stopped asking himself questions.

Rudd press conferences used to be a battle of wills, as journalists lunged and thrust to get questions through the barely perceptible pauses in the Labor leader's relentless self-interrogatory. But now, apart from the occasional 'You know what?', he seems to have kicked the habit.

Mr Rudd's struggle to control his urges in this department will be more than familiar to anyone who has given up smoking and remembers that siren call of addiction, or still feels that glad leap of recognition deep within the treacherous nervous system when someone nearby lights up. At the pub, Kevin has only to overhear a drinker demanding in the course of a conversation 'Do I look like I'm kidding?' for that familiar itch to set in.

But he is being strong. Who knows what technique he is using to quell this powerful urge? Perhaps each morning, before he leaves his hotel room, he takes a deep breath, locks eyes with his reflection in the mirror and interrogates himself for twenty minutes, visiting every topic about which he could possibly ask himself something so as to exhaust the compulsion for the rest of the day.

Perhaps he's just going plain cold turkey – an exercise in white-lipped restraint. Or perhaps he has a sponsor – someone who's been there before, and can talk him down over the phone.

Is there a gum or a patch you can get to help with the self-questioning addiction? We must hope so, if only for the sake of his poor family, who must doubtless feel the brunt of the recovering addict's fraying temper.

Self-questioning is not the only vice of which Mr Rudd has divested himself in recent weeks. Have you noticed that he has also weaned himself off the inquiries? Weeks have gone by since the Labor leader last announced that he would establish a working party, task force, inquiry, peak body or statutory authority. Sure, he did indulge briefly on Monday in the promise of a defence white paper, but to be fair he had already announced that one some time ago, so it can hardly be counted as a relapse.

This is all part of the continuing and relentless self-moulding of the man who hopes to be prime minister come Saturday week. There is, one suspects, very little he would not renounce in order to get over the line.

14 November 2007

LABOR REPROGRAMS ITS RUDDBOT

The Labor launch took place two days after the Coalition's. With John Howard's promises of lavish spending still hanging in the air, the newly retooled Opposition leader took to his own podium and promised to give the masses ... bugger all. This capacity for unblinking reversal confirmed that Mr Rudd was not human at all, but a highly evolved android.

But wait! There's less!

It's difficult to think of anything weirder than a whole theatre full of Labor bleeding hearts cheering hysterically for a man who's just told them he's going to run a knife through social spending. But that's what happened yesterday. The meaner Kevin Rudd promised to be, the more they applauded.

When he defended the Reserve Bank, they murmured warmly; when he reminded the crowd 'I am an economic conservative' they clapped appreciatively; and when he promised not to give them money for their kids' school fees they went bananas. It's lucky Mr Rudd's handlers got him out of there before he started closing hospitals, or he might have been kissed to death. If there's one thing you can say about the Labor Party, it's that it continues to be full of surprises.

The speech itself was an oddly wooden affair, and the Labor leader seemed a little jerky and mechanised in his delivery. This is not an affliction that is exclusive to Mr Rudd, of course; if this election campaign has revealed anything, it is that the art of political oratory is dead in Australia and both John Howard and Kevin Rudd are helping the police with their inquiries. It does lend weight, though, to the developing theory that the Labor leader is, in fact, not a flesh-and-blood Queenslander at all, but a sophisticated humanoid Ruddbot.

Journalists were agog with curiosity yesterday when, having been escorted in practically at gunpoint by the overzealous security goons, we were informed that the launch would be starting forty minutes late. What was keeping Kevin Rudd? An early rumour was that he was waiting for the deputy prime minister, Mark Vaile, to finish his address over at the Press Club in Canberra, in case Vaile said anything interesting.

This theory was quickly discarded, owing to its obvious central flaw.

The real reason for the delay, unrevealed until now, is that there were urgent last-minute recalibrations to be made to the Ruddbot. While out in the theatre the crowd waited impatiently and youngsters in 'New Leadership' T-shirts killed time by gyrating to 'Groove Is in the Heart', the Ruddbot lay prone backstage with his back panel open, while sweating Labor technicians twiddled frantically with tiny screwdrivers to reset him from 'Spend' to 'Scrimp'.

It was a rush job, and there were certain glitches in the finished product as a result. The revamped Ruddbot seemed to be experiencing some problems with upper limb function, for example. When he finally appeared to the throb-throb-throb of a beefy instrumental, both arms hung awkwardly at his sides, and the most he could manage was an occasional shy mini-wave or point as the crowd howled out its welcome.

And one of the Labor technicians must have accidentally knocked his timing circuitry during their frantic re-tooling, because the Ruddbot sped up his delivery as he worked through the speech. By the time he got to the announcement of various 'education revolution' initiatives his pace was such that the terms 'pre-literacy' and 'pre-numeracy' suddenly seemed to have several fewer syllables than we would ordinarily assign them.

But the Ruddbot got all of his messages right. The line about the prime minister being out of touch, the fib about the government expanding Work Choices, the one about it being time for a change – the Ruddbot picked them off relentlessly, like Schwarzenegger gunning down cyborgs as the Terminator.

He is a fearsome piece of engineering, that Ruddbot. Let's hope no one switches him to 'Evil'.

15 November 2007

RED, PINK OR PUCE?

Meanwhile, Kevin Rudd's deputy leader, Julia Gillard, gave us a taste of the political killing machine she was on her way to becoming. In an interview with the ABC's Barrie Cassidy, she charmingly declined to answer any questions whatsoever.

Barrie Cassidy: Julia Gillard, welcome to *Insiders*. Would you describe your hair as red?

Gillard: (Laughs) Barrie, we could sit here all day talking about my hair. I'm just pleased I've got some. Let's leave it at that.

Cassidy: But it is red, isn't it?

Gillard: I can certainly confirm that John Howard doesn't have hair. And Australian working families have noticed that, believe me. And you certainly couldn't accuse Kevin (laughs) of baldness!

Cassidy: Yeah, but yours, it's red. Anyone can see that.

Gillard: Look, to be completely honest with you, I really haven't thought about it. And I really don't think it's the first thing on working families' minds when they get up in the morning and go to work, you know, 'What colour is Julia Gillard's hair?' That's if they're lucky enough not to have been sacked without notice overnight under John Howard's brutal Work Choices regime, of course.

Cassidy: OK, but have a look right now. (Presents hand mirror) What do you see?

Gillard: I see hair that is responsible, that has listened to Australian working families and has a plan for Australia's future. I see hair that is bursting with new ideas; hair that has worked closely with Kevin Rudd and respects the strong leadership he has brought to the Australian Labor Party. I see hair that is mature enough to understand that Australian working families just don't have time for arbitrary political labels like 'left', 'right', 'red' or 'brown'. I see hair that is economically conservative, and deeply attentive to the respected opinions of the Reserve Bank.

Cassidy: (Tearing own hair out) OK. Cut it out. Forget I asked.

The above exchange did not occur yesterday when Labor's deputy leader, Julia Gillard, appeared on the ABC's *Insiders* program in place of her boss, Kevin Rudd, who was prepping for Rove McManus instead. But it might as well have.

Ms Gillard is an exceptionally charming interviewee; she is courteous and clever, she makes jokes, and, for a woman who is no longer a socialist, she retains a certain Soviet capacity for staunch denial of the obvious.

Yesterday, she firmly refused to identify the Labor Party as a 'party of the left'. She refused to concede that the Labor Party's launch was 'delayed', despite the – some would say giveaway – fact that it commenced forty minutes after its advertised starting time. And she cheerfully defended Labor's increasingly not-very-revolutionary 'education revolution', saying nobody expected that a Labor government would be able to change the system overnight.

Listening to this exchange, your reporter was drawn into a reverie about what would happen if Ms Gillard were ever to revisit her 1980s job as the Australian Union of Students' helmswoman. Can you imagine the rallies she'd organise these days? Fearless and bloodcurdling marches on the administration block, demanding an incremental correction of past funding injustices.

You can almost hear their ragged cries. 'What do we want? GRADUAL CHANGE! When do we want it? IN DUE COURSE!' Or a contemporary reworking perhaps of that durable old favourite: 'Two! Four! Six! Eight! Yes, we are prepared to wait!'

In 1871 the American writer Oliver Wendell Holmes remarked that 'revolutions are not made by men in spectacles'. Prescient of him, considering that he spoke eighty-six years before Kevin Rudd was even born.

19 November 2007

FOR THE FAMILY'S SAKE

With the election less than a week away and polls indicating a deep scepticism about the Coalition's leadership succession plan, John Howard took recourse to a desperate measure. He agreed to a joint interview on the Seven Network's Today Tonight *with his deputy and treasurer, Peter Costello. And a horribly compelling piece of television it was, too.*

They've had their tantrums and squabbles; more than your average modern couple. But they've always stayed together for the sake of the economy, and last night John Howard and Peter Costello made a last, heartfelt bid to revive their relationship: televised couples counselling on *Today Tonight*.

Dressed with touching similarity in shirtsleeves and striped ties, the two men perched on gold velvet armchairs for their first joint session. The host, Anna Coren, asked them to say something nice about each other.

'Very high intelligence. A very good sense of humour. He'd make an excellent prime minister', began the prime minister.

Prompted to name the 'qualities, as a man' that he most admired in the prime minister, Mr Costello choked back what must have been a fierce urge to say 'inevitable mortality', and instead said, 'He has the most amazing work ethic that I have ever seen.'

Mr Howard said he thought Mr Costello would be elected unopposed to replace him.

Counselling is marvellous, isn't it? After an awkward beginning, the praise exchange soon began to do its miraculous work.

'I know when the phone rings at 6.30 a.m. that he's watched all of the TVs and read all of the newspapers and he's across all the issues', the treasurer offered, defrosting visibly.

'It's a pretty good marriage. It's lasted a long time!' piped the PM.

And all of a sudden, it was as if they had rediscovered their honeymoon selves, back in those long golden days of 1996 when it seemed that the good times would last for ever. Fond reminiscences, little jokes – they all came spilling out, higgledy-piggledy.

'Of course, real marriages have certain other attractions', honked the treasurer.

To which the prime minister responded with a remark about Mr Costello sometimes not liking some of his spending ideas, which is about as close to ribaldry as the PM gets.

'He likes Holdens and I like Fords. And he doesn't put the cap on the toothpaste', said the treasurer, getting carried away with the romance of the thing.

'He's seriously bright. I mean, he's seriously intelligent – and he's seriously funny', stroked Mr Howard, whereupon his partner stopped giggling and soberly avowed: 'You can't work together for eleven years without having respect, and respecting each other.'

At this point, a tasteful camera might have panned away briefly, so as to allow the couple the privacy of a tearful embrace. But Coren wasn't finished; she wanted to know if Mr Costello felt 'cheated', and whether it would all be going better if he had been given sole custody.

'There are some people who will think he's worse than me, and there are some who'll think I'm worse than him', was all he would concede. The shutters, suddenly, had slammed back down.

20 November 2007

SUCH A CUTE LITTLE PIGLET

Bursting with optimism and promise, the Opposition leader made his closing pitch at the National Press Club.

Opposition leaders are like miniature piglets.

They look so sweet in the shop, don't they? With their whiffling little pink noses and their eagerness to please; with their intelligent eyes and their loving natures and the sales assistant's guarantee that they are fastidiously clean and, moreover, will fetch the paper every morning – what's not to love?

It is only much later on, well after the election's won and the warranty's expired, that you wake up and realise, with a dull sense of unsurprise, that you've got a six-foot grunter digging up your backyard.

Kevin Rudd, at the Press Club yesterday, was adorable. He's planning to hold a press conference after every single cabinet meeting, bless him, and once a month they're going to be held in regional Australia.

In the tradition of *Babe*, Mr Rudd is a cheeky little fellow with big dreams, a new ministerial code of conduct, new rules restricting the amount governments can spend on advertising, new rules dictating when elections can be called. He's going to examine the role of the speaker, and strengthen the role of parliamentary committees. He's going to throw open the doors of accountability and let a little air in.

Mr Rudd is also 'dead serious' about a razor gang slicing though bureaucratic waste, and he excitedly accused the Coalition yesterday of failing to 'apply the meat axe to their own administrative bloating', at which line some among the crowd were seen to push their Press Club beef and mash queasily away.

But all of this is so teasingly reminiscent of John Howard himself, in his own days as a carefree young porker. New advertising guidelines to stamp out 'blatant government electoral propaganda'? Promised by Opposition leader John Howard in September 1995. Independence for the speaker? Waggled temptingly before the noses of voters on 6 June 1995, along with the promise of 'a stronger committee system for scrutiny of legislation'.

Ministerial codes of conduct? Well, that one was promised and it did duly come to pass, but after seven ministers got caught and had to resign, everybody remembered what a nuisance ministerial codes of conduct are and they were abandoned. It's extraordinary how swiftly the appeal of full accountability can fade, once the bunting's packed away.

Mr Rudd may well turn up trumps on his promises, who knows? One hates to receive such dewy-eyed entreaties with a callous heart. History is against him, that's all I'm saying. Those lovely little piglets grow up pretty fast; survival itself demands it, because government is a tough game.

What's the consolation for you, the voter? Just one, I guess; the bigger they get, the more pork they yield.

22 November 2007

JIHAD JACKIE'S SENSE OF HUMOUR BLOWS UP

Mr Howard's campaign was dealt a horrible blow in its closing stages. The husband of retiring Liberal MP Jackie Kelly, assisted by the husband of the Liberal candidate hoping to replace her, led a band of mischief-makers distributing fake pamphlets purporting to be from an extremist Muslim group backing the electorate's Labor candidate. They were caught in the act, and photographed. All hell broke loose.

What could the prime minister have done yesterday, in his last Press Club address of the campaign, to avert the mental image of Jackie Kelly's husband sneaking out and distributing faked-up messages of jihad in the name of the ALP?

What could he have done to erase the soundtrack of Ms Kelly herself tittering on national radio yesterday morning and describing her husband's attempt at secular division of her community as a '*Chaser*-style prank'?

In the midst of her interview with the ABC's Chris Uhlmann, you could hear the call-interruption tones going on Ms Kelly's home phone; who knows which poor Liberal operative was on the other line, his fingers bleeding from stabbing 'redial' in a fruitless, sickening, seconds-too-late effort to get Jackie to put a sock in it?

When campaigns go badly, they tend to go horribly badly, and then in the last week they get worse. Just ask Paul Keating, who in 1996 had his own final Press Club speech wrecked by his treasurer's decision the previous day to release a couple of fake letters that purportedly revealed an agreement between John Howard and Jeff Kennett to slash state budgets.

Those fake letters detonated immediately, messily, and memorably. The Lindsay leaflets were a much clumsier forgery – that's not an unfair assessment, is it, of a supposedly Muslim newsletter that misspells the word Allah? Had the 1996 letters misspelt Kennett, Keating might have had a fighting chance.

The prime minister did all that he could yesterday. He knows he needs to talk more about the future. He says he wants to talk about the future. And you can see him trying to talk about the future; it's just that with a past as long as his is, it involves a hell of a run-up. Not that it would have worked yesterday anyway, given the antics of the Lindsay Jihadists.

'What more can I do?' the PM pleaded, after fielding question after question about it at the Press Club yesterday. 'I have condemned it, I've disassociated myself from it, I think it's stupid, it's offensive, it's wrong, it's untrue. I mean, for heaven's sake, get a sense of proportion!' The audience, its ranks swelled with Liberal grandees, murmured its assent.

When the august Michelle Grattan rose indefatigably with a further question about the leaflet, a subterranean rumble of protest ran around the tables; was it possible that the *Age*'s first lady was herself in danger of attack?

Mr Howard ploughed on, as he has always done. But his campaign seems to have developed a death of its own, despite everything he has thrown at it in the past year. As the Americans might put it: 'The wheel is turning, but the hamster is dead'.

23 November 2007

RUDDBOT WIRED FOR POWER

Election day.

Today, Australia may well elect its first android prime minister. Ruddbot has marched through this campaign like the Terminator, incorporating Coalition policies that suit him and remorselessly amputating Labor sentiments that do not. This is the happy prerogative of the machine.

After unhappy experiments with human leaders (Beazley, Crean, Latham), it is not surprising that Labor finally turned, in desperation, to the world of animatronics. As this campaign has proved, engineering can iron out some of the complications that humanity tends to impart. Let's have a look at Ruddbot's performance in interviews, for example.

In the beginning, the best way to insure the Ruddbot against the ravages of difficult questions was simple; Labor's technicians simply programmed him to ask his own. Thus, every answer to a normal human reporter's question could be augmented by Ruddbot's insertion of a further question, directed at himself, which he could then answer, thus delaying further potentially risky human interrogatory.

Ruddbot was also programmed to default to a safety setting upon detection of certain key words. The safety response 'Um, I'm not aware of those reports. I'll have to seek a briefing' was therefore activated whenever Ruddbot was thrown questions including phrases such as 'Mark Latham has claimed …' or 'Members of the Construction, Forestry, Mining and Energy Union …' Viewers were led through this device to believe Ruddbot had simply not read the relevant paper yet. To those in the know, this is an absurd proposition, given that at five every morning, Ruddbot automatically downloads everything from the *South China Morning Post* to *Sporting Shooter* by means of a cable connected to the ethernet port located discreetly behind his left ear, of which more in a moment. But to the human brain, it seems a reasonable excuse for failing to answer a question.

There are additional basic triggers hardwired into the Ruddbot cortex. Ask Ruddbot about the number of unionists on his front bench, and he will immediately divert into a charming reverie about the fact that his colleagues include academics, small businesspeople, a rock star and an under-employed, Mandarin-speaking diplomat, 'last time I checked'.

And after the unfortunate footage of Ruddbot cleaning his ethernet port during a slow moment in Parliament was broadcast on YouTube, a new trigger was installed; any question including the term 'earwax' is now met with a broad, Muppet-inspired grin and the assurance that he was just scratching his lip. (Poor Ruddbot; his social sensors are still experimental, and he was consequently slow to pick up on the fact that humans do not forage for and consume the residue from their own ears. You live and learn, especially if you're an experimental 'droid.)

On the bright side, cutting-edge research from the University of Cincinnati has developed programs that allow robots to recognise humour and the Labor team has capitalised heavily on these advances. The technology is expensive, but the Shop Distributive and Allied Employees Association dug deep (they don't have senses of humour either) and Ruddbot can now respond credibly to basic puns, which is more than enough to get him through the breakfast television circuit, not to mention – ahem – certain elements of the *Sydney Morning Herald*'s political coverage.

It takes sophisticated circuitry and a steady hand to create a being who can speak passionately about the need for greater accountability in politics while simultaneously failing to submit the bulk of his policies for formal costing analysis by Treasury officials.

After years of careful twiddling, Ruddbot is now a formidably convincing simulacrum of humanity; only informed observers would ever notice his infrequent slips. On *Rove* last Sunday, for instance, he accidentally transposed the names of his cat and his dog, before hurriedly correcting himself. What human would ever make this blunder?

Ruddbot speaks casually of his fondness for Vegemite toast; this is a clever device which artfully cloaks the fact that he actually subsists on a modest diet of Valvoline and WD-40. I once had dinner with Ruddbot years ago and he left suddenly – before the food arrived – when a spot on *Lateline* opened up at the last minute. At the time, I thought him a workaholic. Now I know the truth: he could not allow any human to watch him eat.

Readers, there is not much time. Our best hope lies in Isaac Asimov's Basic Laws of Robotics. First Law: A robot may not injure a human being, or – through inaction – allow a human being to come to harm. Second Law: A robot must obey orders given it by human beings, except where such orders would conflict with the First Law. Third Law: A robot must protect its own existence as long as such protection does not conflict with the First or Second Law.

Let's hope they hold.

24 November 2007

RUDDBOT YEAR 1

NOTHING MAKES SENSE

The Coalition government was duly dispatched. So was John Howard himself, who lost his seat of Bennelong to the former ABC broadcaster Maxine McKew. But the larger surprise was that Peter Costello, at last presented with an opportunity to lead the Liberal Party, instead announced at a reflective press conference, wife Tanya at his side, that he was moving on from politics. National Party leader Mark Vaile felt the same way. All sorts of potential leaders promptly materialised, including Tony Abbott, who made the immortal claim that he had the 'people skills' necessary for the party's top job.

A new rule of thumb has emerged for Coalition press conferences. If the principal appears at the lectern flanked by his wife, it means he's pulling the pin. If he appears solo, it's a dead cert he's making a bid for the leadership.

Australian politics has undergone such a wrenching rearrangement in the past seventy-two hours that there is a dizzy, hallucinatory quality to everything. If you'd told me three days ago that by Monday Tony Abbott would be making a run at the Liberal leadership based on his 'people skills', I would politely have assumed you were smoking something. And if anyone can nominate a more hilarious fib than Kevin Rudd's claim on Sunday that he had found this election 'a humbling experience', I am all ears.

Nothing is making sense.

Just look at the potential field for the Liberal leadership. There's Mr Abbott and his people skills against the duelling egos of Malcolm Turnbull and Brendan Nelson. The former foreign affairs minister, Alexander Downer, that old flirt, showed a tantalising flash of leg yesterday but eventually threw in the towel on the *7.30 Report* last night. His comments during the day were laced with the trademark Downer graciousness and tact.

'You can imagine, after I've been the Opposition leader once before and I've been the foreign minister for so long, I don't sort of leap out of bed in the morning thinking I'd love to be the Opposition leader now. I find it a bit hard to get enthusiastic about it.'

Well, when you put it like that.

It's kind of hard to imagine where he's going to find post-political work with an attitude like that. Can you picture it?

'Mr Downer, thank you for applying for the position of chief executive. The board is pleased you could be here for this interview.'

'Yeah, well, you know. I've been the foreign affairs minister for eleven and a half years, so as you can probably imagine, the prospect of running your two-bit investment bank is not exactly a big thrill or anything.'

Luckily, as Tony 'People Skills' Abbott reminded us on grainy video footage during the campaign, there are plenty of jobs out there, so I guess even chronic recalcitrants are in with a fighting chance.

Kevin Rudd, meanwhile, appeared in Brisbane at Scarborough's Southern Cross College, a school he briefly attended as a boy. The prime minister-elect does seem to have rather a photogenic range of former schools at which he can graciously accept a standing ovation when required. Is it possible that he planned it that way, even from the age of nine?

Mr Rudd announced crisply that to get his education revolution started, he would be requiring all of his MPs to visit one public and one private school in their electorates, and report back to the party's first caucus meeting on Thursday.

Homework! Did you hear that, Class of 2007? Two schools by Thursday and a written report, or it's detention for the lot of you, and make sure your shirt's tucked in.

And that means you, Laurie Ferguson!

27 November 2007

WHO NEEDS PEOPLE SKILLS WHEN YOU CAN HAVE YOUR VERY OWN DYNASTY ON FREE-TO-AIR?

The Liberal colleagues, having watched Tony Abbott spend the election campaign lambasting a dying asbestosis patient, swearing at his Labor counterpart Nicola Roxon on live TV and showing up late to his scheduled health debate, declared themselves underwhelmed by his people skills and Mr Abbott withdrew from the contest.

The departure of Tony 'People Skills' Abbott from the Liberal leadership race can be counted as a major blow for political discourse in this country.

In the very act of withdrawal, he gave us a haunting glimpse of what it is that we are losing. While acknowledging that he does not have the numbers to win, People Skills made it very clear that he expects to be a challenger again for the leadership in the not-too-distant future – a clear vote of confidence in the eventual victor.

Now that all is ashes in the Abbott campaign, I can reveal that this tiny acreage in the *Herald* – in defiance of just about everybody in the parliamentary Liberal Party, if not the broader community – was wedded to the idea of a People Skills leadership.

In the absence of that possibility, it is with a heavy heart that your correspondent turns to the alternative: the need for a new *Dynasty* in Australian conservative politics. And if we're going to have a new Liberal *Dynasty*, then why not adopt a literal approach and elect the Blake and Krystle Carrington of the party, Malcolm Turnbull and Julie Bishop?

Think about the daytime TV viewers who would be captured by – nay, riveted to – this pair. Blake, with his boggling billions, with his patrician good looks, with his effortless poise and his common touch (he catches buses, y'know). Even his dogs have blogs, which probably puts them in the running for a shadow parliamentary secretaryship at the very least.

And by his side, coming from the West, Australia's Texas, Julie

'Krystle Carrington' Bishop. What a marvellous foil she would be. Krystle screams 'expensive', what with the costly sheen of her bob, and the scuff-free, murderous point of her stilettos. After all, she hails from an Australian state where, if you are so rash as to order a cappuccino, the waiter tips you.

Despite her Barbie-doll looks, Krystle is as hard as nails. She knows money. And she was not backward in making the point yesterday (in perfect taste, of course) that seeing as money might be an issue for the federal Liberal Party in years to come, it might be worth having a deputy leader with the key to the piggy-bank state.

It's all so much more encouraging than the race for the National Party leadership, a tussle which in no way looks like endangering the natural status of the Nats leader as the 'rest-stop opportunity' for spectators of question time.

The brief prospect of a Barnaby Joyce leadership was extinguished yesterday, and Victoria's Peter McGauran bowed out despite apparently having the numbers to prevail (in direct and tragic counterpoint to People Skills).

This leaves us with Warren Errol Truss, who at fifty-nine years of age easily satisfies the 'generational change' requirement, being eight full years older than the retiring Nats leader, Mark Vaile. Not quite old enough to be his father, even if he does hail from Kingaroy.

And you thought politics was boring.

29 November 2007

DR STRANGELOVE HAD BETTER NOT STOP WORRYING

Who was the most surprised when Brendan Nelson – former defence minister, former education minister, former ALP member – emerged as the Liberal Party's new leader? Malcolm Turnbull? The press gallery? Dr Nelson himself? There were only three votes in it.

As if the Liberal Party had not done enough to shock and amaze us since Saturday, yesterday it gave us the greatest show yet: *The Resurrection of Dr Strangelove.*

For the last few years Brendan Nelson has eked out a neglected existence crouched among the heavy weaponry of the defence ministry. Driven slowly mad by the lack of media profile, the bodgy accounting and the constant contact with people who wear white shoes, Nelson shrank to a cackling shadow of his former self.

As minister for education (his former gig) he had been all dash, wearing his hair in an exuberant quiff and existing in a state of rampancy that always seemed to correspond directly with his political fortunes. Day after day he enthralled Parliament with shared glimpses of his inner character: his manly contempt for the existence of university degrees in surfing and the semiotics of Britney Spears; his full-sized office poster of Neville Bonner.

Is it any wonder that Nelson's swift advancement in that portfolio won him a prime ministerially sponsored suicide mission to the Department of Defence, whence no Howard minister had ever returned? In defence he affected a buzzcut of paramilitary closeness and disappeared from our screens – so what a brilliant resurrection yesterday was.

However, caution must be urged. Just as someone who has been starving in the desert for a week should never be given a full meal, Dr Nelson should take the return to public life gently. Too many news conferences, TV interviews and magazine profiles could prove too much for a psyche already rendered vulnerable by prolonged neglect.

And what of his medium-term future? Just because you're paranoid doesn't mean they're not out to get you. And the air around the mad doctor already crackles with threats. Malcolm Turnbull, for instance, whose billion-watt smile as he emerged from his three-vote defeat by the doctor didn't fool anyone.

'It's a great result for the party', he lied. 'Brendan and Julie [Bishop] have my absolute commitment and loyalty, as they do of every person in this room.'

Then there's Tony 'People Skills' Abbott. If People Skills were to feature in a TV drama (and it is a gross indictment of the local industry that this has not yet occurred), he would be the principal character in an action series called *The Vocaliser*. Where other politicians have private thoughts that prudence forbids them to express publicly, People Skills doesn't agonise – he vocalises. So when he pulled out of the leadership race on Wednesday, People Skills did not even try to disguise his feelings.

'I'm certainly not ruling out a further tilt at the leadership', he assured the gathered hacks.

Make no mistake – Abbott and Turnbull are about as far from alike as two politicians can be, but on this occasion they're thinking exactly the same thing. They're just expressing it differently.

30 November 2007

ONE FOR THE GIRLS: JULIA GRABS THE BATON AND MARCHES INTO HISTORY

Meanwhile, on the other side of the fence, Julia Gillard continued to make significant progress.

Fellow Australians: do not be alarmed. From roughly midday today, the role of Australian prime minister will for the first time in our history be played by a woman.

Fireworks are not expected; the stockmarket is expected to remain stable, although a sharp spike in PMT jokes is expected on the CGI (cheap gag index). The lady herself, Julia Eileen Gillard, is expected to hold the office until Thursday night.

'I think it's probably a moment that many Australian women will probably stop and reflect on', she said yesterday. 'I think if there's one girl who looks at the TV screen over the next few days and says, "I might like to do that in the future", well that's a good thing.'

The prime ministerial mantle has only belonged to Kevin Rudd for a week and one day, and he has only lent it to Ms Gillard while he is in Bali on the condition that she does not stretch it or spill anything on it.

It's a brief luxuriation in the seat of power that will top off what has undoubtedly been an incredible year for the member for Lalor. After all, it is only six years ago that Julia Gillard was a little-known bit player in Labor's dispirited Opposition, a red-headed backbencher with a penchant for loud suits and a voice that would strip the enamel off a refrigerator. And it is only three short years since she – along with her Labor colleagues – surveyed the wreckage of the Latham experiment and realised tiredly that they were going to have to start all over again.

What is Julia Gillard like? Accounts, as they say, differ.

If you believe the Coalition's recent campaign advertisements, Ms Gillard is a dangerous socialist who will probably use her sixty hours as prime minister to seize the means of production, install Phillip Adams in Yarralumla and oblige every school-age child to memorise the words to 'The Internationale'.

It is often the curse of those thought by the right to be too left that they are simultaneously thought by the actual left to be far too right. And Julia Gillard has always been viewed with borderline suspicion by her own colleagues in Labor's Left faction. When she was immigration spokeswoman in 2004, and presented to the Labor conference her draft policy supporting the continuation of mandatory detention, she received just one lonely vote in a hostile Left caucus of more than 100 – and that was her own.

The acting prime minister has always retained the ability to laugh at herself. She groped her way cheerfully around that self-same 2004 conference in a myopic haze, after her boyfriend of the time – the now minister for small business, Craig Emerson – drank her contact lenses in a horrific bedside-glass-of-water mix-up. She readily lampoons her own paltry housekeeping skills, and confesses privately that her polished wooden dining table has never been the same since she tried to spruce it up with oven cleaner in 2003. And her favourite thing about the Australian people, she says, is their larrikin sense of humour.

'I was standing out at a street stall in my own electorate on one very windy winter's morning, and when you're campaigning at a street stall you stand next to a corflute sign of yourself, you know – a big poster of yourself. And so there I am, windswept and looking a bit bedraggled, and this old bloke comes out of the supermarket, and he looks at me and looks at the sign, and looks at me and looks at the sign, and then finally says: "Taken on a good day, wasn't it, love?'"

Ladies and gentlemen, for two-and-a-half days only: the acting prime minister.

11 December 2007

GET SET FOR KEVIN 08, AUSTRALIA

He's back.

After taking a brief festive break during which he completed his move to Canberra, learned to love cricket and developed a mild man-crush on Hugh Jackman, the prime minister, Kevin Rudd, flew back to the national capital last night in readiness for the first official working week of Kevin 08.

At this level in public life, the distinction between holidays and work can be difficult to spot. Thus, Mr Rudd's last day of holidays yesterday was spent not as an ordinary person might spend such a day (lying about morosely wondering if there is anything clean to wear to work), but as Kevin Rudd would spend it – flying to Brisbane for a bracing discussion of economic policy with the Treasury secretary, Ken Henry, and the treasurer, Wayne Swan. This is all part and parcel of what government press secretaries, with the manic perkiness of the already overworked, have described as a 'working break'.

And at the end of this week cabinet ministers will experience a further workplace innovation: the 'working weekend'. According to a memorandum they all received a couple of days ago, next Sunday will be spent not in quiet reflection as per the Bible's polite suggestion, but in attendance – albeit non-voluntary – at a community cabinet meeting in Perth.

Kevin 08's inbox is groaning with problems not foreseen in the halcyon days of Kevin 07.

Take the banks, for example. Who knew they would turn out to be sneaky sporran-robbers, gouging money from Australian working families? And who knew that one of the first acts of the year of the shadow treasurer, Malcolm Turnbull, would be to accuse Mr Rudd and Mr Swan of being apologists for the banks? Mr Turnbull's muscular attack on the banks would be remarkable even if he had not himself spent four of the past ten years as the managing director of Goldman Sachs.

Whales also have turned out to be a problem – the government has ended up in a wild cetacean chase through Antarctic waters, competing against Greenpeace and the *Sea Shepherd* to find and distract the Japanese whaling fleet. How has this happened?

Cabinet insiders are eyeing Peter Garrett, whose natural affinity with whales may be attributable to the fact that he too is a giant, somewhat endangered mammal with a gift for eerie, discordant song. On Friday Mr Garrett was flown to Antarctica amid some pomp and ceremony aboard the first passenger flight to the frozen continent. But he found his way back.

In the coming weeks, Mr Rudd must also make headway on the rationalisation of the national health system and on the drafting of a cut-price apology to the Aboriginal stolen generations. It is a big ask, but government lawyers are buoyed by Mr Rudd's record; his last known formal apology, delivered to his wife, Thérèse, in 2003 after being 'a bit of a goose' at a New York strip club, appears to have been an unqualified success and resulted in no litigation whatsoever.

Canberra will be full of newcomers in the coming days. The Rudd family pets, Jasper the cat and Abby the dog, are due to arrive at the Lodge this week, although precise details of their itinerary were not available.

And the 2007 crop of new MPs will be in Canberra for formal instruction in the basics of their new life. In a welcome indication that there still burns a spark of humour in the capital, Anthony Albanese has been chosen to lecture them on parliamentary standards.

And the bespectacled Mr Rudd will be at the centre of it all. For a man who confesses to being 'so not cool' in high school, it must be rich fare indeed to have dined with Hugh Jackman and Nicole Kidman on Saturday night at his Sydney pad, Kirribilli House, before returning to Canberra as that city's most powerful resident. The nerds have never had such a revenge.

14 January 2008

THE CURIOUS LOGIC OF NELSONOLOGY IN THE CONTINUING CASE AGAINST AN APOLOGY

Prime Minister Kevin Rudd announced that he would use the first week of Parliament to make good on his promise of an apology to the Aboriginal 'stolen generations'. Some Liberal MPs supported the idea, but many opposed it. New leader Brendan Nelson found himself on the receiving end of a political wedge manoeuvre – a new and unpleasant sensation for the Coalition.

The political wedge shares many attributes with its distant schoolyard relative, the wedgie. Both involve an element of surprise and intense, intimate discomfort; both are designed to expose the target to widespread humiliation and belittlement.

The federal Australian Labor Party has a long history of victimhood on this front; its chief tormentor, John Howard, for many years profited hugely by lobbing divisive legislation towards the Labor ranks and watching them scatter. In the past week, it has been the Coalition's turn to squirm, as its MPs fan out on whether they support or oppose Kevin Rudd's formal apology to Aborigines. Just imagine what fun it must be for Rudd to be on the delivering end of the wedge this time; it's as if the school nerd has, after years of beatings, returned to the playground with his uncle who just happens to be Hulk Hogan.

Mr Rudd and his colleagues have been economical this week with their commentary on what the apology will say. Brendan Nelson, however, has been boundlessly available. As a result, it's been an absorbing week here at the Global Institute of Nelsonology. Ordinarily, one would have expected Dr Nelson to line up with the Liberals who support an apology. He was positive about the idea in 1997 when the original *Bringing Them Home* report was tabled. He told Parliament at the time that he had wept repeatedly while reading the document. He likened the aggrieved Aboriginal parties to medical negligence litigants, who in his experience wanted not money, but 'for the doctor to understand their grief, to understand what they had been through and to apologise for what he or she had done'.

'Let us not be blind to injustice nor deaf to despair', he pleaded with his parliamentary colleagues.

Three years later, Dr Nelson was one of seven Liberal MPs who took part in an insurrection against the then prime minister, John Howard, demanding a federal overrule of the Northern Territory mandatory sentencing laws, which were then imprisoning Aboriginal defendants for crimes as minor as the theft of a packet of biscuits. Nelson has not been historically opposed to the use of symbolism, by any means. We are talking about a man who keeps not one, but two life-sized portraits of Neville Bonner (Australia's first Indigenous MP) in his office. Whose stint as education minister involved stapling the Australian flag to every school-aged child in the land.

What follows below is a rough summary of the arguments advanced by Dr Nelson in daily radio interviews this week as to why an apology is a bad idea.

1. Petrol prices and the economy are far more important than a national apology.
2. We don't claim credit for the Anzacs (clearly, Nelson has yet to meet Howard), so we shouldn't accept responsibility for past national disgrace either.
3. We shouldn't apologise for actions that were well intentioned.
4. An apology might condemn Aboriginal Australia to perpetual victimhood.
5. An apology might condemn white Australians to a permanent guilt complex.
6. An apology might lead white Australians to believe that everything has been fixed.

7. An apology might oblige us further to apologise for the fact that even worse stuff is still happening to Aboriginal children today.
8. It's OK to feel shame about Aboriginal children being removed from their families, but guilt is another thing entirely.
9. Symbolism is important, but not this important.

Dr Nelson insists this is a 'complex issue', and indeed no one who has watched him over the years can deny he has always felt very deeply the challenges of reconciliation; he has travelled extensively and recently in Aboriginal communities, and taken more steps than many of his colleagues to acquaint himself with the realities of life for many disadvantaged Australians. 'What would Christ do, if he were here?' he is said to have asked a neighbour in Parliament during the course of the original stolen generations debate.

But his remarks this week have not been those of a man genuinely undecided on a thorny question; at times, he has sounded more like a man trying to rationalise a decision thrust upon him by circumstance. All the arguments he has advanced are in opposition to an apology, and yet he maintains privately that he could conceivably support one if it were worded satisfactorily.

It's hard to imagine how Nelson could prevent utter bedlam within his party's ranks, should he decide in the end to back the government – particularly among those in the party who voted for him because they were startled by his opponent Malcolm Turnbull's enthusiasm for a formal apology.

Nelson's work this week has been earnest, but hard to follow. In a leader, that is a very dangerous thing.

2 February 2008

GARRETT VENTS HIS INNER GIMP IN PULP FICTION REDUX

Labor's most recognisable face made its debut in question time.

'My question is to the minister for the environment, heritage and the arts', began Greg Hunt, the Opposition front bench's pocket rocket yesterday.

What he should have said was 'Bring out the gimp!'

Because what followed – the question time debut of Peter Garrett – was a masterpiece of snarling savagery that would not have looked in any way out of place in *Pulp Fiction*. We've been waiting for Mr Garrett's leash to be unclipped for some time. Indeed, when he lost the climate change and water management elements of his portfolio to Penny Wong after the election, there were many who wondered if he would ever be let out of his dungeon. But as Mr Hunt found out yesterday, when the dungeon gate swung open and the shaven-headed form of the environment minister hurtled forth in all its repressed rage, Mr Garrett still has plenty to be punchy about.

Mr Hunt's question – quite a rational one – was whether the government's plans to combat climate change would make petrol more expensive.

Veins bulging, Mr Garrett hollered an attack on the Coalition that was almost as full-blooded and throaty as his famed 1990 protest gig outside the Exxon offices in New York.

Come to think of it, I wonder if the ExxonMobil executives (now deeply involved in Australian petrol pricing) remember that gig, and its conciliatory working title *Midnight Oil Makes You Dance – Exxon Oil Makes Us Sick*. And is the prime minister aware that there are 'roids on Mr Garrett's drinks rider these days?

Mr Hunt, who knows no fear, followed up recklessly with a question about partially treated sewage, which made Mr Garrett a bit less angry, but not by much.

The Opposition's Julie Bishop was on something quite different yesterday. Some sort of calmative, perhaps. Ms Bishop has been vocal for months on the need to fight to the death for Australian Workplace Agreements.

And yesterday, for thirty minutes in the Senate courtyard, before a vast throng of fascinated reporters, with a fixed smile on her face, she consumed what for the benefit of family readers we will call a partially treated sewage sandwich. She was cool, charming and professional. She at no point lost her cool. And for much of the time, she made no sense whatsoever.

This is unsurprising, given that Ms Bishop was trying to explain how agreeing to abolish the agreements was pretty much the same as insisting on keeping them, if you thought about it. Who will be disappointed by this Coalition rollover? The Australian Workplace Authority late last year estimated that 9 per cent of workers were on Australian Workplace Agreements.

If they are the same 9 per cent who think Brendan Nelson should be PM according to yesterday's Newspoll, the Coalition is in trouble.

20 February 2009

FOXY DEPUTY HAS HER HANDS ON THE MERCHANDISE

An under-siege deputy prime minister yesterday was forced to fight off cruel, personal suggestions that she is Australia's second-sexiest woman.

That's about as bad as it gets at the moment for Julia Gillard: being pipped for first place in *Ralph* magazine's national totty-off. Otherwise, it's all going pretty well. The past few months have brought her treats galore: a regal new office, death to her political enemies and a mountainous pile of bright orange Work Choices merchandising items with which to belabour her opposite number, Julie Bishop, in question time.

Every day this week, she has tripped happily into the chamber with a new armful of Work Choices bumf, printed in haste by the previous government and since discovered in Canberra's bureaucratic warehouses and shredder queues by the invading Labor army. (Note to all departing governments: if you are going to burn the villages as you retreat, be sure to burn them thoroughly.)

On Monday, it was Work Choices booklets. On Tuesday, it was Work Choices mousemats. And yesterday, Australia's deputy sexpot arrived toting Work Choices folders, pens, postcards and the promise of fridge magnets.

She has generously offered to supplement the Opposition's stationery allowance (and it is a kind offer; in the current round of belt-tightening in Kevin Rudd's Canberra, a wide-ranging pencil freeze can't be too far away) with as much of the Work Choices merch as they can carry.

'Mr Speaker, I am alert and alarmed', she trilled, as Mr Rudd cheerily popped a bright orange ballpoint over the barrier to Brendan Nelson. 'You can't turn a corner in Canberra without Work Choices propaganda cascading on top of you. It's just remarkable.'

Ms Gillard is making hay while the sun shines. She also has the distinct political advantage that none of her own wildly unsuccessful past policy ideas ever reached the merchandising stage. There are no Medicare Gold hotpants, for instance, or Ease the Squeeze mugs still in circulation.

She is loving government, and has quickly established herself as the government's political assassin-in-chief. *Ralph* has reportedly offered Ms Gillard $50,000 to pose for bikini shots. Not everyone is a fan, though. Former minister Eric Abetz (recently voted Australia's sexiest male German-born Tasmanian Liberal senator) yesterday accused the deputy sexpot of being 'arrogant' and 'drunk with power'.

The bikini offer, it should be noted, was not extended to the prime minister, who yesterday discovered that in Australian politics even a 70 per cent popularity rating does not deter national newspapers from calling you a fatso.

Asked about his girth yesterday on radio, Mr Rudd responded with some dignity that he tried to walk or swim several times a week. 'I also try to gym whenever I can', he said.

Which demonstrates that our PM is cutting back on syntactical excess, if nothing else.

21 February 2008

IN THE WILDERNESS, EYEING OFF DAMASCUS

Meanwhile, out of the spotlight, People Skills embarked on a lonely journey of self-evaluation.

It has been easy this year to get lost in the spectacle of frenetic rearrangement within the ranks of the Liberal Party. But like all riot footage, it benefits hugely from a second viewing.

There they all are: Brendan Nelson with his contortions on the apology; the former Howard ministers avidly spilling all to *Four Corners*; Tony Abbott demanding an end to Australian Workplace Agreements ... hang on. Back up the truck.

Tony Abbott, demanding an end to Australian Workplace Agreements?

Yes, indeed. The former Howard minister's personal acrobatics of late have been disguised conveniently by those with whom he shares a stage.

The dazzling smile and intricate footwork of Julie Bishop, for example, as she effected a full reversal of her own views on industrial relations this week, were as horribly compelling as a Little Miss Colorado pageant. It's no wonder we failed to notice 'People Skills' Abbott in the background, easing into a spangled leotard for a few feats of his own. But it's true.

The man who on 28 November last year said of the industrial relations issue: 'The last thing I think we should do is run up the white flag. Work Choices delivered', was this week one of the most aggressive proponents, behind the scenes, of the view the whole thing should be punted. Likewise, his trenchant opposition to a national apology to Aborigines melted puzzlingly into compliance sometime over the Christmas break.

It is tempting but unrealistic to think People Skills has embarked on an elective re-education program, and will burst forth soon in his new guise as Mosman's organiser for the CFMEU. Can it be he is reconsidering his role as honorary president of the John Howard fan club? Either way, the situation has all the outward signs of being, to lapse for a moment into Ruddspeak, a People Skills Crisis.

Abbott has been an MP for fourteen years. He was a minister for nearly ten, and despite his comparatively tender years is one of the most memorable faces of the Howard government. These days, he looks a bit lost.

His two great friends in Canberra were the former member for Parramatta Ross Cameron and the former member for Lindsay Jackie Kelly. Both left public life in cartoonishly disastrous circumstances: Cameron in 2004 amid lurid reports of his infidelity, and Kelly last year in the farcical, pamphlet-festooned denouement to the Liberals' eleven-year custodianship of outer-suburban Lindsay.

Stripped of his mates, his political mentor and his robes of office, Abbott is in a bind. He is too young to be an old fogey, but too senior to be a young Turk, palling around with the newcomers to the Liberal front bench. It cannot make things any easier that the women who shadowed him as health minister for the past five years have gone on to spectacular success, Julia Gillard as deputy prime minister and Nicola Roxon as health minister.

It is very possible that Abbott – whose feminist credentials are not widely recognised – has inadvertently made much better politicians out of these senior Labor women. To the extent Gillard has emerged as a sort of parliamentary Rocky Balboa, Abbott is her Apollo Creed – the adversary who provoked and tested her, then succumbed. Roxon, too, has benefited through cross-promotion of the Abbott Show. Their catfight through fixed grins at the National Press Club last year did wonders for her profile.

Now, in a testament to the quiet ability of parliamentary bureaucrats to be hilarious simply through the medium of room allocation, Abbott is in Roxon's old office, on the outer perimeter of Parliament House's northern ground floor.

The suite, RG62, is modest and far-flung. Queen Elizabeth the Second, whose girlish coronation portrait is a lonely ornament to the walls of its reception area, smiles brightly but must – like Abbott – be wondering what the hell she is doing there. On one view, this office is Nowheresville. On another, it's base camp for a new expedition. There is little doubt the election defeat has prompted Abbott into an ideological spring-clean.

'We have to resist yearning for "ideal" families and "traditional mothers"', he told the Young Liberal convention in a speech last month. As immediate past yearner-in-chief for this sort of stuff, it is possible that Abbott was addressing himself here as much as he was his youthful audience.

He also told the crowd, 'The search for philosophical purity is almost as big a voter turn-off as political insiders speculating about who might make a better leader.'

Much as he might argue the toss, Abbott's obsessive-compulsive interest in philosophical purity is one of the things that have given colleagues the creeps in the past. If he is willing to co-exist with a few philosophical germs, he might emerge from RG62 so much the stronger.

23 February 2008

GLASS OF BINGE THE ORDER OF THE DAY

Binge drinking is such a popular issue at the moment that it has generated a brand new noun.

'I'm just here for a spot of binge', said the Liberal politician I ran into this week at a Canberra bar.

'Another glass of binge?' a journalist colleague had offered, courteously, an hour or two earlier as we stood at a Rabbitohs function listening to Anthony Albanese canvass the dangers of heavy drinking as the drinks trays went merrily round.

Mr Albanese is worried about binge. The health minister, Nicola Roxon, is worried about binge. Kevin Rudd – who among his many achievements counts Australian politics' most celebrated recent episode of goat-faced alcoholic excess – is very worried about binge, and somehow we all kept a straight face this week as he promised a shock and awe advertising campaign to stamp out Australia's alco-pop epidemic.

I can't wait to see the ad. Will it be one of those silhouette jobs featuring the tragic confessions of a raddled binge veteran? In the darkened room onscreen, perhaps we will be able to pick out the dim outline of a bust of Dietrich Bonhoeffer and a modern Chinese print. Cloaked in anonymity, the subject will speak, hesitatingly, his voice croaky with regret.

'My name is Kevin. I am a binger.'

In Canberra this week, it was definitely a bit infra dig not to be worried about binge and prudent observations about moderation in the enjoyment of alcohol were as commonplace at official functions as the acknowledgment of the Ngunnawal people.

Tony 'People Skills' Abbott volunteered that he didn't think it was Australia's biggest problem, and people reacted as if he'd just handed a six-pack to a nine-year-old.

In question time, Rudd declared his unswerving determination to do something about it, and Roxon chimed in with a yucky detail about the lesser-known effects of booze on the small bowel.

The new West Australian Liberal MP, Steve Irons, used his maiden speech to outline the role alcohol had played in his own tragic family history and to call for binge control. Brendan Nelson, who sat supportively beside Irons for the duration of his speech, sprang up spontaneously afterward and hugged him. Actually, 'was hugged by Irons' is probably more accurate; Irons is a big man and the spectacle put one irresistibly in mind of koalas and trees.

Incidentally, Nelson has faithfully attended all his new MPs' maiden speeches and has sat beside each and every one. Perhaps he hopes that, like ducklings, the newly hatched MPs will bond with the first thing they see and thus follow him unquestioningly in the troublesome months that lie ahead. But back to binge.

Such was the interest in the topic this week that when journalists spotted the Family First senator, Steve Fielding, wandering round Parliament House on Thursday dressed up as a giant bottle, we assumed he was taking a graphic leap aboard the binge wagon. It turned out, however, that he was advocating a container deposit levy on plastic drink bottles, which is an entirely different concern.

It cannot be long before binge gets its own lapel ribbon and gala benefit dinner, at which – of course – quantities of top-drawer hooch will be consumed without a sniff of irony.

This is the thing about binge: it's something other people do. The binge conjugation goes something like this: '*I* like to get a bit merry now and again. *You* are a lush. But *they* are binge drinkers.'

This proposition is amply demonstrated by an Alcohol Education and Rehabilitation Foundation survey published in the *Herald* yesterday, which found that only 20 per cent of heavy-drinking men classified their own activities as binge drinking, but 50 per cent were of the view that other Australians drank too much.

The binge conjugation also explains why Canberra can unblinkingly juggle genuine concern about binge drinking with its own rich and continuing booze culture. (Not that many journalists can afford to be especially judgmental about this; we are happy to report the concerns about binge but are just as apt to get smashed later.)

Yesterday, Kevin Rudd called in AFL and netball heavies, among other sporting personages, to come up with some innovative binge-fighting strategies. I am not sure how many cultural cues I am prepared to take from a group of sportsmen who still – if we may draw the obvious inference from the AFL's recent training video on sexual ethics – need gentle prompting before they can answer correctly the question: 'Is it OK to have sex with a mate's girlfriend if she mistakes you for him?'

And why is it always these hard-bodied types to whom governments turn for assistance with binge drinking? When they convene a summit of the Bone Idle, Flabby Booze Hound Advisory Group, we might start to get somewhere.

15 March 2008

HUCK AND HIS AMAZING ANECDOTES

At the Press Club yesterday, Brendan Nelson took us for a little walk through his life.

First of all, we met the freckle-faced boy Brendan, whose fishing expeditions on the Tamar River with his father were interspersed with walks around Launceston's posher suburbs and some stern lessons about the realities facing a child not born into a rich family. (I would like to add that there were madcap adventures, too, with Brendan's best friend Huck Finn, but I would be making it up.)

Next, we met Nelson MD, the cool-headed doctor, encountering his first suicide, his first cot death and a hysterical mother clawing to get to her unconscious eight-year-old son.

And Nelson the disenchanted ALP member of the late 1980s: 'I started on this journey [to Liberalism] twenty years ago, when I got angry.'

Then for a moment it seemed we were meeting Hillary Clinton, when an emotionally charged Nelson declared: 'For some people, politics is a game. To me, it's about people's lives.'

Nelson specialises in anecdotes; the more graphic, the better. Ask him about hospital funding and he will tell you about the ninety-year-old with a gangrenous leg he met last week. Ask him about the regulatory complications in Australian telephony, and he'll give you five minutes on a guy he knows whose son died from an asthma attack because the line was down.

It is not fair to question his actual sincerity about this stuff; he is a man of substantial empathy for those suffering from misfortune. But it is entirely fair to say that Nelson's attention is drawn disproportionately to the Gothic end of the human suffering spectrum. As a result, he is in distinct danger of becoming a tragedy tourist. How else can you respond to a man who, when asked yesterday which parts of Work Choices he thought were OK, rushed straight into a story about finding a father of two hanging in his garden shed after losing his job?

It's important for people to know that suicides happen, or that four-year-olds get raped in some Aboriginal communities (another of Dr Nelson's more frequently repeated anecdotes, which recently beamed out to thousands of school children watching the parliamentary apology to the stolen generations, to some consternation). And it's important that politicians care about them.

But the Opposition leader seems almost to use these stories as a stepladder to the moral high ground. After all, who will side against a desperate mother or a raped child or a man driven to suicide by dreadful misfortune? How can a journalist, having heard the parable of the hanged man in the shed, possibly be so heartless as to come back and say, 'Well, forget the dead guy. Answer the question, please'?

It's not just that Nelson's speeches sometimes deliver too strongly on 'yuck factor', although that is a criticism regularly made. It's that the rush to homily often bypasses the straight answer.

19 March 2008

LA GILLARDINE CRUSHES THE ANCIEN REGIME

The deputy prime minister managed to kill off the Coalition's Work Choices with new legislation. But she wasn't especially gracious in victory.

Work Choices is finally dead.

Yesterday it was seamlessly replaced by a violent new system of repression, as the Rudd Revolutionaries combed Parliament House seeking out and crushing pockets of resistance.

Coalition MPs were all but stopped in the corridors and asked to present their credentials. Those who obediently squeaked 'Long live Australian working families!' were allowed to scuttle away free. But those found in possession of a Work Choices ballpoint pen, or who dared to breathe the words 'A simpler, fairer workplace relations system for Australia', were dragged off to face the vengeance of La Gillardine.

La Gillardine, who before the revolution went by her birth name of Julia Eileen Gillard, showed no mercy yesterday as she decapitated the Howard government's industrial relations system by means of majority vote in a packed House of Representatives.

But victory was not enough.

La Gillardine sought to heap humiliation upon the vanquished by asking them to denounce the deposed regime, and to swear before the Parliament that never again would statutory individual contracts be a part of the Australian industrial relations landscape.

Julie Bishop, a brave resistance fighter who has styled her hair into a helmet to signify the stoutness of her resolve, refused to swear the oath and thus incurred the wrath of La Gillardine.

Tony 'People Skills' Abbott, a wounded veteran of the counter-revolution, told reporters that, in his opinion, the Howard government was 'good for wages', 'good for jobs' and 'good for workers'. In question time, he duly felt the chilly kiss of La Gillardine on the back of his quivering neck.

'The member for Warringah has helpfully laid bare, for every working Australian to see, that it believes being able to be ripped off is good for workers!' she cried.

Alexander Downer, an as-yet unexecuted member of the exiled aristocracy, objected shrilly from his seat.

'Fancy someone disagreeing with you! They should go to jail. What about show trials?'

The government's victory on Work Choices is complete. But the enthusiasm with which they yesterday roamed the perimeters finding and shooting stragglers created more than a sniff of dangerous triumphalism.

La Gillardine is a member of the ALP's Left faction, and therefore has never had the numbers on anything, ever, until now. This may help to explain why power has gone to her head a little this week, and why, having knocked the Opposition to the mat, she cannot stop herself from sinking the boot repeatedly into its inert form.

Please excuse the violence of this imagery. Be assured, it is Walt Disney stuff compared to the rhetoric employed by the government yesterday.

Perhaps somewhere deep within Parliament, far from the public eye – deep, deep down in the catacombs, where the catering trolleys whizz around unseen and the most boring of old documents are stored – a secret bunker exists for the industrial relations resistance, ingeniously sound-proofed using several thousand Work Choices mousemats.

Their ranks are badly depleted. Their old protector has escaped to the US, where he is presently undertaking a speaking tour of duty.

They await a new leader.

20 March 2008

RUDDESE GETS TO THE CORE OF IT ALL

As you pick up your newspaper today, Kevin Rudd will be digesting his first White House lunch with the US president after the first major engagement of his first world tour as Australian prime minister.

As schoolgirls are said to dream of their wedding days, so must Rudd have rehearsed this moment many times over the course of his boyhood in Nambour.

If all goes well, all the formal elements of an Australian prime ministerial expedition to the US will be honoured in the coming days, including the Rose Garden joint news conference and the ritual mangling of the distinguished Australian visitor's name.

Just as Malcolm Fraser became John Frasier, and John Howard became Paul Howard and John Hunt at the hands of the US media, tradition demands that Rudd return from his travels fully blooded, with a new and apparently randomly chosen northern hemisphere name. (George W. Bush's most recent trip to Australia, during which he respectfully referred to us as Austrians, was an innovative and moving variation on this tradition.)

More pressing, however, is the matter of translation. Everybody knows that the PM will take care of himself on the Beijing leg. But on the English-speaking parts of the grand tour, there's a big chance some of his favoured idiomatic expressions will cause difficulties.

It's not just the likelihood that he will at some stage offer to sort out some major NATO tangle 'on the verandah in Brisvegas' over a 'cuppa' and an Iced VoVo, which to the northern ear might sound dangerously like a specialised nuclear device. What about the other Rudd favourites? How will we break it to an enchanted European trade official that the phrase 'core business', in untranslated Ruddese, does not necessarily enjoy the same weight as it might in normal English? And consequently, that the undertaking 'Your widget exports are core business for my government' might not in practice carry quite the degree of thrilled exclusivity as the words imply?

A quick review of the past few months reveals that many items are 'core business' for Rudd. Good economic management in general is 'core business', as you would expect. Inflation, too, is 'our biggest challenge, and it's core business'. Climate change has been 'core business' from the beginning, and was formally decorated as such in the prime minister's official statement announcing his cabinet, to which Penny Wong turned out to be absolutely core.

But there's much, much more to the core than that. Speaking in South Australia, Rudd confided that water management was 'core business for the people of South Australia, and therefore it's core business for us as the national government'. Preventative health, too, turns out to be 'absolutely core business'.

Housing? 'Core business.'

Binge drinking? 'I can think of no more core business.'

Simon Birmingham, an industrious young Liberal senator from South Australia, compiled a list after the last election of matters Rudd had declared to be his government's 'first' or 'number one' priority. Education, defence, inflation, economic management, climate change and co-operative federalism were each separately pronounced to be the single most important task facing the new administration.

Nearly everything you can think of is 'core' in some way. The continuation of free-trade talks with China is a 'core business of government', according to Rudd. But no snub should be inferred by the Americans from these words because the US alliance is, happily, also 'something that I regard as core business'. As are affordable childcare and the pleasantly vague goal of 'keeping trust with the community'.

You would think John Howard's misadventures with the words core and non-core might cause tiny bells to ring in the inner ear of the new prime minister. But he has already sunnily referred publicly to areas of budget spending that are 'not core business for the nation, which we can take the axe to'.

Intriguingly, the Rudd agenda contains cores within cores. Some of them appear almost interchangeable and rearrangeable, like those fridge magnet sets where you can compose your own erotic poem or Shakespearean sonnet. Climate change, for instance, is 'core business for national economic management'. And budget spending cuts are 'core business when it comes to inflation', which as we know is already itself core business.

We can only hope that the day is not too far distant when we will hear that an education revolution is core business for free-trade talks with China, or that binge drinking is core business for climate change.

All of this, in any event, adds up to a salutary warning: if Rudd ever opens a fruit and veg shop, go for the bananas. The apples will be all core.

29 March 2008

NERD POWER GOES GLOBAL

Oh, Lord. We've created a monster. Before we sent our Ruddbot out into the world, he was our nerd. Now, after two weeks of exposure, he's everyone's favourite nerd, and we are having to acclimatise ourselves to a new and vertiginous feeling, whisperingly reminiscent of nausea. It's the dawning realisation that sometime soon, our prime minister will be photographed by Annie Leibowitz, and there is bugger all we can do to stop it.

The Ruddbot has been feted all over the globe this week. In Britain, the *Guardian* gave him a full-body massage, admiring his mastery of China and comparing him favourably to their own man, Gordon Brown. 'He is everything the British prime minister wants to be, and is not – a king nerd who has crushed conservatism at home', the paper opined.

The Ruddbot will have loved the *Guardian* article, even though it doesn't sit too well with his private plan, which is to *be* conservatism at home. The 'king nerd' thing won't bother him, either. That's the big thing about nerd chic; once you've nailed the chic bit, you stop minding so much about the nerd bit.

'The world needs more leaders like this', breathed the *Independent*, a newspaper so achingly right-on that it was once guest-edited by Bono, a celebrity whose own endorsement of the Ruddbot can surely be but a heartbeat away.

And now k.d. lang has got involved. She's the Canadian chanteuse who became extra famous in 1993 when she was photographed in a barber's chair for the cover of *Vanity Fair*, being shaved by a lingerie-clad Cindy Crawford. Currently touring Australia, lang this week described the PM as 'fearless' and 'very, very graceful' in his interventions with the Chinese on the subject of Tibet.

(Of course, strictly speaking, Kevin Rudd has no need for extra support from foxy, trouser-suited androgynes, given that he's already travelling with one – his climate change minister, Penny Wong. Apart from being seriously clever, 'k.d.' Wong is also – barring any startling retrospective revelations about Amanda Vanstone or Bronwyn Bishop – Australia's first federal minister to be a bona fide lesbian pin-up.)

We should probably brace ourselves for further celebrity endorsements, particularly now that the Ruddbot has established himself internationally as a friend of Tibet. Tibet can draw a Hollywood crowd faster than a freshly opened jeroboam of Cristal.

And mark my words: everybody who whinged at Christmas about the Urban-Kidmans having dinner at Kirribilli will be wishing for the good old days once Richard Gere and Goldie Hawn are flipping their fair-trade beanburgers onto the prime ministerial barbie.

Let's look at what spawned this wave of adulation. First, the PM mentioned Tibet directly as a 'problem' – a piece of plain speaking that earned him a diplomatic rebuke from the Chinese. Second, he told the Chinese there was no way Australia would allow the tracksuited 'torch guards' following the Olympic beacon to be in charge of security during the Australian leg. Sensibly, the Chinese do not appear to have arced up about this one: perhaps they have checked out the stats on past clashes between the Ruddbot and short guys in tracksuits.

But the fact our prime minister can create global love-waves simply for mentioning Tibet and politely telling Chinese bouncers they won't be needed is a massive tribute to the enduring power of the developed world's China syndrome. Rudd is being congratulated for fearlessness not because the words were especially cheeky, but because everybody automatically accepts China's reputation for extreme unreasonableness and fits of temper. Thus, he wins points not so much for what he said as for the fact he said anything at all; it's the same awed respect you might pay to Russell Crowe's telephone operator, or Naomi Campbell's manicurist.

No other country is accorded the same deference as China. Japan is obliged to remain sanguine as armed Australian boats chase theirs around the Southern Ocean, which you couldn't imagine if the Chinese suddenly developed a taste for Peking porpoise. When George W. Bush addressed Parliament in late 2003, he was heckled by the Greens and subjected to protest petitions signed by dozens of MPs. But nobody gave President Hu Jintao a hard time when he spoke in the same chamber just one day later.

It seems inevitable, given China's rapid pace of development and its elevated exposure this year thanks to the Olympics, that this international culture of acceptance will change. And if Kevin Rudd can be at the pointy end of that process, then he will look like a very clever nerd indeed.

12 April 2008

FLYING IN THE FACE OF FURRY YOGHURT

Who takes the workaholic award this week – Kevin Rudd or Cate Blanchett?

In the field of competitive international multi-tasking, this is a grudge match of *Alien versus Predator* proportions. The actress is showing up to the 2020 Summit on Saturday even though she has just given birth to her third child. Mr Rudd is still pinging around in the hyperactivity stratosphere after three weeks of intensive international diplomacy, which seem to have left him completely unblunted by jet lag of any kind.

What does the ordinary person do, upon arriving home from a demanding three-week work trip? Call in sick for a few days. Watch telly. Nervously avoid the reeking, yet-to-be-unpacked suitcase and the fridge full of furry yoghurt.

Not our PM, who had barely shimmied out of his in-flight pyjamas on Sunday before he was addressing a group of Australian youth and announcing the nation's first female governor-general. Yesterday, he nipped to Sydney to harvest ideas from the Jewish community. They are unable to attend this weekend's summit due to a pre-existing commitment, Passover, which, in their defence, had been in the diary for about 3000 years.

And today, Mr Rudd will proceed to Penrith for community cabinet and its now customary speed-dating side event, where ministers and members of the public enjoy ten-minute interludes full of bracing policy debate, at the end of which they are at liberty to exchange phone numbers.

A hardworking prime minister is the kind of prime minister you want, it is generally agreed. But this whirl of activity is starting to look a tiny bit obsessive-compulsive. Kevin Rudd never just phones anything in. Take the world trip, for example. Not only did he visit as many countries and leaders as he could pack in, but he devised a special shtick for each stop.

In the US it was frank talk about Iraq and that we now want a seat on the United Nations Security Council. In Bucharest it was a reproach for European countries for failing to do more in Afghanistan. In Britain it was the slight waft of a republic. In China, of course, it was Tibet, and the prime minister's last act before flying home was to deliver a mild slap to Pakistan for taking its eye off the ball, Taliban-wise. (Poor old Pakistan. How do you explain to the world's greatest multi-tasker you have had a few things on recently?)

Last week, Kim Beazley remarked that Mr Rudd would have to slow down a bit, as it would be impossible for him to sustain the blistering pace he has set his staff and himself. And it is fair to say that if it had been Prime Minister Kim Beazley behaving like this, we would already have had a crack team round at the Lodge with a tranquilliser dart gun by now, under the assumption he had gone rogue.

15 April 2008

THEY MOVED KEVIN AND EARTH ON THE ALTAR OF CHEESINESS

Early in his term as prime minister, Kevin Rudd convened his Ideas Summit, an opportunity for Australia's 'best and brightest' to submit their big ideas on how Australia might be advanced more fairly. Or, as a non-political friend of mine observed, viewing TV footage of movie stars and bigwigs milling around the PM, a chance for Kevin Rudd to throw the 21st-birthday party he'd never had.

Picture Vatican II, with Kevin Rudd playing the role of God. That'll give you a fair idea of what this weekend was like.

Much like God at Vatican II, the prime minister was not – technically – a participant at the 2020 Summit. But to pretend that the event was not all about him would be absurd.

Apart from being his idea, the entire program was suffused with Kevinism, as delegates tried each in their own little way to achieve the ultimate state of grace, or Kevin on Earth. There wasn't a souvenir stall out the front selling stamped wafers, splinters of the original Nambour farmhouse or authorised reproductions of slightly-too-short chinos, but there might as well have been.

It started out on Saturday morning, far too early, with a flurry of butcher's paper as all the groups got everything down preparatory to horse-trading. Over in Economy, the facilitators were provided by McKinsey, so those participants were required to write their big ideas down on paper and parade around holding them up, so as to attract like-minded colleagues. This meant that Lindsay Fox, the transport magnate, had quite a lonely time of it. He was the only person with 'intermodal transport' written on his bit of paper, and interest seemed pretty thin.

By Saturday night, the groups had assembled big piles of policy wood. The challenge, overnight, was to whittle them down into passable graven images of the prime minister.

The Productivity group did well – their top idea by the end of the summit was Kevin Rudd's idea, which was to integrate health and other services into childcare centres.

The Economy group did even better; their offering was nothing more than a glittering treasure-trove of inquiries, investigations and reviews, for which our prime minister has a widely reported weakness. Interestingly, the Economy group was about the only one to emerge without a specific proposal for tax. They wanted a 'comprehensive review', which is what economists and high-wealth individuals say in mixed company when what they really mean is 'lower taxes'.

Almost all of the other groups had tax ideas – mostly about new taxes that could be imposed to fund their ideas. New junk-food taxes to fund healthy food initiatives, fuel taxes to fund public transport, and so on. All in all, it conformed pretty well to the universal conjugation of the tax argument, which classically goes like this: 'I think that the things you like should be taxed more, in order to fund the things that I like.' The Creative group felt that 1 per cent 'creative dividend' from every federal department should be spent on the arts; nobody put their hand up to break the news to the Department of Agriculture, Fisheries and Forestry.

The prime minister himself, over the course of the summit, was on the whole a benign and twinkling deity. He materialised beamingly from time to time, to kid around with the participants or to drink tea. Cameras followed him everywhere, and every time they drew near he would immediately begin the sincere, talking-intently-while-chopping-the-air performance that is widely demanded from prime ministers filmed talking to people at public events.

On one visit to the Economy group, he arrived among a standing group of summiteers and promptly seated himself on the floor. He did not wash anyone's feet or anything, but the 'Suffer the little economists to come unto me' theme was obvious enough nevertheless.

Like Vatican II, the 2020 Summit demonstrated to us that our language is changeable; the favoured little sayings of John Howard now seem far away and hopelessly antiquated, as out of favour as Latin Mass. We have officially said goodbye to 'mateship', 'the things that unite us are bigger than the things that divide us', the 'barbecue stopper' and 'the pub test'. Kevin Rudd, having famously failed the pub test himself, has done away with all that.

We are now in the era of 'partnerships', where we 'tackle' things together, and we try to ensure that the arts and the economy don't live in separate 'silos'.

'These are false polarities', the prime minister said as he bestrode the lectern at summit's end. 'We can carve out a different way forward.'

What, between the false polarities? Or just wherever you like, ignoring the polarities, given that we already know them to be false?

Clichés were welcome – the cheesier, the better. At the opening session, it took the prime minister about four seconds to make reference to 'opening up the windows of democracy, and letting in some fresh air'.

But this is the Year of the Nerd. It's OK to be cheesy.

21 April 2008

HEADING OFF A STINK AT THE PASS

A nation unaccustomed to following the intricacies of Western Australian Opposition politics was nonetheless gripped in mid-2008 by the allegation that Liberal leader Troy Buswell had once, in front of select colleagues, knelt down to sniff an office chair recently vacated by a female adviser. This invited a most unwelcome series of mental images, and made me wonder how a trained spin-doctor might have managed the matter on Mr Buswell's behalf.

When is it right in politics to 'fess up? It's a pretty complicated equation. On Monday, the unfortunate WA Liberal leader, Troy Buswell, acknowledged, after initial vague denials, that he had in fact sniffed the chair of a female staffer back in 2005.

How does a man come to find himself in this situation? Could it have been better for him to admit it earlier? Pre-emptive action on these sorts of stories is like preventive healthcare: it seems like too much trouble until it's too late, when it starts, in retrospect, to look very sensible indeed.

Tony 'People Skills' Abbott, who this week made a welcome return to frontline politics after a period of something very much like introspection, is himself an astute practitioner in this area. In 1997, as he was preparing to sue the writer Bob Ellis for various claims in Ellis's pulped book *Goodbye Jerusalem*, Abbott undertook a controlled detonation of the news that he had fathered a child out of wedlock while at university.

He told the story to the columnist Christopher Pearson, who wrote it up for a Queensland newspaper, the *Courier-Mail*. If you don't count the soap opera that was to burst forth years down the track, in which the missing boy was first discovered to be working as a cameraman in Parliament House, and then found to bear no genetic relationship to Abbott at all, this controlled-release strategy was pretty successful on the whole. In disclosing the news early, and on his own terms, Abbott avoided any potentially toxic accusations that he had been trying to hide it.

But pre-emptive action is not always advisable. How could even the most brilliant of damage-control merchants possibly have engineered the harmless detonation of the chair-sniffing incident? How would Buswell, even aided by the most understanding of interviewers, ever achieve the correct tone of casual insouciance while mentioning the one time when possibly he might have sniffed a chair in front of a roomful of colleagues?

It's not even that chair sniffing is such a grand crime in the scheme of things. It's just that it's so brilliantly weird, and – much like the term 'pleasure horse industry' – creepy for reasons that you would actually prefer not to summon into your conscious mind.

The problem with the chair sniffing incident is that its disclosure in any form raises the question: 'Why?' – and I'm not sure it's one that many of us really want answered. Buswell is best advised, now that he has acknowledged and apologised for it, to leave well alone.

Some politicians, when eager to make a clean breast of things, err on the side of over-disclosure. The British Liberal Democrat MP Mark Oaten, who for a short time in early 2006 was a candidate for the leadership of his party, made no attempt at denial when a London tabloid, the *News of the World*, felt it was time to acquaint voters with the news that he had for some time been paying a London rent-boy to dress up in football gear and oblige him regularly in a 'sex act too revolting to describe'.

Oaten gave subsequent interviews about the events and about the extent to which he had been overwhelmed by life as a politician. At one point, he claimed to have been thrown off course by the loss of most of his hair while still in his thirties. His wife, Belinda, also gave interviews in which she described her feelings about the revelations and charted the gradual rehabilitation of their relationship. The pair of them could not possibly have been more open and honest. But Oaten was finished, of course, just as one is forced to suspect Buswell is finished.*

Straight adultery isn't necessarily a hanging offence politically – just ask Bob Hawke or 'Bonking' Boris Johnson, whose celebrated infidelities did not stop him from being very close to becoming the next lord mayor of London after Thursday's poll.

A suicide attempt is survivable.

So is shooting somebody. Mr Buswell's predecessor, Paul Omodei, stood down as deputy Liberal leader in 2005 after accidentally blowing his adult son's thumb off as part of a poorly thought-out manoeuvre during a rabbit shooting trip.

It wasn't terminal, though. Resisting what must have been quite a strong temptation, given his qualifications, to run for the US vice-presidency, he returned to the fore of the WA Liberals in early 2006, this time as leader. And there he stayed, until he was unseated by the chair sniffer late last year, for reasons unrelated to the shooting.

Son-shooting is survivable because an average human being can easily imagine the circumstances under which such an accident could plausibly occur. Chair sniffing – well, that's a different story altogether.

**He wasn't finished at all. He became WA treasurer.*

3 March 2008

AN ASHES LOSER'S BATTY NUGGETS

John Howard emerged from retirement to offer some post-match analysis.

One of the most popular anecdotes circulating around the Liberal Party after the election loss last year came out of John Howard's Parliament House office, in the days after the former PM encountered his electoral Armageddon.

One Howard staffer, newly jobless, was visibly upset as he packed his boxes, and Howard – working nearby – spotted his distress. Wandering over, the defeated PM placed a reassuring hand on the young man's shoulder.

'Don't worry', he said softly. 'I'll be all right – really.'

People aren't always on the same wavelength, are they? Towards the end of the Howard era, some of those around the venerable J. Winston sometimes wondered if he was even on the same wave as his troops – hell, the same ocean, on bad days. And Wednesday night found the great man again alone on his boogie board, paddling about happily in a lagoon far, far away in a universe where he didn't even lose – not really, anyway.

Speaking to the 1200 loyal NSW Liberals who paid $250 a plate to honour him (a handsome turnout, although the phrase 'good money after bad' must have skipped across at least some of their minds as they climbed wearily into their dinner suits just one more time), Howard spoke enthusiastically of his advisers.

'One of them said to me tonight, you know, in a Test series, 4-1 is a triumphal retention of the Ashes, and it's probably a reasonable metaphor that I find very, very agreeable.'

Dear old thing, he hasn't even got the stats right: the 1987 defeat by Bob Hawke brings it to 4-2.

But this new perspective must have come as a substantial relief to those present who had feared this Rudd thing was going to turn out to be permanent. Once the Australian Electoral Commission has been brought around to the Ashes model of representative democracy, convincing Kevin and the team to hand back the keys to the Lodge should be a snap.

A better cricketing analogy might be this: John Howard is the captain who beat his own team to death, then returned to coach the corpse.

Many of Howard's peers made video appearances, most notably George W. Bush, heavily disguised as Alf from *Home and Away*, who said, 'You're a digger who is simple, direct and tough. And you have never let this cobber down. Flamin' heck, you bloody galah!' (OK. Maybe I made the third sentence up.)

And Tony Blair, who said, 'It's a real pleasure and privilege to give this tribute tonight, to say how lucky I was to have him as a friend and ally.' This might sound lukewarm in comparison to Bush's message, but when you consider that Blair hasn't used a verb in a sentence in years, the festival of conjugation contained in those scant lines can be appreciated for what it really is: a rare Fabergé egg of a tribute.

Those three gents – Howard, Bush and Blair – have a lot in common, such as coming to power at roughly comparable times, and being on the same side against Iraq, al-Qaeda, France and the other major global loons.

The other thing they share, of course, is the painstaking precision with which each has prepared a dainty dog's breakfast for his successor. Just ask John McCain, as Barack Obama makes hay. Or Gordon Brown, as the Tory fop Boris Johnson chunters merrily into the mayoralty of London. Or indeed, ask Brendan Nelson, who finds himself in awkward possession of a leadership he would never have held had Howard's succession plan been better organised.

Actually, they did ask Nelson on Wednesday night. Sky News's David Speers, who perhaps had not been briefed on the Howard speech and thus had missed the inside Ashes skinny about how the election wasn't really lost after all, asked Nelson outside the event whether the Howard–Costello hostilities had contributed to the Coalition's election defeat. 'Well, look – I'm not going to get a, you know, retrospect-o-scope out on that', was Nelson's stern reply. Fair play to him.

Nobody else was using the retrospect-o-scope that night – least of all Howard, who instead delivered some canapé-sized, thrillingly batty nuggets of advice.

'Rage against Opposition! Work as hard as you can to get out of it as soon as you can! Be proud of what we've achieved! Don't take any cheek from the other side!'

'Cheek, John!' the diners might well have chorused, had they not been too well bred. They seem to have forgiven him for stringing them along, then abandoning them to the chair-sniffers and the bra-snappers of Opposition. But in some quarters it could be viewed as entry-level cheek; to give advice on Opposition to those in whose consignment there you have been directly instrumental.

10 May 2008

MR SOMERSAULT

The Rudd government's first budget, in May 2008, was trailed extensively in advance in quite terrifying terms by the prime minister and his treasurer, Wayne Swan, who warned that it would be full of tough measures and spending cuts. When it appeared, the document was far more benign than expected, which necessitated some extremely fancy footwork on the part of the Opposition. Particularly the shadow treasurer, Mr Turnbull.

Malcolm Turnbull is taller than he looks – easily five eleven. And while by no means fat, he is hardly a stripling. Which makes it all the more impressive that he yesterday managed such an audacious, high-speed, midair triple-axel on matters budgetary. It would have been the envy of any serious figure-skater.

Mr Turnbull's planned routine was entirely different: a muscular choreographical work called *There Is No Inflationary Crisis*, set to an appropriately indignant Wagnerian overture. This work, rehearsed exhaustively in public last week by the spangled and enthusiastic shadow treasurer, denounced the government for its vile pretence that inflation in Australia is any sort of problem, and expressed stout opposition to the idea of spending cuts.

He was ably supported by the lithe form of his leader, Brendan

Nelson, who nearly a fortnight ago performed a breathtaking impromptu version of his solo spoken-word show about the importance of maintaining the Baby Bonus as a universal entitlement – a work well known among the arts community by its working title, *Every Sperm Is Sacred.* (Nelson's other major works, *I See Dead People* and *Five Dollars' Worth of Petrol*, are still awaiting a corporate sponsor.)

You can appreciate the position in which both men found themselves, then, when budget night brought a document whose spending cuts did not live up to the savagery promised in the pre-budget promotional material.

Dr Nelson seemed a little deflated yesterday. Questioned by the ABC's political correspondent, Chris Uhlmann, in the morning, he refused to have an opinion on the installation of a $150,000 cut-off for the Baby Bonus.

'Well, we'll just have a look at the fine print on this', was the best he could manage.

Mr Turnbull, however, was ready for the performance of his life.

Whatever else anyone might say about the member for Wentworth, he is certainly enthusiastic. There is about him nothing of the faintly hangdog air that used to hover around shadow treasurers in the long dark days of Labor's Opposition.

Skating forth with aplomb onto the ice, he executed his stunning reversal with a fixed and debonair smile that never wavered – not once – as he gave Australia his new routine, *This Budget Is Inflationary!*

The finance minister, Lindsay Tanner, had a different view. In his pinched, cynical way, he thought perhaps Mr Turnbull was using a body double. 'The member for Wentworth has cloned himself!' he cried, adding for clarity that there was 'no truth to the rumour that he used his ego as the stem cell'.

For sensible Coalition comment on the matter of the Baby Bonus, we were forced to turn to the venerable Wilson Tuckey, a father and long-standing turf expert, who did not hesitate to disapprove of the new means test.

'I've been in the racing business for many, many years and we tend to look at the high achievers as those that should have foals', he said.

Good news for high-income earners. Bad news for the poor, whose children will be melted down for glue when Wilson is PM.

15 May 2008

YOU SAY BUDGET, HE SAYS BOOZE

The handful of savings measures in the budget – a new luxury car tax, for example, and an increased levy on premixed alcoholic drinks – were opposed by Dr Nelson and his followers, as the Doctor himself announced in a characteristically soulful speech to the House of Representatives. Petrol prices were at the time experiencing a sharp peak, so Dr Nelson threw in a promise to cut fuel excise. This pledge was later abandoned by the Coalition.

As every unpopular school kid knows, there are a couple of ways to deal with being a reject.

One tactic is simply to get used to it. Stay in your room, develop weird obsessive interests, and eventually go into politics.

The other is: throw a giant party and hope for the best.

Brendan 'Nine per cent' Nelson last night went for plan B.

His dream budget is a thrilling, hedonistic $6-billion affair, and nearly everyone is invited. Dr Nelson's Budget Reply party will be fully catered, with about 42 million bottles of premixed boozy delights. Jerry-cans of cheap petrol will be provided.

There is every chance he will throw in some luxury cars, although you'll have to show up to find out; the invitation also holds out a strong hint of cheaper computer software and tax-deductible sandwiches.

The party has a good chance of popular success.

For one thing, Dr Nelson's folks are out of town, more or less permanently. John Howard and Peter Costello, who would no doubt have been horrified by the plans, are no longer in a position to reiterate their views on why cutting petrol excise is a dumb thing to do.

For another, it has simple appeal; what's not to love about cheap booze and petrol?

Choice of words is always important in politics. In Thatcher's Britain in the late 1980s, the Iron Lady's decision to introduce a new council tax caused widespread pandemonium, and led to her eventual demise. You could tell pretty much where anybody stood on the issue, just from what they labelled it as. Thatcher loyalists stoutly insisted on calling it 'the community charge'. Everybody else called it 'the poll tax'.

Something very similar is happening to Tuesday's budget. If you are a member of the Rudd Revolution, you refer to the document as 'this inflation-fighting budget'. If your heart lies with the Nelson Resistance, however, it is 'this high-taxing, high-spending budget'. Rudd Revolutionaries speak ringingly of the budget's 'luxury car tax', but Brendan Nelson last night rebadged it as a 'Tarago tax'.

And if you read the budget in the original Ruddese, you will find that it imposes an excise increase on 'alcopops' – a term which has the effect of making premixed drinks sound like fizzy, frivolous items, almost certainly purchased by effeminate Sydney types and fifteen-year-old girls with too much pocket money and thus just begging to be heavily taxed.

Nelson Resistance fighters do not generally recognise 'alcopops'; they tend to refer to them as 'ready to drink' beverages, or 'RTDs'. An 'RTD' sounds like a new model of four-wheel-drive ('I was out shootin' pigs in my new Ford RTD') and evokes a rather more manly drinker, much more the sort of chap Dr Nelson wants to win over.

In the hands of Dr Nelson last night, the spectre of the pissed fifteen-year-old vanished entirely and the new tax became 'a one-dollar slug on responsible Australians who happen to enjoy a premixed Bundy and Coke or Scotch and dry'.

16 May 2008

LOYAL WORKHORSE ESCAPES KNACKER'S YARD – FOR NOW

A seasoned factional figure is forced to atone for an offence against his Supreme Leader.

Martin Ferguson has been a member of the Labor Party for forty years.

He is an earnest and hard-working MP, and an influential factional figure within his party.

Some of Labor's sharper practitioners, mocking Mr Ferguson's occasional tendency to mumble, call him 'Marn' behind his back, but there is no disputing that the man is Labor to his bootstraps. If you were undertaking a stage production of *Animal Farm*, you could do worse than casting Mr Ferguson in the role of Boxer.

Yesterday, Mr Ferguson was called upon to make a public self-criticism. His letter of several weeks ago, advising colleagues that he thought Kevin Rudd's 'Fuel Watch' plan would hurt people in western Sydney, has been leaked, and Mr Ferguson was therefore required to dissociate himself in no uncertain terms from his own views.

The prime minister's own attitude to what the Coalition is optimistically calling 'Fuelgate' is one of professed nonchalance.

'I think actually having an exchange of views and having a debate where you have a complete embrace of different points of view is the way to go', he told Parliament smoothly on Tuesday. 'We are actually pretty relaxed about having a debate which has different points of view. We do not seek to suppress different points of view.'

Poor Mr Ferguson. It was even worse than he had feared. As all the prime minister's colleagues know, Mr Rudd reserves the expression 'I'm actually pretty relaxed about that' for moments of particularly uncontrolled private rage.

As Boxer approached the dispatch box yesterday, the prime minister looked on with chillingly neutral eyes. A tiny spasm seemed briefly to pass across those disciplined features, as Mr Ferguson referred to petrol prices as 'this little problem'. But good old Boxer was soon back on message.

'Those cabinet discussions have been and will continue to be robust debate, because the best policy comes out of a free and frank exchange of ideas', he recited several times. 'As a result of that process and on the evidence of the ACCC, I was convinced that there was a better way forward.'

The rest of question time proceeded as it normally does; government MPs popped up to implore ministers to expand upon the theme of the government's magnificence, and ministers responded by reading out page after page of prepared statements. Free and robust debate! A frank exchange of views!

Comrade Ferguson's capitulation suggests that discipline is as crisp as ever in the Ruddocracy. But the increasing disarray in the Dear Leader's papers suggests intriguingly otherwise.

Mr Rudd has always spread out his papers in question time, constructing neat piles which he rearranges and tends with all the assiduity of a pensioner at bingo. But in recent days, his piles have become noticeably dishevelled. There were eighteen yesterday, as best we could count – although counting them was difficult because they spilled into each other. At one point, he dragged up another chair and had three new piles going on that, plus another stack propped up behind the brass clock that adorns his desk.

The whole effect was unsettling in its disorder; kind of like the scene in *A Beautiful Mind* where you finally get to see inside John Nash's shed and it's a flapping mass of newspaper clippings, and you finally understand the true extent of his condition.

29 May 2008

NO TANTRUMS, NO KICKS: MS DEMURE LEAVES HER SEAT QUIETLY

The member for Robertson, Belinda Neal, occupied an enormous newsprint acreage at about this time, owing to an outing she undertook to Iguana Joe's, a family restaurant in her electorate, with husband John della Bosca, then the NSW minister for education. Staff alleged that the pair had been rude and aggressive, with Ms Neal at one point posing the immortal question 'Don't you know who I am?' Denials and recriminations ensued, as well as much reportage about Ms Neal's history of temper tantrums. From the safety of an overseas assignment, the prime minister ventured the opinion that Ms Neal should undergo counselling. We had our first glimpse of her when Parliament resumed.

In the past week, a certain notoriety has built up around the person of Belinda Neal. So alarming are the accounts of her exploits that at this point a genuine bombshell about the member for Robertson would probably be that she likes kittens, or has a secret knack for flower arranging.

A hushed, expectant silence preceded her arrival in question time yesterday. Would she be wheeled in, cursing and spitting, restrained on a trolley like Hannibal Lecter? Would she be gnawing on the shinbone of some poor unfortunate Pizza Hut delivery boy who forgot the garlic bread?

But as regular attendees will tell you for nothing, anticlimax is a regular feature of question time.

Neal, demurely attired in pink, arrived and took her place without kicking anyone. She did not meet anyone's eye, but calmly unpacked her laptop and absorbed herself in business unknown.

Brendan Nelson asked the prime minister about petrol prices. Neal tapped away at her keyboard.

A Labor backbencher asked the prime minister about safety nets for workers. A Liberal daredevil yelled in response: 'What about safety nets for the staff at Iguana's?' but Neal didn't even flinch, let alone throw anything or curse. Her state of heavy-lidded docility was like that of a python on a school visit; perhaps her handlers allowed her to gorge on baby rats before question time.

Ten questions were asked and answered, and it was as if 'Iguanagate' had never happened. Then Julie Bishop, the deputy leader of the Opposition, climbed to her feet. Something in her manner – her tautly muscled gait, perhaps, or the defiant set of her jaw – told us that she was going to tackle the member for Robertson.

We tensed in our seats. Bishop is in a lower weight division than Neal, but she works out; anything could happen.

'Will the prime minister assure this house that neither he, nor his office, nor any of his ministers or their officers, were involved in any way in the preparation of the statutory declarations of the member for Robertson's staff regarding [the Iguanas] incident?' Bishop asked.

Neal cocked an eyebrow, but she did not need to raise even the eyebrow in her own defence, because Anthony Albanese leapt in swiftly to have the question ruled out of order.

Albanese is in a position to take a broad view of this affair. Apart from being the leader of government business in the chamber, he is also said to have been personally punched by the member for Robertson during a Sydney University Student Council meeting in the 1980s.

In vain did the Opposition try to move motions compelling Neal to explain herself; Albanese stepped in and crushed every attempt.

One of the votes compelled Neal to vacate her seat; she did it without a murmur. The member for Solomon gave her a kiss on the cheek. In some sections of the Labor Party, blood is still thicker than water.

17 June 2008

DON'T DARE DRINK TO THE HEALTH MINISTER'S HEALTH

The Rudd government's obsession with binge drinking continued.

In the good old days, health ministers were never healthy. You used to have marathon lunchers in the job, such as Graham Richardson and Michael Wooldridge. Florid men, who looked as if one more carafe of claret would land them in serious coronary distress. Men whose interest in the health system was implicitly guaranteed by the fact that they were but a sclerotic heartbeat away from needing it in a big way.

Nowadays, all that's changed.

The last Howard health minister, Tony Abbott, is addicted to endorphins and you can barely move in Parliament House without seeing him streak past in the briefest of shorts, on his way to the gym.

Kevin Rudd's first health minister, Nicola Roxon, has a disappointingly youthful complexion and a seriously judgmental approach to booze. In the Rudd government's battle against binge, she is Booze Boadicea, riding out in search of sin. Yesterday in question time, she fixed her clear, teetotaller's eye on the temporarily empty seat normally occupied by Paul Neville, the National Party's MP for Hinkler.

'I am sorry that the member for Hinkler is not here because I have to confess that, when I was walking the halls of Parliament in the last few weeks, I walked past the member for Hinkler's office', she said, through pursed lips. 'Imagine my surprise, coming across in the window of the member for Hinkler's office a life-sized bear. It was not just an ordinary bear; it was actually a white polar bear. It was quite a famous bear – the Bundy bear, the only bear in the country which has his whole life committed to promoting alcohol.'

In vain did Neville later plead that Bundaberg is in his electorate. His card has been marked.

Meanwhile, further information has come to hand on the Brand Turnbull market-research affair. Wayne Swan revealed to the chamber on Tuesday that he had become aware of some secret focus group research that took place in Melbourne last week, in which punters were rounded up and asked what they thought of the shadow treasurer's website, résumé, budget-reply speech and the general cut of his jib.

Yesterday, Swan was able to furnish Parliament with some of the responses.

'An empty vessel. You don't know what he stands for. No real substance. He uses situations for his own advantage. He bleeds people dry', a pleased treasurer recited to the house, while Turnbull himself smothered a happy little smile (he loves to be talked about, whatever the terms).

Mr Swan was too polite to read out some of the other responses; the *Herald* understands one of the respondents described Turnbull as a 'succubus', which suggests that the entire focus group session may have been conducted in Monash University's classics department. Turnbull could not fairly be described as a mythical female demon who sleeps with mortal men and saps them of their life force, but there is no doubt that the criticisms reported by Mr Swan were quite personal in nature.

'Brendan was in the focus groups!' piped the finance minister, Lindsay Tanner, giving voice to the suspicions of many.

19 June 2008

IF ONLY THEY WERE ALL LIKE RAIN MAN

Brendan Nelson is vexed to the point of apoplexy by the prime minister's reliance on speaking notes. 'Word for word!' he will often hiss disgustedly as Kevin Rudd folds his script and resumes his seat after an answer in question time.

To be fair to Rudd, Nelson's own accomplishment in this department is rare to the point of freakishness. It is not unusual to see him speak for half an hour, unaccompanied by aids or props of any kind. He laces his oratory with detail both complex and obscure; within one sentence, he might canvass the GDP of Swaziland and then mention the bloke who runs the Mudgee IGA, just to show he's not faking it.

His obsession with memorising facts and figures, while he was education minister, quickly earned him the nickname 'Rain Man'. If criticism is to be made of him, it's that the richness of his gift makes his disdain for those not similarly blessed seem a bit curmudgeonly, like Ian Thorpe sneering at anyone obliged to use floaties.

But on the question of question time, he has an excellent point. Question time has two elements. The first question, and alternate questions thereafter, are delivered by the Opposition to the government and tend to have a confrontational air: 'Will the treasurer now apologise to hard-working Australians for his vicious, low-minded budget?' and so forth.

Questions two, four, six, eight and continuing even numbers all the way up to twenty are asked by government backbenchers and answered by their frontbench betters. As a rule, they are more caressing in tone. At times, they move shamelessly into heavy petting. 'Perhaps the unnervingly handsome foreign affairs minister would be good enough to outline for the house just how completely this government dominates the world stage?'

I don't think I'm breaching any state secrets in disclosing that ministers throughout history have rarely been taken by surprise on these even-numbered questions. All governments do it – pepper question time with craven, boot-licking little inquiries from aspirational backbenchers, giving ministers the opportunity to deliver carefully prepared sermons describing just how lavishly their own skills outshine those of the previous administration.

Howard's ministers used to do it, too, but after six months of the Rudd government it's now pretty clear that this lot is worse. Mark Latham's Labor used to read books aloud to children; Rudd Labor reads cheat-sheets aloud to Parliament, and they are shameless about it. I can't think of a single minister who doesn't bring a prepared speech to the dispatch box with them when answering a 'Dorothy Dixer'; most of them simply spend several minutes morosely reading the answer out word for word, then sit down.

There are minor variations. Julia Gillard brings a script but departs from it occasionally. So does Wayne Swan, despite his early reputation for awkwardness. The minister for youth and sport, Kate Ellis, likes to memorise little passages so that she can look up and smile at crucial points. 'We are well aware of the importance of sport and the Olympics to Australians', she sparkled on Thursday, causing hearts to beat faster amid some sections of the Coalition benches (the minister for sport is rather a good sort).

The finance minister, Lindsay Tanner, writes his answers in longhand on foolscap pages, in black ink. What is most puzzling is there are so few crossings-out on the Tanner scripts. When preparing for question time, the finance minister clearly is capable of dashing off a cogent argument with very little by way of reversal or change of heart.

So why can't he just do it on his feet? Why can't any of them? Even the prime minister reads his Dorothy Dix answers out pretty much word for word. There's no sense of debate, no sense of spontaneity, no reason at all, really, why they shouldn't just table the damn speeches and let the Hansard reporters out early for afternoon tea.

It is possible that my annoyance at this phenomenon is inflated by the fact that I regularly have to sit through it. But a federal minister is a well-paid creature retained by the voters of Australia to pay exclusive attention to one particular allotted slice of public policy. Is it too much to ask that they should be well enough informed to speak knowledgeably about their slice when required?

During the Howard era, these same Labor faces used to jeer at junior Coalition ministers who were incautious or nervous enough to bring prepared speeches with them to the dispatch box in question time. 'Page two!' they'd chorus, when Jackie Kelly or Larry Anthony reached the end of their first page of notes.

Back then, cheat-sheeting was a sufficiently unusual event to warrant special ridicule. These days, they're all at it.

21 June 2008

HOW BLOWTORCH WAS DISEMVOWELLED

Martin Ferguson returns to the public eye – this time entrusted with a crucial mission.

A long time ago, in a galaxy far, far away, the leadership of the *Star Ship Australia* became increasingly vexed about the relentless advance of fuel prices.

The ship's captain, Kev Solo, a hardworking half-human, half-android famed for his silver helmet, found himself for the first time the object of accusatory cries from his subjects, for whom filling the family space-hopper had become a costly trial.

And so Kev Solo sent out a warrior, by the name of Martin Ferguson, to go forth to the galactic council on fossil fuels in Jeddah, Saudi Arabia. A Jeddah Knight, in other words, to do battle with OPEC, the evasive oil-producing forces of the East.

Ferguson is a galactic skirmisher of some experience, who combines the doggedness of Chewbacca with the speech patterns of Yoda. It is said of Ferguson that he was the only English-speaking delegate to the Jeddah summit to require an English interpreter, so confounding is his ability to form entire sentences without the use of a single vowel.

The Jeddah Knight was sped on his mission by the ringing words of his leader, who spoke recently of the need to 'apply the blowtorch to the OPEC organisation'. But as Shadow Admiral Brendan Nelson and his fellow members of the loyal Galactic Opposition wasted no time in pointing out yesterday, the blowtorch wielded by our Jeddah Knight was something of a fizzer.

The expected chest beating did not occur. As debate raged during question time on the poop deck of *Star Ship Australia*, Kev Solo at no stage repeated the line about the blowtorch. Perhaps he has had occasion to rethink the wisdom of applying a naked flame to that much fuel, even if it is just a rhetorical one.

Kev Solo may be hasty, and sometimes incautious with his words, but there is no denying that the Force is strong within him. Yesterday, for instance, he was able simultaneously to put words into Ferguson's mouth (an inherently risky venture; you're very unlikely to get them back in the same condition) and make them match the underwhelming communiqué from the Jeddah meeting. All of this was accomplished using only the powers of telekinesis – mind control – and without having to hear from Ferguson at all.

The Jeddah Knight himself will not return this week. He has been packed off to the Australian–American Leadership Dialogue, an event from which it will take him several days to strip the vowels.

Kev Solo went on to give us a second glimpse of the Force yesterday, demonstrating his well-developed powers of precognition.

'May I refer the member to the statement I made at the end of next week?' he said, in response to a question from Joanna Gash, the member for Gilmore.

Meanwhile, Ferguson's forbearance won plaudits from some unexpected sources.

'Apparently, Martin Ferguson was too sensible to repeat his leader's idea that he could put the blowtorch on OPEC', Wilson Tuckey said.

Tuckey is a visiting life-form currently resident in Western Australia. You may remember him from his brief appearance in the original *Star Wars* movie – in the bar scene.

24 June 2008

RIVERS FLOODED – IN GOBBLEDEGOOK

The premiers met in Sydney to commemorate an agreement with the federal government on the management of the Murray–Darling. Or is that what they were commemorating? Reading the mangled prose of the meeting's much-hyped communiqué, I really couldn't tell.

Finally – a breakthrough. At Thursday's Council of Australian Governments conference here in Sydney – more commonly known as a premiers' conference – the floodgates at last opened, thanks to a landmark agreement between the Commonwealth and state leaders.

Years of blocking tactics, of pinched parochial interest, of parched downriver deprivation gave way, and massive environmental flows of jargon were released. A great gout of gobbledegook burst forth, flooding through the great river system, bringing life and cheer to its shrunken tributaries and thirsty creeks.

Intergovernmental agreement! A Whole-of-Basin Plan! Vehicles for long-term reform! Interstate regulatory arrangements! The re-engineering of the Lower Lakes!

Riverside communities, who for years have eked out an existence whittling clothes pegs out of dead river gums, leapt up in astonishment as the silvery torrent thundered towards them, restoring life and colour to their desiccated world.

Children who had lived their whole lives without so much as glimpsing a real, live 'framework for action' romped and splashed in the shallows, and the more adventurous – unbidden, and perhaps answering some long-dormant, atavistic instinct – made rafts. Wet laundry plastered the rocks on the banks, and dragonflies zoomed around in the sunshine, while individual buzzwords sparkled like fish between the reeds.

Across the raddled marshes that the river had hitherto worn like a salty scarf, whole crops sprang up – waving green pastures, promising rich future harvests of polysyllabic words such as 'intergovernmental' and 'regulatory'.

The prime minister, Kevin Rudd, applied his full bodyweight to the levers, opening the sluices ever wider.

'Last time we had a memorandum of understanding which is based on principles', he reminded the stragglers. 'We now have an intergovernmental agreement which we have just signed in front of you.'

The NSW premier, Morris Iemma, in the new spirit of co-operative federalism, selflessly diverted his own natural flows of bureaucratic blatherskite to join those of his comrades.

'The other key issue that New South Wales has wanted addressed has been the transfer of risk, and the management of risk, when it comes to liabilities, and any future change in liabilities as a result of a nationwide cap, and the determination of those levels', he gushed.

The meeting's formal communiqué was itself a rich environmental flow of fatuity. You may remember (or, more likely, you may not) that the last time the premiers' conference was held, in Adelaide back in March, it issued a communiqué announcing: 'We have for the first time in the basin a co-operative and accountable governance arrangement, which will enable genuine whole of basin water management to restore the environment and ensure sustainable agriculture in the future. Significantly, COAG also agreed that providing for critical human needs will be included in the basin plan.'

Thursday's communiqué confirmed that this latest meeting was much, much more advanced. 'COAG signed an intergovernmental agreement (IGA) on Murray–Darling Basin reform that establishes the new governance of the Murray–Darling Basin. Notably, the IGA includes arrangements for critical human needs, comprehensive and consistent trading arrangements across the basin and the transition of the Murray–Darling Basin Commission to the new Murray–Darling Basin Authority.'

How is this July agreement different from the March memorandum? It's been signed.

Much mention was made of the 'projects' worth $3.7 billion that were approved at Thursday's meeting – the re-engineering, piping and other fiddling that will occupy the states in the next 'five years plus', which is the slippery timeframe nominated by Rudd when invited to do so by Kerry O'Brien on the ABC on Thursday night.

'That's absolutely new – $3.7 billion worth of projects', Rudd had earlier assured journalists at the press conference after the premiers' meeting. Well, yes and no. The existence of the $3.7 billion is not new – it's part of the old Howard government $10-billion plan, which the Rudd government has topped up and refitted for its own use in a sort of governmental *Pimp My Ride* exercise. But the actual projects have not been identified before; this is the factor which allows the prime minister the rhetorical wiggle-room to call the spending 'new'.

Now that Rudd has revived the premiers' conference, we are reminded of the magical theatrical opportunity the press conference afterwards provides – an opportunity for nine adults to gather and blather to highly trained journalists for upwards of half an hour, without once making anything clear.

Struggling to keep his head above the brine, one journalist shrieked, 'Where in this agreement does it say anything about more water?' – or words to that effect. It was tricky to hear him above the roar of the torrent. Water, it turned out, was another matter entirely.

'Well, one of the things that you can't do as prime minister is make it rain', Rudd reminded the questioner, tartly.

Fair enough. But who needs rain, now the river folk can gulp down pints and pints of political pidgin?

5 July 2008

NO NEED TO PANIC AS DR WONG ADMINISTERS CPR

At the National Press Club, Penny Wong unveiled the Rudd government's answer to what its leader once termed 'the greatest moral challenge of our time'. No wonder it deserved its own acronym.

No more 'emissions trading scheme'. As of yesterday, it's now called a carbon pollution reduction scheme. A CPR scheme, in short.

The title imparts a convenient tone of emergency, just in case we weren't getting that clearly enough from Kevin 'The End of the World Is Nigh' Rudd.

Australia, lashed to a gurney, is bursting through the double doors into emergency, its vital signs ebbing, its temperature catastrophically elevated and its fluids dangerously low.

Happily, it's Dr Penny Wong's shift. Wong has the calm, blank face and steady hands of a good trauma surgeon. Outlining Australia's unilateral course of tough love yesterday at the National Press Club ('Hold still. I'm afraid this is going to hurt quite a lot'), the climate change minister's tone never wavered, even as she reiterated the grim global tidings which we have all learned to dread, thanks to Garnaut and Stern and their fellow prophets of the apocalypse.

'This is not an emotional plea to abandon our self-interest in favour of ecological concerns', she said, emotionlessly.

This, no doubt, is why Kevin Rudd gave her the hardest job in the cabinet. Wong's soothing, slightly mesmeric bedside manner is impressive. ('Now, I want you to close your eyes, open your wallet and count backward from 2013.') After years spent as a backroom negotiator for the Labor Left, Wong is herself virtually immune to pain of any kind, and you would certainly never be so foolish as to play poker with her. In an uncharacteristic and temporary lapse into rhyme, Wong claimed during her speech that the green paper was intended to communicate the government's 'dispositions and preferred positions on emissions'.

A beat of silence followed, and others beside your correspondent may have been plagued by the lyrics of a Young MC tune, 'Bust a Move': 'On a mission / and you're wishin' / someone could cure your lonely condition ...'

Dr Wong had good news for heavy polluters: they will be eligible for transitional assistance. This does not mean that power-station owners will be 'reskilled' to work in tourism or encouraged to leave the industry with dignity and devote themselves to the composition of lilting blues songs. Nor does it mean Australia's aluminium smelters will be reopened as a chain of niche bed-and-breakfasts any time soon.

It turns out to mean money in the form of free pollution permits and – in the case of coal-fired power stations – a specific line of welfare called the Electricity Sector Adjustment Scheme. This goes in part to show that no matter how sclerotic and dysfunctional the NSW Right is, it still maintains some grip on the Rudd government's neck-scruff.

Dr Wong is inflicting pain, all right. But she has morphia available, and she's not afraid to prescribe.

17 July 2008

DR DISCLAIMER'S GOOSE IS COOKED

Meanwhile, circumstances for the Opposition leader continued to worsen. Climate change was an issue already dividing his troops, and Dr Nelson's attempts to please everyone did not improve his aura of authority.

The problem for Brendan Nelson is that it will be hard, from now on, to take anything he says seriously.

Very few of his colleagues seem to. In the past few weeks, as Nelson set about erecting a new philosophical platform for the Libs on climate change, his shadow cabinet simply followed along behind him, tactfully dismantling his efforts every day after sundown.

The most surreal part of this routine is that his opponents don't tend to disagree with him openly. Instead, they simply pretend that he hasn't spoken at all, or that whatever he's said has been catastrophically misinterpreted. This produces some bizarre moments, such as on Sunday when the Opposition spokesman for the environment, Greg Hunt, under questioning from the ABC's Barrie Cassidy after a week of increasingly hysterical public division within the Libs, began an answer: 'Well, firstly, everybody in their public statements has been absolutely clear about where we're at.'

With respect to Hunt, who may well himself have been quite clear at regular intervals, this was about as convincing as Amy Winehouse kicking off an answer with: 'As you know, if there's one thing I simply cannot bear, it's recreational drug-use.'

But you can understand why the colleagues might retreat into denial. Nelson has a strange approach to problem-solving, in which he operates both as canary and mine shaft. When confronted with a twisty political or philosophical conundrum, he'll dabble with both sides of the argument, always passionately, sometimes angrily, and occasionally simultaneously.

His delivery is often backfilled with personal anecdote about poor or blighted people of his direct acquaintance; this tends to muddy the waters and prevent a clear view of his opinion.

On the questions of the national apology and climate change, it became clear over a period of months that what Nelson was actually doing was conducting an argument with himself. For a leader to argue with himself in public is bad enough. But what makes it worse is that he keeps losing. The substantial result is that colleagues of Nelson's have stopped responding to what he says. Nelson now needs a permanent asterisk above his head for the purposes of any broadcast, with a discreet disclaimer down the bottom of the screen: 'Views expressed are the opinion of the speaker at this moment. They do not necessarily represent the views of the Liberal Party. They do not necessarily represent the views of the shadow cabinet. They almost certainly will not represent the views of the speaker by about ten past four tomorrow afternoon.'

This is bad news for any politician.

But it could be worse. Imagine if Dr Disclaimer were actually your GP. The first consultation would sound something like this.

'Good morning. First of all, I'd like to acknowledge the traditional owners of this surgery. And the great Australians, from the prime ministers to the graziers to the bloke who runs the Wendy's in Launceston (G'day, mate!), who have made this nation the proud, big-spirited place it is today. On my way into the consulting rooms today, I was stopped in the street by a little old lady. She was carrying a tin with three dollars' worth of petrol in it. And she said to me, "Brendan" (I always ask that people call me Brendan) – "Brendan," she said. "I'm not rich or important. I don't have a medical degree. But I've got this rash on my arm. Can you help me?" And that's what this health system is all about. And if I ever forget that little old lady, if I ever turn my back on her, then you can go ahead and repierce my ear, because you'll know I've given up. In your own case, I'm absolutely convinced it's a cold. Which is not to say it's not cancer.'

You might be forgiven for feeling confused. By the second consultation, you'd be dead, and probably featuring in one of Nelson's famous reveries about dead people he has known.

One of the surest signs that Dr Disclaimer's goose is cooked came on Thursday night, when Hunt returned to the airways to praise him so effusively that no doubt could possibly remain of his imminent demise.

'Brendan Nelson will lead us to the election and he will do that because he is a very driven individual with a passion for Australia, a passion for the challenges that mums and dads and pensioners face. He is not taken by the rich and famous, the high and mighty. He actually enjoys and loves going to ... whether it's the Camden or the Campbelltown or the Berwick or the Pakenham shopping centres', Hunt insisted during a *Lateline* interview.

This is politics, where the richer the praise, the cooler the corpse.

2 August 2008

MADONNA, NELSON AND THE PETER PRINCIPLE: THAT'S POLITICS

The new session of Parliament brought the swearing-in of the new Senate, allowing the senators elected in November 2007 to take their seats, and exterminating the Coalition's majority. Having for three years been commanded by John Howard's lieutenants, the upper house was now at the mercy of a clutch of Greens, an anti-gambling campaigner and a man who periodically dresses up as a fizzy-pop bottle.

The Senate is back. It's been a long time between drinks for the poor old upper house, forced for the past three years to live in legislative drought, unable to meddle with anything or have inquiries or do any of the things that senates like to busy themselves with.

But as the rickety balance-of-power equation was hammered into place yesterday, you could feel life returning to the place, like the Serengeti as the rains arrive. Dusty senators stirred and stretched. Greens grinned from seemingly every corner. Nick Xenophon and Steve Fielding, the costumed campaigners, commandeered whole benches to themselves and took up action stations. The stirring theme to *Hawaii Five-o* blared forth in all its tinny splendour.

This was a mistake – the South Australian Labor MP Nick Champion, who had his phone accidentally run over last week, now finds it impossible to turn off, and it was his persistent ring tone that thus provided the backing music as he looked on from the bleachers. But it was beautifully apt, given the catchphrase for this Senate looks like being 'Block 'em, Danno!'

Any celebrity who has experienced troubled times knows you can swing the mood at an event simply by turning up with a stunning date, and Brendan Nelson demonstrated this principle perfectly. He and Peter Costello were the talk of the chamber as they sat close, sharing jokes, talking intently with the slightly exaggerated hand gestures characteristic of people who know they're being watched. It was the biggest public show of unity since Madonna and Guy Ritchie last faked one.*

What did it mean?

It can't have been good news for Malcolm 'Deep Throat' Turnbull, who is still recovering from the revelation – delivered by *Four Corners* on Monday night – that Conrad Black considers his judgment a bit dicey. When someone who lives in a Florida correctional facility questions your judgment, you know you're in trouble.

With the new Senate duly launched, we all trooped down to the House of Reps for question time, and were surprised to find that Kevin Rudd had turned into John Howard. Having happily promised a profusion of new ideas in Opposition, Mr Rudd is discovering that it's another thing entirely to get big ideas through unco-operative Senates. The Coalition's going to knock over his alcopops, siphon away his condensates and nick his luxury cars, leaving him nearly $6.2 billion poorer and a hell of a lot grumpier.

If you closed your eyes and listened, it could have been Howard himself griping about lousy political opportunists and economic vandals and 'uncertain global economic times ahead'.

Wayne Swan chimed in: 'They [the Coalition] choose to stand up for people buying luxury cars but not for lower interest rates for working families. They are not with the working families of Australia who are getting the tax cuts that they made them wait years and years and years for.'

'You voted against them in the Senate', reminded Joe Hockey helpfully.

**Brendan and Peter didn't last. Neither did Madonna and Guy.*

27 August 2008

IF ONLY OUR MOB COULD SAY BOO TO A MOOSE

Yesterday was a tough day to be an Australian political reporter.

In America, joyous reporters swarmed like ants over Governor Sarah Palin, the Republican vice-presidential nominee, who zooms in her snowmobile across the caribou plains with rifle at the ready and her youngest children – Twig, Block and Tackle, or something similar – snuggled into a papoose at her side. Whether Governor Palin turns out to be a triumph or a disaster, who can avoid being fascinated by a woman who prefers to catch and cook her own moose?

In question time it was horribly difficult to forsake the inevitable daydreams of such journalistic riches and concentrate instead on our own big-game specialist, Kevin Rudd the jargon hunter, who stalks through the bureaucratic jungle in quest of phrases so devastatingly banal that barely anyone can survive them.

'If you look at the challenges which many businesses have had in securing not just lines of credit but also affordable credit, it has been a real challenge out there, as it has been for Australian households', the PM began, as reporters drooped.

The minutes ticked drearily by as everybody waited for the day's big announcement – a Reserve Bank rate cut – and the prime minister gave us a numbing lecture about infrastructure.

Hmmm. Perhaps it would be worth moving to Russia, where Prime Minister Vladimir Putin on Monday saved five journalists from potential mauling when, on a tour of a Siberian national park, he shot an escaped Ussuri tiger with a tranquilliser gun.

It's probably a sin to covet thy neighbour's prime minister. But as the dusty plains of Rudd's verbiage spread out unendingly before us, it was hard not to yearn for an exotic and distant legislature where public figures might occasionally gun down a big cat in question time, rather than just droning on about capital expenditure.

Whoops!

Raised voices snapped attention back to Parliament, where – interest rate cut duly announced and gloated over – a controversy had broken out. The shadow assistant treasurer, Peter Dutton (the member for Dickson), had called the prime minister a rude word.

The speaker didn't hear quite what it was.

The leader of government business, Anthony Albanese, demanded a withdrawal.

The speaker concurred.

But what was the rude word?

Tony Abbott flowed slyly to his feet and suggested that Albanese could perhaps repeat the word, so as to facilitate the retraction process.

The Liberal frontbencher Christopher Pyne, something of a Portia, delivered a brief but stirring speech likening the persecution of Dutton to the witch trials of Salem.

'Requiring the member for Dickson to withdraw something, when nobody actually knows what it is, is ludicrous and reflects poorly on the house itself', he pleaded movingly.

Seven minutes passed in this fashion, as Liberal grandees queued up to propagandise on their new, united cause: Free the Dickson One.

'I ask the leader of the House to identify the offending word', commanded the speaker at last.

Albanese declined.

After some further huffing and puffing, the member for Dickson withdrew his remark.

And what was the offending word?

'Idiot.'

Oh, for the caribou plains.

3 September 2008

IT'S A COMPELLING COCKTAIL: CLEAVAGE AND AUTHORITY

Torrid as our own political times were in Australia, it was impossible to ignore the escalating drama in the United States, where Barack Obama eliminated Hillary Clinton to stand as presidential nominee for the Democrats, and John McCain responded by enlisting a truly stunning vice-presidential candidate from Alaska.

Even at a distance of 13,500 kilometres, Governor Sarah Palin has a remarkable effect on the conservative male.

After the live broadcast of Palin's convention speech on Thursday, Parliament's corridors in Canberra were full of slightly flushed, giggly Coalition blokes who could speak of little else.

'Bring on Sarah Palin!' hollered an excited Joe Hockey during question time in Canberra on Thursday, clearly pining for Alaska as he endured an eight-minute prime ministerial lecture on matters budgetary. (Of course, Joe Hockey has an understandably deep historical connection with 'hockey mums' – he was raised by one.)

As has been widely reported, Palin is a former beauty queen who hunts.

'As an immigrant, I'm not saying I came to the United States purely to meet chicks like that, but it was certainly high on my list of priorities', enthused the conservative commentator Mark Steyn this week.

It's not just that, as one-time potential Republican candidate and TV star Fred Thompson pointed out, 'She's the only candidate who knows how to field dress a moose.' It's something more; a compelling cocktail – authority plus maternalism, with a hint of cleavage.

Matron's back.

And she's hot.

And she's armed.

Call it the dominatrix effect; it's the same element that used to turn grown men into fawning, wobbling supplicants before the former British prime minister Margaret Thatcher. Her one-time junior minister, the late philanderer and diarist Alan Clark, was an admirer of Thatcher's 'pretty ankles'. He reported intoxicatedly after one meeting with her that he'd 'got a full dose of personality compulsion, something of the Fuehrer-Kontakt'. (Granted, Clark was a fairly extreme character. He spent much of the 1997 general election campaign being pursued by a South African judge whose wife and two daughters Clark had bedded, in what even his critics were forced to admit was a remarkable feat of multi-tasking.)

François Mitterand described Thatcher as having 'the eyes of Caligula and the voice of Marilyn Monroe'. Silvio Berlusconi only last year called her '*una bella gnoccha*' – roughly translated, it means 'a nice piece of pussy'. Trust Berlusconi, the Italian prime minister and super-spiv, to take things too far.

But why does a perfectly serious female politician – and no one could accuse Thatcher of being anything but – get these reviews? Even Bill Clinton, much of whose electoral success could be attributed to the subliminal sexual note in his personal magnetism, never got this sort of talk from the opposite sex, and he spent half his term with his pants around his ankles.

Neither 'side' of the feminist 'debate' has dealt particularly elegantly with Palin. The National Organisation for Women has no time for her because she is the wrong sort of woman – an attitude that cannot but diminish that organisation. Staunch Republicans, meanwhile, find themselves awkwardly borrowing the language of the feminist movement to condemn Palin's critics as sexist. But while half of the Republican movement protests that Sarah Palin is being targeted or ridiculed because she is a woman, one suspects the other half, like Mark Steyn, secretly dreams of being field-dressed by her.

Tony Abbott, for the record, admits that he finds Palin 'electrifying' and likens her to Thatcher. But he bridles at the suggestion that her gender has anything to do with the piquancy of her appeal.

'I think you might be suggesting that men are incapable of taking a female politician seriously', he says. 'We, conservatives, are always thrilled to find people who are not, if you like, the usual suspects. She's an attractive woman. But the fact that she is an attractive woman is no more significant than the fact that Barack Obama is a handsome man.'

The thing that makes Sarah Palin so fascinating is not so very different from what makes Obama fascinating. Palin is a Republican fantasy candidate – mother of five, pro-life, brilliant speaker, gorgeous and a good shot. In exactly the same way, Barack Obama is a fantasy Democrat candidate: family man, brilliant orator, he grew up poor, he's flawlessly educated and he's black for good measure. For all the bickering about records and experience, these two are pretty evenly placed – nobodies who came from nowhere, armed with little more than striking life stories and an amazing ability to fire the imagination.

In Australia, we do things more quietly. Our revolution has involved little of the breast-beating to be observed in the US, but it's undeniable that a revolution is under way, thanks to the unshowy leadership of Kevin Rudd.

Yesterday, our first female governor-general moved into Yarralumla. Our deputy prime minister, who poses no threat to the moose world, is nevertheless looking more and more like the backbone of the government. A proportion of cabinet's big jobs have gone to women, including Nicola Roxon, the first woman in Australia to combine a federal cabinet portfolio with the parenting of a young child.

It's not sexy, but it's worth a quick round of applause.

6 September 2008

THE CRUEL TRUTH: MR RIGHT JUST DIDN'T FANCY YOU

Dashing the hopes of fantasists everywhere, Peter Costello confirmed that he was indeed leaving politics.

So here we are. After the longest and most politically erotic Dance of the Seven Veils modern observers can bear to recall, the last scarf has wafted to the floor.

Peter Costello stands before us, exposed. And it turns out he's exactly the person we've always known him to be.

'I'm leaving', he declared on that tumultuous day in November last year. 'I'm not challenging', he reiterated last month at a Liberal senator's office-warming party. And all the shimmying about in between – months of coyness, an eyelash-flutter here, a dropped bra-strap there – amounts to nothing. He meant what he said, and he really is going.

There's no turn-on like genuine lack of interest, as they say, and Peter Costello's silence this year has proved utterly bewitching to some of his colleagues.

Modern chick-lit is full of advice about what to do when the man of your dreams doesn't call. Maybe he's just really, really busy. Maybe he's afraid of commitment. Maybe he's shy, or tongue-tied, or so in love with you he can barely speak.

Maybe he's secretly planning an incredible holiday for two, where he whisks you away by limousine to the airport and a private jet will be waiting, and there'll be flowers everywhere, and you'll touch down in Paris, and he'll take you to the Tuileries, and there'll be a glass of Cristal with a diamond in it the size of a pigeon's egg.

Sick with yearning for Costello, some Liberals have resorted to this degree of fantasy in recent months. Some journalists, too. The best conspiracy theory going around of late was that Costello never intended to retire at all; that his announcement last November was a strategy, giving him cover and a chance to scribble out his memoirs while some other poor boob bumbled into the leadership and got peppered with duck-shot for a bit.

According to this theory, Costello's close buddies have been in on the scam all along, honour-bound to insist that as far as they knew, Costello was planning to leave as promised, and never breathing a word about the exciting secret plan.

The great thing about this conspiracy theory is that to a believer, it was logically impossible to disprove. The more Costello's chums averred this year that they thought Costello was probably fair-dinkum about being on his way out, the more vigorously the believers nodded their heads: 'Well, they would say that, wouldn't they?'

When Costello let it be known that he wouldn't challenge Brendan Nelson, even this was not enough to kill off the conspiracy theory; it simply sprouted whole new crazy branches of speculation, in which Costello would somehow stand back while Nelson was executed, then accept the leadership, to uncontrollable applause.

Paris, flowers, a handsome avenger and a happy ending.

For the lovesick Libs, today is the day on which a horrible possibility becomes apparent: Maybe he's just not that into you.

11 September 2008

NOW YOU'VE GONE AND MADE HIM MAD – REALLY MAD

Malcolm Turnbull, chief tormentor of the troubled Liberal leader, travelled to Venice with his wife. Dr Nelson seized the opportunity to call a snap leadership ballot.

It's taken Brendan Nelson a long time to get mad.

But mad he was last night – madder than most of his colleagues had ever seen him. The Liberal leader is a famously temperate bloke. He comes up smiling in the face of almost anything: rancid polls, internal Liberal double-crossing, horrible things written in newspapers. He could be the Face of Valium, such is his ability to remain calm amid extreme provocation.

So he had two things working for him last night: the element of surprise, and the element of rage. The combination had a dizzying effect. 'He went through every emotion, with the possible exception of humour', one Liberal said. As Liberal MPs reeled out of the meeting, even Turnbull supporters were crediting Nelson with his best performance to date.

Most dived into offices to start the frenzied, excitable exchange of phone calls indispensable to the leadership spill process. There is nothing like Parliament House the night before a leadership challenge. A thrill of possibility tingles in the air. Knots of senators form in the gloom, then melt away on approach. Wild rumours whip around the building, then blow themselves out. Photographers crouch in dark corners.

Last night the big-game target was Malcolm Turnbull, returned all golden and sun-kissed from Italy, where he has been hanging out with his wife and virtuously not doing the numbers. Is it possible his best behaviour will be rewarded with defeat?

In question time yesterday, Turnbull did not utter a squeak – just sat there and watched while Nelson worked himself into a rage about the plight of the aged. Pensioners, Nelson declared during a towering piece of oratory, were now forced to eat baked beans and jam sandwiches, and it was all the fault of the Rudd government.

'That is what they are living on when you are at the UN General Assembly and the Parliament sits at the cost of $1 million a day!' he bellowed at the PM. He did not venture an analysis of what pensioners ate under the Howard government, which decided against a pension increase just over a year ago.

Nelson was flanked in his attack by his shadow minister for the ageing, Margaret May, who swept to the dispatch box to remind the prime minister that bread, coffee, lamb, electricity, butter, gas, prescription drugs and petrol had all ballooned in price. May did not mention citrus prices, but did not need to, as she had prepared for her moment in the spotlight by donning a jacket covered with fluorescent orange and lemon slices.

If there were pensioners in the party room, Nelson would be home and hosed.

17 September 2008

YOUR MOST HUMBLE SERVANT LETS HIS MINNOWS DO THE TALKING

Despite his impassioned oratory, Dr Nelson was toast. Bowing to what many of them had long seen as an inevitability, the Liberal party room elected Malcolm Turnbull as its leader. Mr Turnbull, who only weeks into Dr Nelson's leadership telephoned him and demanded that he resign because 'You're just no good at it', took the opportunity to praise his predecessor.

Malcolm Turnbull's victory press conference was already quite advanced (he was seven words in) when he uttered the first untruth of his young leadership.

'Well it's a great honour and privilege – humbling – to be elected today to lead the federal parliamentary Liberal Party.'

Accounts of the Turnbull ego do differ across the broad church of the Liberal Party. Some argue it is Milky Way-sized, while his intimate admirers and defenders (whose ranks are fast swelling with opportunists) argue it could probably be squeezed into Wembley Stadium. The chances of him finding anything about yesterday genuinely humbling, however, are about as good as Zimbabwe's new power-sharing agreement panning out well.

Broadcasts of these events really should feature a hand-bell, rung any time the speaker gets carried away into untruth by the emotion of the moment.

'Brendan has led the party through very difficult times. He's done that very well', Turnbull avowed later in the press conference, for example.

Ding-a-ling!

'I am a great believer in communication and consultation …'

Ding-a-ling-a-ling!

'I have learnt over the years that you cannot achieve anything working by yourself.'

DING-A-LING-A-LING-A-LING!

Turnbull's great task is to convince everyone that the headstrong, arrogant Turnbull is yesterday's news. Now, he's Your 'Umble Servant, and he stands ready to help.

Turnbull does additionally have something of a money problem. He's got too much of it; side by side yesterday, he and Julie Bishop looked like the Blake and Krystle Carrington of the Liberal Party. It's an awkward fit for the present political culture, in which the hard-luck story is king, and any candidate unlucky enough to have enjoyed a happy and comfortable childhood in a stable family unit starts very much behind the eight ball.

Fortunately for Turnbull, he was abandoned at the age of eight by his mother, who probably had no idea all those decades ago just what a handy future political service she was rendering her son.

So armed with his hard-luck story and the admiration or at least resignation of his colleagues, Your 'Umble Servant made his way to question time.

Now the old Turnbull, given one nationally televised hour to spar with Kevin Rudd, would have hogged the whole thing for himself, and probably tipped in some of his own cash to give the catering and draperies a bit of a lift while he was at it. Your 'Umble Servant, however, played it quite differently.

He asked two questions, both on the global financial crisis, and then sat back, allowing all of his minnow backbenchers a chance at the kill. Fran Bailey asked about the Goulburn River, Patrick Secker fretted about the Keith Community Hospital and Russell Broadbent (don't worry, you're not supposed to have heard of any of these people) discharged a strong interrogatory line concerning the high-tensile powerlines at the Wonthaggi desalination plant.

In political terms, this question-time technique is akin to Turnbull donning a T-shirt saying 'It's Not All About Me'.

But it was about him, and the government did not hesitate to disinter the old story about Turnbull seeking a Labor Senate vacancy in 1994.

'We have seen a former Labor Party member replaced by someone who wanted to be a Labor senator', squawked Anthony Albanese. (Turnbull later declared the story 'quite untrue', but his smile was rich as pound cake.)

Brendan Nelson and Peter Costello – the man who wanted the leadership but couldn't keep it and the man who could have got it but didn't want it – sat quietly on the back benches.

17 September 2009

IT JUST DOESN'T PAY TO KICK THE FAMILY FIRST SENATOR

Family First senator Steve Fielding, elected to represent Victoria in 2007 after the Victorian Labor Party committed a righteous cock-up of its preference planning, did some dreadful things to the government's legislation in the upper house. The government pretended it didn't mind.

Time marches on. Yesterday, the political ghost of Alexander Downer was laid to rest even as Kevin Rudd was in New York visiting the United Nations (an organisation Mr Downer detested in office, and for which – in a pleasantly irrational twist – he now works). The new member for Mayo, Jamie Briggs, took his oath just before question time.

'Traditionally, the member for Mayo goes to lunch about now!' advised the Labor member for Longman, friendly Jon Sullivan.

And Belinda Neal has officially been taken out of the whips' freezer. She was allowed to address a demure question about economic management to the finance minister, Lindsay Tanner, who was happy to receive it.

'Make sure you get it right, Lindsay!' warned the Opposition spokesman for education, Christopher Pyne.

Neal's new diplomatic skills seem to have rubbed off on some of her senior colleagues.

The troublesome Family First senator, Steve Fielding, has a little toy shopping trolley, which he used to fill up with cornflakes and go trundling about the corridors in happier times, demanding unit pricing in supermarkets. (These days, he's mostly holed up in his office, which is starting to resemble the Waco compound.) Privately, Wayne Swan and Nicola Roxon would like to take Senator Fielding's little trolley and snap it into a hundred pieces.

In fact, it would be a rare government minister who doesn't have a little wax doll in the top drawer, wearing kooky glasses and a short-sleeved shirt with a tie, and stuck full of pins. In the shooting gallery that the Senate has become, nearly no one is immune from the rogue pot-shots for which Senator Fielding is swiftly becoming renowned.

But publicly, they are full of love for the Victorian senator. The more of their legislation he guns down in the Senate, the nicer they are to him. Call it the art of Fielding compliments.

Nicola Roxon couldn't have been sweeter about Senator Fielding yesterday morning, barely twelve hours after he'd cost her about $300 million by summarily executing her Medicare-levy legislation. Instead, she trained her barrels on the Liberal Party, blaming it for the defeat rather than the man who triggered it on Wednesday night.

Julia Gillard, likewise, yesterday praised the Senate's rag-tag minority band for its record of excellence in the field of responsible economic management, making much of the degree to which the cross-bench senators outshine the Coalition in their devotion to such matters.

Wayne Swan soon chimed in.

'We thank the Greens, we thank Senator Xenophon, we thank Senator Fielding; they've got more economic responsibility in their little fingers than the Opposition has in its entire body', he enthused.

Laboratory tests were not immediately available on any of the little fingers involved, so we will just have to take the treasurer's word for it.

But the tactic on Senator Fielding is clear: Be nice to him, in case he does something even worse.

26 September 2008

STEP RIGHT UP FOR THE $20-BILLION RED-SPOT SPECIAL

Kevin Rudd and Wayne Swan announced their solution to the galloping financial crisis transfixing the whole world: Let's spend everything we have.

Could this crisis get any stranger? We're now in a state of confirmed international fiscal panic, but there's money everywhere.

Six months ago, Kevin Rudd and Wayne Swan were heavily involved with two mysterious women – one called Budgetary Prudence, and another one called Inflation Jeannie, whom they were keen on stuffing back into some kind of bottle. Everyone was most insistent that Australia should be saving all its pennies for tougher times. Yesterday, all that went out the window.

'Those tough times have come, and we are well positioned to act in anticipation of them', declared Mr Rudd, with the slightly alarming blend of conviction and nonsensicality on which we have come to depend in his historic public statements.

That's right, working families: if I may translate from the original Ruddese, it's time to spend the surplus. Prudence be damned. If you can think of a good way to spend $20 billion, then step right up.

If you have a plan to irrigate the Red Centre by means of snowballs propelled by a series of giant pea-shooters ranged around the Antarctic, don't be shy – just ask Kevin for the seed funding.

Looking for funding for your chip-fat-fuelled personal jet-pack? Get yourself to Canberra.

Got a madcap scheme to put bags on the bottoms of cows to catch their gaseous emissions?

Actually, whoops – scratch that. We're already funding the bovine bottom-bags.

Even as the prime minister spoke, a faint drumming sound became audible, reminiscent of wildebeest stampeding across the Serengeti. No prizes for guessing what it was; hordes of lobbyists, descending upon the capital to share their ideas about how to blow a gazillion bucks, pronto.

Nation-building is the new national security. It used to be that to prove your patriotic love for this great country, all you had to do was uncomplainingly surrender your right to habeas corpus. Nowadays, you have to be cool about personally underwriting the government's guarantee that by the end of this decade, no Australian bank will live in poverty.

Also, you have to be really, really enthusiastic about nation-building.

Yesterday, the Opposition suggested that the surplus should be spent on tax cuts for Australians. Mr Rudd was utterly withering in his response. It was as though the Libs had turned up to an Ashes decider wearing Barmy Army outfits.

The humble taxpayer, watching question time yesterday, could be forgiven for feeling a bit disjointed from all of this. We know there's a crisis, because we've seen it on television. But apart from some nervous near-superannuants and those with speculative share-holdings, there aren't too many Aussies who have felt any actual pain yet, and for plenty of home-owners, the global financial crisis so far looks like kind of a nifty way of getting an interest-rate cut.

Their greatest risk of injury at this stage is getting hit on the head by a falling wad of government hundred-dollar bills, or hearing-damage from Anthony Albanese noisily digging a Paris-style metro under the nature strip.

14 October 2008

HE'S EXCITED: BIG KEV, OUR SIRE OF STIMULUS

Feeling stimulated yet? The prime minister certainly was.

Want longer lasting economic growth? Dr Kevin Rudd (Bachelor of Applied Fiscal Stimulus) has a miracle treatment for you.

It only costs $10.4 billion, and it'll do wonders for anybody suffering from underperformance in the boardroom department. It doesn't overlook the 'P' Spot (pensioners), either.

It's stimulatory, it's exciting, and it's huge, because as Dr Rudd knows all too well, size really does matter. And best of all, you know it works; just have a look at the doc himself. Kevin Rudd has never looked more stimulated.

This is one of the most intriguing aspects of the financial crisis. With the global economy tanking, the dollar taking a graceful swan-dive and Australian taxpayers being drawn inexorably into a minefield of fiscal liability, the prime minister should be a hollow-eyed, gibbering wreck by now. Instead, he looks better and better the worse things get. Stimulated? He's looking positively politically priapic.

Gone is the obsession with pointless detail, the formalised dithering of the notorious Rudd Review Regime. Just think of those long months we spent groaning over his short attention span, his lack of political narrative, his inability to construct a sentence in English. The problem is obvious, with hindsight: He simply wasn't getting enough stimulus at work.

Now that there is a genuine mess to sort out, the obsessive compulsive elements of the Rudd personality become super-useful. Now that we actually need a control freak who never sleeps and can't stop telephoning Dominique Strauss-Kahn, our decision as a nation to elect Kevin Rudd last November is starting to look sort of prescient.

Some key Ruddbot features remain, of course. The relentless self-questioning, for example: 'Why is this necessary?' he demanded of himself halfway through yesterday's announcement – before answering himself at length. And he's still the country's leading mangler of metaphor: 'There are going to be some bumps on the road yet – it's not going to be smooth sailing.'

Normally when a government is doing well, one can safely assume that the Opposition is doing poorly. But that's another funny thing about this crisis – Malcolm Turnbull is having a very good month, scampering along just ahead of the eight ball most of the time, and maintaining a creditable degree of public modesty. Yesterday, he resisted the temptation to dance around chanting 'I told you so' about the pensioner payments, even though every fibre of his being must have been shrieking from the effort.

The Opposition's lot during a national crisis is a hard one. Mostly it involves a lot of meek nodding, and not making a squeak lest accusations of unpatriotism be levelled. Wayne Swan demonstrated yesterday during question time that the government would not hesitate to hurl accusations of unpatriotism; with nary a sniff of provocation he accused those opposite of failing the country with their lack of commitment to the crisis. Possibly, he is still smarting from the years of being called a terrorist-sympathiser by John Howard, back when the roles were reversed.

'Confected outrage, Swan!' called Joe Hockey from across the chamber.

A bit rich, given that Hockey himself is honorary life president and foundation ticket-holder of the United Outrage Confectioners' Guild. But you can see his point.

15 October 2008

PM GOES OVER THE TOP IN BATTLE OF BULGING PAYSLIPS

Kevin Rudd now speaks with the clipped air of a military tactician.

He doesn't spend money; he deploys it.

He doesn't enter a room; he advances into it.

And he certainly never has anything quite so mundane as a plan – not any more, now that things have taken a new and dangerous turn. It's always a strategy.

Yesterday the prime minister advanced into the National Press Club to address a hastily convened audience of interested patrons (most of whom had been obliged to deploy $100 to attend).

It was faintly surprising to see him arriving at the building by means of an ordinary Commonwealth car; given his current star turn as a wartime leader, one half expected to see him arrive on an elephant, like Hannibal.

But he wasted no time in identifying a common enemy.

'The champions of extreme capitalism have been found to have feet of clay', he declared. 'As a government and as a nation, we must respond to the twin evils which are at the root of this malaise – greed and fear.'

What exactly is extreme capitalism? Is it anything like extreme frisbee? The prime minister's rhetoric was red-hot, but his definitions were pretty hazy. Deliberately so, you'd have to think; the PM needs to blame a guilty party for the global financial crisis, but it would be foolish to name anybody in particular. Much like the term 'militant Islam', 'extreme capitalism' coalesces our feelings of anger and condemnation, without offending anyone actually in earshot – extremists of all varieties being notoriously reluctant to classify themselves as such.

'*I* am a battler', the enterprise conjugation might go. '*You* are an entrepreneur. But *he* is an extreme capitalist.'

How rich do you have to be to qualify as an extreme capitalist, anyway? What about Ahmed Fahour, CEO of the National Australia Bank, sponsor of the Press Club, earner of a package worth $7.9 million last year, and possessor of an admirably blank countenance as he sat in the audience yesterday during Mr Rudd's critique of corporate excess? Does *he* qualify?

On the precise definitional matter, Mr Rudd himself is slightly constrained. If the prime minister were forced at gunpoint to nominate a specific wealth threshold for 'extreme capitalism', personal and professional factors would dictate that it be somewhere above Thérèse Rein's net worth, and somewhere below Malcolm Turnbull's.

But Mr Rudd has nevertheless unleashed a fusillade of fighting words, the general sense of which is that he is planning to combine international reform of the Basle Capital Adequacy Requirements with strong action at home – namely, asking the Australian Prudential Regulatory Authority to think of something to do to constrain outrageous corporate salaries.

Sort of an Aussie special with a Basle garnish, if you will.

'We will be urging the G20 to commission an action agenda in collaboration with the International Monetary Fund, the Financial Stability Forum and the Basle Committee on Banking Supervision on the best means of implementing this initiative, preferably by the end of this financial year', the PM declared.

Take that, fat cats!

16 October 2008

HENRY STAYS CALM IN A HAIRY SITUATION

The atmosphere of fiscal crisis allowed the rise of a new national megastar: Treasury secretary Ken Henry, whose square-jawed good looks and intriguing personal habits made him a popular study among journalists.

As a marsupial buff of some repute, Ken Henry must have been thrilled to land before the Senate standing committee on economics yesterday.

Henry's hobby is the conservation of the 113 remaining northern hairy-nosed wombats in the Epping Forest. (He is also the man of the minute in national politics; already this week he has been quoted extensively by the prime minister, and the Opposition leader has wafted the suggestion of his dismissal through the Reps chamber like a cheap perfume.)

Yesterday, Henry's lead inquisitor on the economics committee was a live Tassie Devil – Senator Eric Abetz – whose whirling, spitting hostility brought to mind the cartoon critter by Warner Bros. Senator Abetz made a lot of noise as he tried to get Henry to admit he had received a letter from the Reserve Bank governor, Glenn Stevens, expressing concern about the government's bank deposit guarantee scheme.

But Henry was giving nothing away. George Brandis, the shadow attorney-general, whose hobbies include the study of lying rodents, tried his hand from time to time, but likewise could not dent the indomitable will of the Treasury secretary.

Tempers frayed.

Liberal senator Mitch Fifield began to talk ominously about 'the powers of the Senate', which is classic senator-speak for 'Don't forget we can put you in jail, China'.

Soon it appeared everyone was shouting at each other, except for Henry himself, who was temporarily forgotten in the fray.

It was all too much for the chairwoman of the committee, South Australian Labor senator Annette Hurley. She called a recess and the senators trooped off into a neighbouring burrow to fight among themselves for a bit. Henry's sidekicks rushed in to give their man a rub-down and words of encouragement.

There was little need, though – notwithstanding several hours of heavy attack, Henry looked as fresh as a daisy. He even looked sanguine about the possibility of imminent incarceration; one of his lieutenants offered him a little travel toothbrush but he waved it away confidently.

After ten minutes, the door to the room containing the senators opened – the shrieks and sobs of the warring tribes could clearly be heard – and Barnaby Joyce emerged, shaking his head.

'My wife runs a kindergarten', he said. 'It's better than that lot.'

Joyce, as a pure-blood National, should probably be on Australia's highly endangered list slightly ahead of the northern hairy-nosed wombat; at least there are 113 of the wombats, which is more than you can say of the pedigree Nat.

When the session resumed, Joyce asked Henry whether Treasury had done any modelling on the government's $10.4-billion rescue spending package. Henry smoothly handballed the question to David Gruen, his star macroeconomist (a classic manoeuvre, known in estimates lore as the Gruen Transfer). Gruen confirmed that no modelling had been done. Joyce went bonkers, but Henry remained impassive.

In waddled the loveable National Party senator Ron Boswell, whose generous girth, shambling gait and distinctly hairy nose might prove distracting to a wombat enthusiast of less than iron will. But Henry didn't so much as turn a whisker.

He's good.

23 October 2008

HAIL TO THE CHIEF: KEVIN LEAVES US SPEECHLESS

After the Obama victory, high-flying political rhetoric enjoyed a brief resurgence in some parts of the Australian body politic.

After England reclaimed the Ashes in 2005, British schoolchildren stampeded to sign up for junior cricket coaching.

When Paul Mercurio wowed the world in *Strictly Ballroom*, Australian interest in the long-dormant art of exhibition Paso Doble went through the roof.

And now that Barack Obama has been elected to the US presidency, everybody wants to be an orator.

Not Kevin Rudd, it should be said. When he delivered his formal acknowledgment of the US election result to the House of Representatives yesterday, the prime minister sounded as though he was reading aloud from the agenda for the National Association of Metallurgists' annual general meeting. Only our prime minister could take an event like the election of the first black president of the United States and describe it with all the excitement of a bored automotive mechanic listing off things that have gone wrong with your car.

But Malcolm Turnbull has the bug, big-time. His oratory yesterday moved onto a discernibly higher plane. Unlike Mr Rudd, Mr Turnbull did not mutter his words absently into his notes, like a preacher padding while he looks for the right passage in Corinthians. He projected. He gesticulated. His voice was deep and textured.

'What we have in common, which Barack Obama personifies, is that we are two nations that define themselves by commitment to common political values', the Opposition leader mused richly. 'There is no person who can look into the mirror and say, "That is an Australian face" or "That is an American face". The United States is a nation of choice, a nation of immigration – just as our nation is.'

Are we witnessing the emergence of a new force in Australian oratory? It's a pity that 'Malcolm X' is already taken. Maybe he could be 'Malcolm Cap-Ex'?

Mr Turnbull's passion was undimmed even when he turned his thoughts to the slightly more mundane matter of our friends across the Tasman. He congratulated the incoming New Zealand prime minister, John Key, with lyricism and panache; he couldn't have been more enthusiastic had Mr Key been the first chimpanzee elected to lead a Western democracy.

Meanwhile in the gallery, eyes were irresistibly drawn to a horrid little growth on the upper lip of the shadow minister for employment participation, training and sport, Andrew Southcott. In some light it looked like a shadow; in others, a smudge. But inquiries confirmed the mild mark in fact constituted Dr Southcott's efforts in the charity enterprise known as Mo-vember.

Poor Dr Southcott.

Some men can grow moustaches overnight. The member for Gippsland, Darren Chester, for example, has effortlessly sprouted a luxuriant horseshoe number that would render him very comfortable indeed in the *Police Academy*'s Blue Oyster Bar. Others try their very best and at the ten-day mark still look vaguely like pornographic film-makers. But Dr Southcott is persisting, and has so far racked up $210 in pledges.

The audacity of hope!

11 November 2008

GENERAL RUDD WAGING WAR ON EVERYTHING

Kevin Rudd caused a few grimaces on Tuesday by using Remembrance Day to declare 'a war on unemployment'.

Yesterday, he repeated his fighting words, and the manager of Opposition business, Joe Hockey, could stand it no longer. He marched to the dispatch box. There is something about Hockey's burly frame and carriage that conveys the faint impression, even in peacetime, of a military greatcoat.

'I refer the prime minister to his 2007-declared war on drugs, his January 2008-declared war on inflation and yesterday's declared war on unemployment', he began, then produced a sheaf of newspaper clippings, from each of which he read in turn. 'I also refer the prime minister to his 2007 "war on whalers", the February 2008 "war cabinet to fight disadvantage", his February 2008 "war on downloads", his March 2008 "war on pokies", his May "war against doping in sport" and his October "war on bankers' salary deals".

'Prime Minister, how goes the war on everything?'

It was a good point.

Words are like bullets, said Bill Hayden once, referring to the art of foreign diplomacy. And the same applies to domestic politics. But our PM isn't a sharp-shooter; he's more of a carpet-bomber. Mr Rudd specialises in a rapid-fire barrage of armour-denting jargon, designed to exhaust and disorient the enemy.

A classic fusillade was unleashed yesterday in response to a question from the Opposition trade spokesman, Ian Macfarlane, on the $6.2-billion car industry assistance package. (This is a key skirmish in the war on unemployment, in which the government's strategy is to buy motor-industry jobs at the rate of nearly $100,000 a pop, at which prices you'd be better off getting nationalistic pensioners to knit 'em instead.)

The PM attacked mercilessly, with a wall of sound that included references to 'a path of active interests that has conditionalities attached' and 'a specific co-investment ratio'. Pity Macfarlane, who dropped back into his seat like a spent casing at this impenetrable onslaught.

A brief ceasefire occurred at 2.52 p.m., when the PM was asked by Hockey why the government was bailing out ABC Learning, and Rudd actually answered the question with a simple and comprehensible response. A ceasefire!

Journalists danced and kissed each other in the corridors. Was it our imagination, or did the sun seem to break through the clouds of death and gunpowder hanging over the House of Representatives? But our hopes of armistice were premature; hostilities resumed straight away.

It must be said that the PM's brutal style is lent some deadly finesse by his finance minister, Lindsay Tanner, who – with Wayne Swan on furlough in Washington – has excelled this week.

Hockey can talk all he likes about Rudd's wars on pokies, executive salaries and whalers, and it's true the prime minister has skipped between them with all the strategic agility of a trained mercenary.

But there's only one war for which Rudd would sacrifice everything – it's the Bore War, and he's winning.

13 November 2008

WHEN KEV'S AWAY, KILLER GILLARD COMES OUT TO PLAY

There really isn't any doubt any more about whether the deputy prime minister, Julia Gillard, has the killer instinct. The problem tends more to be how to drag her off the victim's body.

When the curtain rose on question time yesterday, Ms Gillard sat calmly in the prime minister's chair (its customary occupant having set forth for Washington). Ms Gillard greeted her inquisitors with the quietly confident air of a $10,000-an-hour alimony lawyer arriving at her first bout with Eddie Murphy.

Her first question came from Malcolm Turnbull. How did the acting prime minister feel about the fact that one of her own backbenchers – the blushing member for Dawson, James Bidgood – had said that very morning that there was 'no question the prime minister was indiscreet' in his recent dealings with a certain US president?

Ms Gillard rose crisply and delivered a scathing and precise attack on the Coalition's own history of insulting US presidential candidates; cheeky, given that the air is still blue with her pal Mark Latham's thoughts on the subject.

Then Joe Hockey popped up with what looked an absolute slam dunk. What did the acting PM think about the exploits of her Victorian ALP fellow traveller Dean Mighell, of the Electrical Trades Union? Mr Mighell was reported yesterday to have blown $80,000 of his members' money on a lollapalooza trip to London featuring lavish meals, first-class accommodation and an unexplained call to a transvestite hooker called Suzana.

Mr Hockey was also interested to know if the Labor backbencher Mike Symon, who is a former sparky and ETU official, could shed any light on the affair.

Ms Gillard was not amused.

How dare Mr Hockey besmirch the good name of Mr Symon? How dare he interfere so crassly in a matter that was very properly before the Australian Securities and Investment Commission? Had the manager of Opposition business no shame?

After five minutes of this, Ms Gillard had officially achieved the impossible. Faced with Joe Hockey and a guy who has reportedly milked a vast bucket of union dollars to fly sharp-end to London, douse himself in Dom Perignon and finance calls to a feisty she-male escort professional, she succeeded in making Joe look like the grub.

Ms Gillard's colleagues cheered. As well they might – you wouldn't want to get on the wrong side of this chick.

Later she unblinkingly answered a question from Warren Truss concerning urinary dipsticks.

One suspects that Ms Gillard has seen rather a lot during her time in politics, including the odd urinary dipstick. Hence her composure.

Kevin Rudd has had a shocking week, twisting awkwardly on the hook of his all-too-obvious indiscretions concerning a certain telephone conversation with the wildly unpopular American president. But the true moribundity of his performance didn't really become clear until yesterday, when Ms Gillard demonstrated – cogently, ably and without a speaking note to be seen – that in the right hands, question time can be easy.

14 November 2008

MUCH IN COMMON, THERE'S NO DENYING IT

Last year's election campaign was all about Kevin Rudd convincing us that he could more or less reproduce John Howard's government, only without John Howard at the helm. And it worked.

But good Lord, they're similar sometimes.

Cartoonists used to depict Howard with that little lower-lip jut that spoke so eloquently of the stubbornness that people close to the former PM knew so well. And Rudd has it, too, that stubbornness.

In June the PM made a minor blunder in a parliamentary answer, getting the Government's projected inflation rate wrong by 0.5 percentage points. It wasn't a big drama; anybody else would quietly have corrected the record at the end of the session, as countless politicians have done on the occasion of a slip-up.

But the PM didn't. And when he was challenged repeatedly by the Opposition in question time the following day he dug in, refusing to acknowledge he'd expressed a view that was any different from his budget documents. It was a bizarre spectacle: watching a man fight to the death to avoid owning up to a complete triviality. And it was Rudd's first major experimentation with the intricate political art of DBO: Denial of the Bleeding Obvious.

John Howard's career highlight in DBO came in February 2003, when he spent several weeks denying that he had committed Australian troops to the approaching Iraq war, despite having deployed about 2000 of them to the Gulf already. This really was world-class DBO, champagne DBO – the kind of DBO that makes even hardened reporters sit back, rub their eyes, and think, 'Hang on. Am I going mad? Am I missing something here?'

Kevin Rudd's mastery of DBO is a work in progress. But as he stonewalled questions this week about whether he or his staff had leaked details of his 10 October phone conversation with George Bush, Rudd showed some precocious talent.

Obviously the leak came from Rudd or his office.

It's bleeding obvious.

But asked over and over where the information had come from, Rudd over and over just denied the accuracy of one detail in the leaked account.

'On the question of my conversation with the president of the United States, the leader of the Opposition will be aware of my earlier answers: that is, that the purpose of my call to the president of the United States was to discuss the relevance of the G20 to the global financial crisis. Secondly, the president of the United States was entirely aware of the role of the G20.'

In DBO, the grandmasters' handbook is clear. When you can't answer a perfectly simple question on the grounds that you almost certainly will incriminate yourself, simply substitute a new question, and answer that instead.

Rudd stuck to his guns, and obfuscated for Australia. You could almost see the lower lip jutting out.

Which brings us to another thing that John Howard and Kevin Rudd have in common. George Bush.

Labor figures used regularly to accuse Howard – mostly in private, but occasionally and spectacularly it spilled out in public – of being a lickspittle to George Bush. Howard used his friendship with Bush to make himself feel important, or so the critics used to say. But Rudd, too, is borrowing plumage from the American president to feather his own nest. The only difference is that Howard sought to win political points by being chummy with Bush; Rudd seeks – possibly subconsciously – to demonstrate his own status by showing how easily he can snub the man.

It reminds me of that brilliant old joke about the guy in the Chairman's Lounge who spots Kerry Packer and approaches him.

'Mr Packer, you don't know me, but I am an utter disciple of yours – my ambition is to be just like you one day', the man gushes.

'Could you do me a huge favour? My business associates are over there. If you could just come over when I'm standing with them and say "G'day, Steve!" it would just make my day – my life! Please?'

Packer, in a good mood, agrees.

Five minutes later, the man is standing with his mates when Packer strolls over.

'G'day, Steve!' he booms, proffering his hand.

'Piss off, Packer', snarls Steve. 'Can't you see I'm busy?'

15 November 2008

SERVICE OK – NO BOTS ABOUT IT

The first anniversary of the Ruddbot's accession to power being only days away, I wondered how his manufacturers would assess his first twelve months of service.

An open letter to the people of Australia from Prime Animatronix Pty Ltd, manufacturer of the Ruddbot™.

Congratulations again on your purchase of Ruddbot™.

Here at Prime Animatronix, we value our clients. And as part of our post-sales service package, Prime offers a comprehensive (and complimentary) twelve-month warranty check on all prime ministerial androids supplied to Southern Hemisphere customers.

Prime has already conducted significant market research among stakeholders, and we are pleased to report that, in general, your Ruddbot™ appears to be performing within the 'reasonable' to 'fair' band.

His first twelve months in service appear to have been free of major malfunction.

Your Ruddbot™, as should have been explained to you at point of sale, is a completely unique and experimental piece of machinery.

He is designed to evolve.

During the survey process, some stakeholders expressed concern about certain changes in vocabulary and behaviour.

This is perfectly normal – please, do not adjust your Ruddbot™ .

The phrase 'End the blame game!' for instance, was an in-store promotional feature exclusive to last year. It was designed to be succeeded by other subtle variations, such as 'Eleven and a half years of neglect!' and 'Economic vandals in the Senate!'

Some features of Ruddbot™ cannot be altered.

The machine's fondness for slightly too-short trousers, for instance, is not a design specification; it is a genuine synthesised human weakness, and as such is unlikely to change.

And in response to overwhelming stakeholder curiosity on this point, we are obliged to confirm that the haircut is also a fixture.

Ruddbot's technicians have designed him to be excitingly responsive to changing economic conditions. He is the first android to feature this function, and we are justifiably proud of his performance this year.

Just twelve months ago, as you will recall, one of Ruddbot™'s most impressive political manoeuvres was his counterintuitive promise to rein in social spending.

His campaign repertoire was dominated by powerful rhetoric about the Howard government's 'drunken sailor' expenditure habits, with special attention to regional pork-barrelling schemes and much mention of the 'Fishing Hall of Fame'.

It is a tribute to Ruddbot™'s sophisticated evolutionary software that he has seamlessly revised this approach in the face of global financial crisis.

The conversion from 'Down with regional pork-barrelling!' to 'Come here, Mr Mayor – I've got a couple of million bucks here for you to spend on whatever you like!' took only months to effect.

More importantly, from a manufacturer's perspective, it was accomplished without any physical retooling of hardware; that is to say, it was a genuine 'human' transition on the part of Ruddbot™ himself, which is a very exciting breakthrough indeed.

From a starting point of irreproachable fiscal conservatism, Ruddbot™ has now successfully convinced a grateful nation that patriotism demands the greasing of every mayoral palm on the continent. (Even Wollongong benefited from the largesse, which must – given that nobody even had to remove their undergarments – be the easiest money that particular council has made in some time.)

We trust you will have noticed your Ruddbot™'s near-infinite capacity for work. This is why every standard Ruddbot™ comes with a complimentary back-up chief of staff, designed for fuss-free substitution when the factory original peters out at about the eleven-month mark.

According to our notes, your Ruddbot™ was licensed in November last year with the standard 'David Epstein' attachment but by now should seamlessly have transferred to the 'Alistair Jordan' model. (Please contact our toll-free number if you have experienced any transitional difficulties.)

Of course, there are a few teething problems.

We are well aware of Ruddbot™'s tendency towards garbled language on occasion, and the difficulties being experienced with his 'delegation' function. Our technicians are attending to these problems.

We are also working very hard on devising a program to protect against the notorious 'Blabbermouth' virus that appears to be attacking some elements of the Ruddbot circuitry during and immediately after bilateral discussions with foreign leaders. We appreciate your patience in this matter, and trust that a satisfactory result will be achieved.

On a final and, somewhat, regrettable note, confusion seems to have arisen in some stakeholder sectors about the question of legal liability for certain public remarks made by Ruddbot™.

For the sake of clarity, Prime Animatronix would like once again to draw attention to its point-of-sale disclaimer, and remind clients that the company is in no way responsible financially for the undertakings of any of its androids.

Specifically, with regard to the 'Computers for Schools' scheme, Prime is sorry to hear that your children don't have a computer yet, but cannot be responsible for providing computers to disappointed parents.

Further, the 'Education Revolution' is not a registered trade mark belonging to Prime, and the company cannot therefore entertain any of the proposed litigation under the 'misleading and deceptive conduct' provisions of the Commonwealth Trade Practices Act.

Once again, congratulations and thank you for choosing Ruddbot™.

22 November 2008

DEFIANT SHOW AS PAWNS EYE BISHOP'S MOVE

With the Liberal leadership settled for the time being, party white-ants turned their attention to the deputy leader and shadow treasurer, Julie Bishop. Something of a whispering campaign was conducted, in covert criticism of her abilities. Ms Bishop, however, is rather resilient, and possesses a secret weapon.

Nobody gives 'looks' quite like Julie Bishop can.

The Liberal deputy leader is carefully co-ordinated in everything she wears, from the heels on her feet right up to the expression on her face. But the expressions are easily the best. When the shadow treasurer 'looks' at you, you know you've been 'looked' at.

The Bishop repertoire ranges from shocked innocence through pouting reproach to pure hate. Each has a specific use. Each is unforgettable.

The shadow treasurer entered question time yesterday wearing 'Hillary Clinton'. 'Hillary Clinton' is a dazzling, defiant, diamond-hard smile, whose wattage tends to be in inverse proportion to the direness of the circumstances at hand. It is an expression employed when everything around the wearer is falling apart, and she'd really like everyone to change the subject; Bishop donned the very same expression this year for a press conference after her colleagues voted to abandon Australian Workplace Agreements, against her express advice.

At present, Bishop is the victim of what Ken Kesey once called a 'pecking party'. She's made a few blunders, non-terminal in nature, and her enemies are reciting them over and over again until they take on the sound of war drums in the distance. After all, Bishop is the shadow treasurer, and she is surrounded by people who think they would be good shadow treasurers; it's premium pecking party territory.

She has, of course, other expressions for happier times.

There's a pouting, teasing one, 'Britney', which she occasionally uses to taunt her opponents. As education minister in the Howard government, she used it memorably on Kevin Rudd in February last year.

'One thing I can say about the leader of the Opposition: he has not had an original policy thought on anything, let alone education', she said. 'He talks about his education revolution. Naughty boy! You stole that idea, didn't you?'

On that occasion, she accessorised 'Britney' with a wagging forefinger, and got on all the news bulletins.

But it was yesterday, after the shadow treasurer asked a question of Wayne Swan, that we really saw something special.

As she sat down, some Labor backbencher called out something about plagiarism.

Bishop turned – and there it was – 'Blue Steel'! A flash of pure poison, deep and savage.

'I *beg* your pardon?' the shadow treasurer hissed, as her tormentors whooped and cackled.

As you can imagine, Julia Gillard is thoroughly enjoying her opponent's discomfiture. And yesterday, she couldn't resist the chance to sink her own dainty ankle-boot into the fray, taunting Bishop about her claims to have been educated at Harvard Business School. A bit rich, reckons the Deputy PM; Bishop was only there for six weeks.

'The truth is she was there for a summer program, for a course that now costs $60,000', Gillard mocked. 'That is $10,000 per week, $2000 per day …'

There was something a bit icky about this attack. Gillard is a hungry political carnivore, and no doubt about it. But yesterday it looked horribly like she was killing for sport.

2 December 2008

RUDDBOT AND CO. TAKE A PRODUCTIVITY RISE

Christmas. Where has the time gone? Same place as the entire global economy, I guess. But a multipartisan era of ceasefire is about to descend upon the Australian political scene. Even the indefatigable Ruddbot is planning to power down for the Christmas break.

He has promised to take a couple of weeks off and return to the national stage only in the event of a legitimate national emergency, like a blown light bulb in Committee Room 2R1, or Craig Emerson breaking a nail.

Wayne Swan is also taking a holiday; that is to say, he's moving his desk to a beachside location in Queensland and will restrict himself to a few hours' work in the mornings and afternoons, occasionally slipping out of his tie for a dip.

As you can probably imagine, many Rudd ministerial spouses are now facing a novel dilemma. After reintroducing the children, how does one best entertain someone whose past year has been a blur of reviews, task forces, constant concern for working families and – above all – decision making that is not only timely but also decisive? In the spirit of the season, here are a few ideas about how they might occupy their leisure time.

Kevin Rudd: Will spend several days compiling a dictionary of all the words he has invented over the past year – a *Little Rudd Book*, to be distributed to the family and anyone else who's interested.

The *Little Rudd Book* will feature all the latest Rudd words including 'passthrough', 'brekkers' and 'maximalist', which was born just this week at the National Press Club in the following entrancing reply to a question from the *Financial Review*'s Laura Tingle: 'Australia, in the negotiations, will be ambitious and working hard to bring about a maximalist agreement.'

He may also undertake a chocolate-making course, which if successful will yield a small but intriguing new product line: Kevin Rudd's Reforming Centres.

Julia Gillard: Will receive a thoughtful gift from her ever attentive other half, Tim Mathieson: a giant replica Opposition frontbencher fashioned out of dried pigs' ears. Ms Gillard will spend a happy January gnawing and tearing at it, and digging holes in the garden.

Stephen Conroy, minister for communications: Will spend his entire holiday waiting patiently and uselessly by the phone, not aware that the single remaining maintenance worker retained by Telstra has – acting on higher company orders – already whippersnipped his home line.

Nicola Roxon, health: Will also have an extremely quiet break. News of her campaign against binge drinking has spread so efficiently that she is no longer invited anywhere.

Anthony Albanese, infrastructure: Will have a creative and fulfilling Christmas period nutting out how to gift-wrap a motorway, a football stadium, an urban metro system and six Lifelong Learning Centres, and how to get them all under the tree.

Peter Garrett, environment and the arts: Will spend the break avoiding artists and environmentalists. Known to have enrolled in a recreational logging course.

Ken Henry, Treasury secretary: Will devote his time and energies to caring for a small and desperately threatened population of Australian mammals, whose vulnerability requires close attention and hand-feeding around the clock to prevent extinction. Once he's finished with the cabinet, though, he'll get back to doing what he can for the northern hairy-nosed wombats.

Penny Wong, climate change: Scheduled to disappear for several weeks. Informally her office will let it be assumed that she is acclimatising to Copenhagen, but actually, she will be in Las Vegas, where her famed poker face rakes in millions in a single evening at the MGM Grand's high-roller room. Colleagues were snobbish about her abilities until they realised that Wong is now Australia's only remaining growth area in national revenue.

Stephen Smith, foreign affairs: Will set up a replica desk and pretend to be foreign affairs minister, dictating long letters that don't go anywhere and making sure all the pencils are tidily arranged in order of decreasing length and sharpness. From time to time, he will get a briefing from the PM's office about what's actually going on.

Whoa – hang on a second. That's his real job! He's not taking a holiday.

20 December 2008

ALSO STARRING ...

FREAKISH POWERS OF A FORMIDABLE OPERATOR

Some people are born with an innate ability to sing; some to paint, or dribble a basketball. Such is the randomness of creation's miracle. But what are the odds that Penelope Ying-Yen Wong, born in Kota Kinabalu, Malaysia, on 5 November, 1968, would enter this world with a God-given knack for politics?

She was barely eighteen when she seized control of the campus Labor Club at the University of Adelaide; her methodical destruction of the existing power structure there gave an early glimpse of her freakish powers.

Colleagues now describe her as 'relentless', and this word sums up her progress through the federal parliamentary Labor Party, of which she has been a member for just five years. She is calm, groomed, and virtually unflappable. She has a sharp intellect. She is a forensic Senate operative in the John Faulkner mould. She is a lesbian. She is a practising Christian.

And now she is one of Kevin Rudd's most senior cabinet ministers, charged with driving an international consensus on climate change and a domestic consensus on water management. It's a huge ask, by anyone's standards.

Penny Wong did not always intend to be a politician, even if it looks that way in retrospect. Her initial plan was to be a doctor, and to work for Médecins Sans Frontières; she won a spot in medical school in 1986, deferred it, and then left for an exchange year in Brazil, where she volunteered at a hospital – and quickly changed her career plans.

'There was a bit of a problem with blood', she explains briskly.

This is an important revelation, as it might be the first and last recorded example of squeamishness in Penny Wong.

Arriving at the University of Adelaide in 1987 as a first-year arts student, the politically conscious Wong dabbled with a couple of environmental groups and the left-wing group CISCAC – the Committee in Solidarity with Central America and the Caribbean. (This group was founded and run, incidentally, by fellow arts student and enthusiastic campus Trotskyist David Penberthy, who has since moved to the beating heart of Australian conspicuous consumption – Sydney – where he edits the *Daily Telegraph*.)

Pragmatic Wong, however, was never going to be a very committed Trotskyist. In 1988 she swivelled her gun turrets towards the Labor Club, which had been colonised two or three years earlier by George Karzis, a cheerful right-wing headkicker who has since worked in senior advisory roles for state and federal Labor politicians.

'I ran it as a non-factional group', recalls Karzis from his Adelaide legal office, breaking off to laugh uproariously before adding: 'That is, there was no other faction than mine.

'Penny arrived in 1988. By the following March, she had organised the numbers and there was the largest ever Labor Club meeting – the Union Theatre was packed to the rafters. It was an unfortunate display of branch stacking – by both of us. She was trying to take the club over and I was trying to defend it. And she won! I have to concede, I backed the wrong horse.'

Wong remembers: 'We had these big fights about who would control the Labor Club. I mean – really. Look, I think with the benefit of hindsight we probably got much more wound up in student politics than we really needed to, but isn't that what you do when you're young?'

It's true that in student politics, where practitioners subsist on a rich diet of reality-free political theory and too many standing orders, things can often get out of hand. What you tend to end up with is a riot of ballot-stuffing, vote-rigging, dirt-digging and amateur character assassination, washed down with endless schooners of beer.

The thing about Penny Wong, however, is that few such tales of outright excess exist.

'To her credit, there are no funny stories involving Penny Wong', is how one alumnus of the vintage puts it.

Another – her former Labor Club colleague Amy Barrett, who is now a lawyer in Sydney – says Wong was not given to skullduggery.

'The rest of us would be running around, putting up posters, but she would be talking about serious number-crunching deals, preference flows, stuff that made you think – this is really serious business', she says.

Wong called people 'comrade'; she was intensely organised; her attention to detail was rigorous. If a comrade was spending long hours campaigning, Wong might arrange for a set of course notes to materialise in that person's pigeonhole, just so they didn't get too behind.

'She was totally focused on politics, right from when she started', says Kris Hanna, another comrade who ended up in the South Australian parliament – he now serves as an independent, having defected from Labor several years ago. 'She was methodical, serious and committed – in the left, she was known as 'Penny the Prefect'.'

In fact, Wong's generation of Adelaide University student politics produced an aberrantly large crop of professional politicians. Senator Natasha Stott Despoja was a contemporary, as was Wong's then boyfriend, Jay Weatherill, now a senior minister in Mike Rann's South Australian government. Other contemporaries include the South Australian transport minister, Pat Conlon, the federal Liberals' Christopher Pyne and Andrew Southcott, the Labor senator Anne McEwen, the new member for Port Adelaide, Mark Butler, and the South Australian speaker, Jack Snelling.

Wong worked part-time as an organiser for the Construction, Forestry, Mining and Energy Union through the concluding stages of her law degree, but still managed to graduate with honours.

She formed a deep alliance with the 'Bolkus Left' – a sociable grouping of ambitious youngsters around the then senator Nick Bolkus, who was a mentor to Wong and whom she thanked in her maiden speech in 2002. Conlon, Butler, Weatherill and Wong were the most promising of Bolkus' protégés, and all are still on the rise.

But the group suffered a wrenching split in 2003, on the matter of Bolkus's own future in the Senate. He wanted to stay on, but was defeated by a coalition of friends and foes. Wong's failure to defend her mentor caused some hard feelings, which persist in South Australia to this day.

'Penny's made a lot of sacrifices to get where she is. Mainly of other people', says one party to that upheaval. Her defenders say this attitude is unfair, and that Wong, already in the Senate, did not advance at Bolkus's expense; Bolkus declined to comment this week.

Certainly, Wong is known widely within the party for her driving ambition and her lack of squeamishness about the hard and unattractive side of factional business, of which she saw plenty through the Crean/Latham era.

'She is very into the politics. But she has a sort of dignity and authority about it', Hanna says.

Like Julia Gillard (a friend), Wong has answered internal critics with the most crushingly effective retort available in politics: performance.

Butler, who remains factionally close, describes her as a cool political operator ideally suited to the task set for her by Rudd. Butler is the former secretary of the Liquor, Hospitality and Miscellaneous Workers' Union in South Australia; he has also served on Labor's national executive committee and is viewed as an exceptional talent federally for Labor (a fact which would no doubt have puzzled his great-grandfather, the 1920s Liberal premier Sir Richard Butler, were he still around).

Wong worked for Butler as a legal officer for three years at the union before she won Senate preselection, and was a barrister and solicitor at the Adelaide firm Duncan and Hannon for three years before that.

Butler says she has a forensic brain and a gift for cross-examination; he describes her appointment as a 'brilliant' move on Rudd's part. 'Climate change, water, emissions trading – they're all about getting across some really difficult technical detail, then getting into a room and negotiating hard. They are just her major strengths', he says.

Wong's negotiating skills were proven in 2003, when as a new senator she wangled affirmative-action rules through the federal party during the infamous 'special rules conference' called by Simon Crean.

Conlon, whose relations with Wong are chillier since the split, nevertheless describes her as 'intelligent, and focused on her goals', and says he has 'no doubt at all that she will be a success in the role'.

As a politician, Wong is not naturally gregarious; at least, not to the degree that many of her colleagues are. She is serious of demeanour and conservative of appearance, given neither to drinking nor excessive frivolity. A periodic flirtation with cigarettes is about as close as she gets to formal vice.

Mark Latham, who met her in 2000 at Labor's national conference in Hobart, made a spirited attempt to have her referred to thenceforth as 'Wongy'. It didn't catch on.

But in private she has a warmth and humour which belies her reputation; there is a touch of goofiness, if you can imagine that. There is a hint of it in her smile, which is shy and engaging; she is striking to look at, and photogenic, but hates having her picture taken.

Over the course of last month's election she served as Labor's federal campaign spokeswoman, proving to be articulate and surefooted; on being asked anything about her private life, however, she gets tongue-tied. She seems genuinely puzzled by the idea that anyone would be interested in the fact that she is Australia's first lesbian cabinet minister, and the first Asian-born cabinet minister, for that matter.

'If it means that we … as a nation … if it shows that we are a nation where people can achieve things just on their abilities, then it is a good thing', she says, with rare hesitance.

Wong brought her mother, Jane Chapman, and her partner, Sophie Allouache – a former University of Adelaide Students' Association president – to Monday's swearing-in ceremony at Yarralumla.

'Is she out?' wondered her old comrade Barrett, with interest, when contacted this week. Technically, Wong was never really 'in'. She has never sought to disguise or advertise her sexuality, which – after her undergraduate experimentation with the opposite sex – has long been settled in its present orientation.

When Wong won preselection for the Senate before the 2001 election (she replaced the retiring Keating government veteran Rosemary Crowley), the joke went around that she would never have been able to contest a lower-house seat, being not only a woman, but Asian and gay to boot. Wong gently disagrees, but says she never thought of a House of Representatives seat in any event: 'I actually think that the house of review is the chamber where more detailed legislative work is done.'

Nevertheless, she has made some references in the past to the marginalisation she and her younger brother, Toby, experienced while growing up in Adelaide, and her maiden speech was a passionate denunciation of the politics of racial division.

The two young Wongs moved from Malaysia to Adelaide with their mother when Penny was eight; their father remains overseas, though he and Penny keep in touch. Toby, a bright and charismatic boy, went on to work as a chef in Adelaide while Penny pursued her political career. Toby turned thirty on the day his sister was elected to the Senate, in the middle of the bitterest race election this country had seen in the course of the siblings' lives. Ten days later, he took his own life.

Wong does not discuss the circumstances of this dreadful blow, beside an enigmatic promise to him in her maiden speech: 'Your life and death ensure that I shall never forget what it is like for those who are truly marginalised.'

She leaned heavily on her faith after her brother's death, and remains a committed worshipper in the Uniting Church, although religion is another subject she is loath to discuss. 'It's a very private matter. I suppose I think people have very different ways in which they express their spirituality. I have mine. It's deeply personal, and it has sustained me at difficult times of my life.'

On her brother: 'The only thing I'd want to say is how much I missed him the day I was sworn in.'

8 December 2007

THE FORBIDDEN ALLURE OF RED JULIA

Something very strange is happening to Julia Gillard. After years of being hyped as the hard face of Australian socialism, she's become something very, very surprising: a right-wing pin-up.

What is it about La Gillardine, the implacable, unflappable executioner of John Howard's industrial legacy, that causes such pandemonium in the hearts of certain conservative males?

I noticed this the other day during the ABC's *Insiders* program, when my fellow panellist Andrew Bolt, of Melbourne's *Herald Sun*, interrupted his ordinarily reliable flagellation of the Australian Labor Party with some words of admiration for 'DPM', as the prime minister fondly knows her.

'Hello, hello, hello', I thought. 'What's all this?'

Further investigation reveals the situation to be far more serious than I had suspected. 'I have nursed a secret passion for Julia Gillard, but only now is it safe to say so', Bolt wrote in a giddy, confessional rush in February last year. 'She has the mouth of Paul Keating but the eyes of Megan Gale, and the one just enhances the other.'

Before you panic, you should know that Bolt here is adapting an old comment once made about Margaret Thatcher (another shiver looking for a conservative spine to run up), who was once described by the French president François Mitterand as having 'the eyes of Caligula and the mouth of Marilyn Monroe'.

The Bolt–Gillard thing started out in the usual schoolyard way, with Gillard accusing Bolt in 2003 of 'pure and simple propaganda' and Bolt offering in print to buy the then Opposition immigration spokeswoman 'some pills for her alarming paranoia'. For years after that, Bolt called her 'the Left's Julia Gillard'. The chosen prefix told readers all they needed to know about what the writer thought of the subject.

But something's changed. Is it Bolt, or is it Gillard? In his 2008 confessional, Bolt explains that 'Gillard went from put-down to pin-up simply by applying the finest make-up: a powdering of pure power'. But Kevin Rudd's been slathering that stuff on for a year and a half, and it doesn't seem to have inspired anything like the same response down at 'Still Not Sorry' HQ.

My Melbourne friend is by no means the only right-wing bloke experiencing these turbulent and unpredictable urges. Even my dad, a South Australian sheep and grain farmer whose political views have scant natural intersection with those of the Labor Left, was sufficiently captivated by Gillard last year to name one of his chickens after her; the Julia Gillard of the Crabb chook house is a personable bird of reddish plumage, with leadership tendencies and a disinclination to lay eggs.

When some loudmouth subsequently told her about the chicken, Gillard wrote a note to Dad declaring that she 'could not imagine a greater honour'.

Whether Dad would vote for her, I don't know. But like most Australians, he is drawn to any politician capable of having a laugh at their own expense.

Tony Abbott is probably the foundation member of conservative Australia's secretive 'Juliaholics Anonymous' chapter, whose members come together now and again to reassure each other that just because they search every crowd for a flash of copper hair and dream of the firm tread of DPM's sturdy ankle-boot in the small of their backs does not mean their commitment to a decentralised system of workplace relations is any the less.

'I think there's an authenticity about Julia Gillard which Kevin Rudd lacks', Abbott sighed last month, helplessly; he cannot lie, poor dear, any more than he can forget the lass who shadowed, then eclipsed him.

Piers Akerman, too, has caught a mild variant strain of the Julia flu.

'PSSST. Want to know a secret? I agree with Julia Gillard on the need for greater transparency in our education system', he wrote in August last year. 'She almost blushed when I told her this on Sunday.'

The *Australian*'s Greg Sheridan praised the 'grace, eloquence and stature' with which Gillard addressed the US State Department in Washington last year, though to be fair to Sheridan, he was specifically applauding her warm words about Alexander Downer, on whom the writer has a far more established crush.

How can a woman who featured in those grainy Coalition advertisements just two short years ago as a hatchet-faced union moll possibly now find herself the object of even secretive conservative admiration? The simple truth is that she never really was the person in the grainy ads, as just about anyone in the ALP would tell you. Real Labor lefties split their sides laughing back then to see Gillard portrayed as a dangerous socialist, because they knew from experience that the ambitious member for Lalor was about as pragmatic as they come.

Silly sensationalist reporting about Gillard's membership of a group called Socialist Forum missed the point about who she had become, and how. Prodigious natural ability and her strategic alliance with first one right-wing Labor leader (Simon Crean) and then another (Mark Latham) swung her up through the monkey-bars of the parliamentary Labor Party and amassed her sufficient influence to anoint a third: Kevin Rudd. She does not intend to grow old as one of those Labor pollies of whom it is said that they could have made a terrific leader had they not had the misfortune to be from the Labor Left.

In opposition, Julia Gillard was a hard-headed and astute operator. In government, she is a political killing machine; a locomotive of a woman whose sense of humour humanises her unstoppability.

No wonder it titillates the Tory blokes to lash themselves to the tracks.

9 July 2009

STOP AT NOTHING: THE LIFE AND ADVENTURES OF MALCOLM TURNBULL

Malcolm Turnbull is standing in the Business aisle of a Qantas flight, fiddling with his BlackBerry. We've just touched down in Sydney and are halfway through a discussion about military butlers, or 'batmen', on which topic his assistant, Nick Berry – a former army man – has offered certain insights. Turnbull is googling, trying to look up the etymology of the word 'batman', but his gadget won't work fast enough for him to find the answer before the queue of passengers behind him – polite, for the time being – builds into one of those quietly angry mobs you see from time to time on freshly landed planes.

'It must be French', Turnbull mutters, to no one in particular.

Then he snaps back into the real world and notices a gentleman hovering tentatively at his right armpit. Accurately gauging his concern, Turnbull retrieves a suitcase from the overhead locker for the man and throws in a dazzling smile. The man looks utterly delighted.

Turnbull tends to switch on and off. You can be in an absorbing exchange with him and then notice that he has gone quiet, his conversational contribution reduced to the occasional sonorous 'Mmmmm'. Then you realise that he's twiddling away at the BlackBerry, or he's jammed the Bluetooth earpiece in his ear and is vetting phone messages.

Real-life conversations with Malcolm Turnbull, however, are worth sticking around for. In Canberra, you are considered well read if you've consumed everything on offer about Australian politics. If you've read about American and British politics as well, you are thought something of a don; knowledge of European politics implies the definite possibility that you might fancy yourself. Many, like John Howard, are voracious readers but restrict their consumption largely to their own professional field, with occasional excursions to the history shelves. Howard's ideal novel, one always suspected, would concern the policy adventures of a deeply principled, perhaps slightly built prime minister with a thing for cricket and an eagle-eyed wife.

Turnbull, however, has a taste for poetry and literature, and a tendency to veer away from politics at any and every conversational opportunity. His life before politics has done several things for him. First, it's made him very rich. Second, it's made him some enemies. Third, it's given him an inexhaustible supply of dinner-party anecdotes.

'Malcolm is a colossal name-dropper', says one former cabinet colleague. 'He won't just offer an opinion on economic policy – he'll always preface it with something like "As I was saying to Tim Geithner the other day …"'

Name-dropper, yes. But to be fair, he has excellent material. 'Six Degrees of Malcolm Turnbull', in which any famous person in the world can be connected to Turnbull within six steps, would be a feasible party game. John F. Kennedy? OK: from Kennedy we make an easy leap to his showbiz friend Frank Sinatra, and thence to Sinatra's fellow rat-packer Humphrey Bogart. Who starred in *Casablanca* with Ingrid Bergman, who was leading lady in *Gaslight*, which also starred Angela Lansbury, whose cousin Coral ten years later gave birth to her first and only child, Malcolm Bligh Turnbull.

At times, the Turnbull life story seems almost to have the silvery impermanence of cinema, and you suspect somewhere behind it all is an old-time Hollywood screenwriter, artfully inserting plot twists and complex little synchronicities for the benefit of the audience. The screenwriter (let's call him Irv) has relied, for the fundamentals, on a classic rags-to-riches theme.

Smart boy, not much dough, abandoned by his mother at eight, left alone a lot as a kid, sent to boarding school, loving but absent father, forced to rely on own brilliance. Brisk university life, period of feckless womanising, moonlights as brilliant young journalist, snapped up by grumpy tycoon. Rhodes scholar, famed barrister, fabulous clever wife, adorable family, filthy-rich banker, substantial philanthropist, stormed into Parliament, breezed into cabinet, seized the Liberal leadership … and that's as far as we've got.

Don't think that this is a mere fairy story, either; Irv's clearly worked with Orson Welles, for there's plenty of darkness too. Our hero is flawed: he is impatient and mercurial, and his life is littered with people who cannot forgive him his victories, feeling them ill-gotten. It's as though he has a poisoned sword. The wounds he has inflicted on others don't seem to go away; they tend to canker and are nursed bitterly by the injured, sometimes for years and years. Perhaps he's not a gracious winner; perhaps it's that. He certainly does not like to lose.

Unlike most practitioners, Malcolm Turnbull was not made famous by politics. He was famous already, having reaped abundant headlines as Kerry Packer's Boy Friday, as the cheeky advocate of the *Spycatcher* case, and as the captain of the doomed ship HMAS *Australian Republic.*

Turnbull was not, like some of his colleagues, driven to enter politics because of some galvanising injustice that nagged and fretted at him. He did not storm into politics to strike a blow for small business against Paul Keating, as many new Liberal MPs did in 1996. Quite the reverse; the mid-1990s found Malcolm Turnbull discussing, with various Labor figures including Keating, the prospect of his recruitment as a Labor parliamentarian. 'Initiated by Keating!' protests Turnbull, who says he refused the approach. 'Initiated by Turnbull!' insists former ALP powerbroker Graham Richardson, who once wrote that Turnbull asked him in 1993 for a Senate spot but legged it on being told about the tender delights of grass-roots ALP membership. When Turnbull finally did enter politics, it was on the other side, to join a long-established Liberal incumbent, John Howard.

So what is he doing in politics? This is a question that has occupied colleagues and staffers in countless happy hours of speculation since his arrival in Canberra. Unlike Howard, Turnbull does not seem to be haunted by nameless inner cravings for major structural reform; the teenage Turnbull, one imagines, went to bed dreaming of one day becoming prime minister, while Howard's night-time reveries were complicated affairs in which he single-handedly dismantled Australia's system of centralised wage-fixing.

Turnbull was driven into politics partly by aptitude and ambition, partly by a sense of public service and partly, one suspects, by the gravitational pull of fate. 'A force of nature' is how the Reverend Tim Costello once described him, and this is a variation on an oft-repeated theme among colleagues, many of whom, from the moment of his nomination for the Sydney seat of Wentworth, have viewed Turnbull as a sort of galloping inevitability – something to be *got through*, like puberty or chickenpox.

*

The writer Tom Keneally says Turnbull – with whom he has a warm if slightly scarred relationship dating back two decades to the birth of the Australian Republican Movement – is driven by a genuine feeling of obligation to spread his good fortune around.

'I always felt that he was, particularly in the late 1980s and early 1990s, a minority among the new rich in that he had the feelings of *noblesse oblige*', Keneally says. 'He wouldn't be out of place as a Venetian Doge.'

And there is indeed something of the Italian Renaissance about Turnbull, preposterous as that sounds. He and his wife Lucy are compulsive givers to charities, hospitals and church enterprises. Recently he handed a personal cheque for $50,000 to the Sydney Cancer Centre at a function, asking to remain anonymous (this story did not come from Turnbull). He gave another $50,000 to charity at the 2007 Press Gallery Midwinter Ball. Most years, the Turnbulls give away somewhere in the region of $500,000. Turnbull is a patron of the arts, classically libertarian in his political tendencies and imbued with a passionate love of language. His sense of his own obligation to society is sincere, though at times you do have to smother a laugh.

'I felt the best thing I could do was to write a useful book about why Australia should be a republic', Turnbull wrote grandly in 1999, on the origins of his republican odyssey. 'I made arrangements with my publisher, Sandy Grant. Then, in the manner of most authors, I became distracted with other matters.'

The painter Lewis Miller was commissioned by Lucy and Malcolm Turnbull in 1994 to paint portraits of the family. Miller spent a week with the Turnbulls on their farm at Scone, where Turnbull's father is buried.

Miller chose to depict Malcolm and Lucy in close profile on two separate canvases, in the style of Piero della Francesca's famous diptych *The Duke and Duchess of Urbino*. In the background, rather than della Francesca's Marche landscapes, stretches the land around Scone.

The reference is a deliberate one. The Duke of Urbino – Federico da Montefeltro, known as the 'Light of Italy' – was a poetry-loving, library-building sort of cove, a giver of alms to the poor and a nurturer of young artists, among them the young Raphael. The Light of Italy and his wife, Battista Sforza, ruled together over Urbino in enviable private harmony; their relationship of equality (rare for the times, particularly when you consider that the duchess married at thirteen) is reflected in the perfect symmetry of della Francesca's beautiful work.

It is easy to see how Miller was seized by his theme. There is no question, for instance, that Lucy Turnbull is the most important person in her husband's world (all right then, pedants: *second* most important). She has helped him with all the biggest deals of his life, not just as a supportive spouse but as a lawyer, businesswoman and politician in her own right. Turnbull constantly defers to his wife's judgment, citing her ceaselessly in conversation and even in shadow cabinet, where his 'Lucy thinks ...' is a familiar refrain. 'I have a sense of us, rather than of me', he says. 'I regret every minute I am not with her. We are very, very close – in some respects we are two individuals but also we are one entity.'

*

Turnbull, in many ways, is the kind of prime minister you'd want Australia to have: clever, outrageous, fearless and interesting. By instinct, he is a discloser; you don't very often hear him engaging in the kind of psycho-babble that is the curse of modern politics, and of which Kevin Rudd is a master.

His colleagues sometimes talk about 'Bad Malcolm' and 'Good Malcolm'. Good Malcolm is charming, attentive and utterly engaging. Good Malcolm is careful to consult with his colleagues and reminds himself constantly that he must not be overbearing or dictatorial. Good Malcolm is tremendous fun. Bad Malcolm, however, can be anywhere on the scale from distant to vicious, none of it good. Bad Malcolm is well known for blowing up at his staff.

Turnbull – like Kevin Rudd – tends to exhaust his staff at a greater rate than the average politician. Many are drawn to Turnbull for the invigorating experience of working closely with a significant intellect; for some, it's too bruising an experience. Speech drafts deemed unsatisfactory, briefings deemed inadequate, too many engagements in the diary: these are triggers that regularly trip Bad Malcolm's temper, although such outbursts are sometimes followed by the contrite appearance of Good Malcolm. Bad Malcolm has a habitual note of bitter sarcasm that never fails to wound. One former employee remembers thinking that Turnbull didn't have much insight into his staff's capabilities.

'He wasn't really interested in the tools he had; he just worked to bully them into getting the job done. If they were inappropriate for the job, he'd just keep bashing them against a rock until they were finished.'

Turnbull has many gifts, but one of the most useful must surely be his ability to inject energy and enthusiasm into a room. In Launceston, during a trip to Tasmania, he knocks over three radio interviews early in the morning and then arrives at the city's new Australian Technical College. At the end of the session (a jobs forum), one ponytailed girl – she is perhaps fifteen – raises her hand diffidently and catches Turnbull's attention.

'I live in Bridgeport, and I had to move to Launceston to go to school', she says, in a tremulous voice. 'When I go to university, I'll probably have to move to the mainland. It's really hard to have to leave home. Can the government do anything to make it easier?'

Turnbull's face undergoes a queer rearrangement; a mixture of empathy, pain and nostalgia dances across his features.

'Well, you don't want to make growing up too easy, do you?' he says, awkwardly. As the audience laughs, he recovers his balance and tells the girl: 'From the moment you leave your mother's womb, you leave a position of warmth and quiet and you come screaming and squalling into the world. But I have to say, there isn't a grownup in this room who doesn't look at you and see what an exciting time you have ahead of you and wish that we were your age again. Don't be daunted.'

Afterwards, Turnbull remains devastated by the girl's question; by its heartbreaking vulnerability and trust.

'What could I say?' he exclaims, waving his arms. 'I didn't even want to say anything – oh, I just wanted to burst into tears.' His eyes, alarmingly, are filling with tears even as he remembers the girl. For all his toughness, Turnbull is extraordinarily susceptible to pathos.

To change the subject, he whips out his BlackBerry.

'Do you want to see something funny?' He scrolls through the device. 'Here – I call this the Madame Bonaparte shot!' It's a picture of Lucy Turnbull, reclining on a couch majestically, with two terriers perched alertly on her hip and shoulder. She looks regally beautiful, and Turnbull holds the device back at arm's length, squinting proudly. 'Can you imagine – looking like that at fifty?'

*

There are two lessons to be learned about Malcolm Turnbull from his role in the receivership, sale and restructure of the Fairfax media empire in the early 1990s. The first is that Turnbull has limitless determination. The second is that he is virtually unbullyable.

By late 1990, Fairfax was heavily in debt, to the tune of $1.1 billion to the banks and $450 million to US junk-bond holders. Turnbull offered himself to the junk-bond holders as an advocate, working principally on the basis of a success fee.

By dint of ceaseless nagging, coaxing, blustering and persistence,

Turnbull parlayed his bond holders' interests into a seat at the table of a most influential bidding consortium, which included Kerry Packer and Conrad Black. Packer, Black and Turnbull met in London in mid-1991 to seal the agreement, which included an undertaking from Turnbull's bond holders that they would deal with no other bidders. They called the consortium Tourang.

But the group struggled to prevail, partly due to the public suspicion of Packer's interventionist tendencies as a proprietor, and partly because Tourang did not have quite the rails run it expected in Canberra, where a divisive leadership transition from Hawke to Keating was eroding the influence of the Packer intimate Richardson, of whom much had been hoped.

Fairfax journalists, too, rallied against the prospect of Packer's involvement. Within the Tourang ranks, fissures emerged between some of the gargantuan personalities involved. Trevor Kennedy, the Packer intimate and good friend to Turnbull, was ejected. Packer grew close to a pair of American advisers who told him that Turnbull's continued presence on the Tourang team was a threat to its viability. Turnbull expected a loyal defence from his old boss but – finding none – quickly swallowed his hurt feelings and switched tactics with an extraordinary display of mercurial cunning.

He has never publicly discussed what came next.

It is well known that Packer's presence on the Tourang consortium was skewered sensationally in November 1991 by the leaking of some notes, made by Trevor Kennedy upon his arrival in Tourang, that demonstrated Packer's intentions towards Fairfax to be distinctly more interventionist than his bellicose public avowals gave regulators to believe. Much more recently, it has been reported that Turnbull himself was the shadowy figure who slid into Australian Broadcasting Tribunal chairman Peter Westerway's car one night in a quiet North Sydney street and slipped him a paper bag full of diary notes.

In a car once again, this time driving along Tasmania's Highway One from Launceston to Hobart seventeen years later, Turnbull at last supplies the narrative of that spectacular denouement.

'It was fairly tense', he begins, somewhat superfluously. 'I regarded what Kerry was doing as absolutely … it was not only stupid but it was contrary to everyone's interests. And he was taking the view that because he was bigger and richer than me, he could run me into the ground. So I rang Kerry Packer and I had a major row with him. I said, "If you want to do this, this is it. This is the end. There is no stepping back from this. This is war."'

Asked about the particulars of his threat to Packer, Turnbull's answer is straightforward: 'I told him I'd get him thrown out of the deal. I never make threats I don't carry out.' But he has to be pressed quite hard to vouchsafe the exact nature of Packer's response.

'He was fairly upset about it', is the way he puts it at first. Pressed further, he says: 'I can't recall.' He even lapses briefly into Italian in an attempt to change the subject – '*Avanti, siempre avanti!* (Onward, ever onward).' But eventually, he spells it out.

'Kerry was, um, Kerry got a bit out of control at that time', he says. 'He told me he'd kill me, yeah. I didn't think he was completely serious, but I didn't think he was entirely joking either. Look, he could be pretty scary.'

Once the disclosure is out, Turnbull warms to the narrative task.

'He did threaten to kill me. And I said to him: "Well. You'd better make sure that your assassin gets me first because if he misses, you better know I won't miss you." He could be a complete pig, you know. He could charm the birds out of the trees, but he could be a brute. He could be like that. But the one thing with bullies is that you should never flinch. My father taught me that if someone threatens you with violence, you never, ever succumb. The minute you do, someone will say: "Oh, so-and-so threatened to belt him and he buckled."'

Packer, it has been reported, did like to keep a firearm close at hand. The prospect of Australia's richest man flattening himself in a doorway in order to unload a few rounds into Turnbull on his way back from the gym does stretch the imagination somewhat. But there is no doubt that the late Mr Packer was full of surprises. As Turnbull puts it, he was scary.

'He was a difficult, mercurial guy. He could be quite capricious. I had a row with him once, about something he was doing – I can't remember what. I said to him: "Kerry, this is a very bizarre way to run a business." He leaned back and said: "Ah. But what you overlook is that I am a very bizarre person."'

The die being cast, Turnbull went about his business and delivered the papers to Westerway on the evening of Sunday, 25 November 1991. Westerway, even when told of Turnbull's admission, will not confirm the identity of the man who slipped into the passenger seat of his car, beyond saying that he was a public figure known to him, who had telephoned earlier in the day.

Westerway says his source told him, as he handed over the copy of Kennedy's notes, that 'he [the source], his wife and family were all at risk'.

'He had a genuine apprehension', Westerway recalls of his informant. 'Whether it was well based or not, I have no way of knowing.'

On the Tuesday, Westerway announced an Australian Broadcasting Tribunal inquiry into Tourang. And on the Thursday, Packer withdrew from the consortium. Turnbull only regrets one action at that time: telling Lucy, who was understandably horrified by Packer's threat.

As is so often the case with Turnbull, there is a postscript. Packer and Turnbull, furious with each other, did not speak for two years, although Turnbull spoke to Packer's wife Ros from time to time. Finally, the two men effected a rapprochement: lunch at Beppi's, a tycoon-infested East Sydney Italian restaurant. The rift finally seemed healed a year before Packer died, when one summer night the ailing mogul and his wife made a rare excursion for dinner down the road to the Turnbulls' place. The two couples sat on the terrace with a handful of friends until 3 a.m., without a trace of rancour; Lucy Turnbull remembers it now as a warm and happy goodbye.

*

The Kennedy notes skewered Packer's involvement in the Fairfax bid because they revealed Packer had lied to the parliamentary inquiry about the extent of his planned involvement in Fairfax. But Turnbull did not leak the notes to defend the integrity of the parliamentary record, or to strike a blow for freedom of the press.

He leaked them, according to his own graphic account, in order to teach Packer a lesson.

Had Packer not decided to cut his protégé loose, are we to assume that Turnbull would have remained peaceably complicit in the deception? In fairness to Turnbull, the leaking of the documents and the ousting of Packer from the Tourang bid did work in favour of Turnbull's clients, the junk-bond holders. With Packer out of the consortium, Tourang's was a much easier bid for the government to approve, and approve it they did, ensuring the satisfaction of the US creditors.

But this story crystallises something about Turnbull that obsesses his critics, and even bothers some of his supporters in quiet moments. Turnbull is an opportunist – a brilliant, charming, savage gun for hire. A lawyer, when all's said and done, with a considerable gift for argument combined with an unbelievable degree of persistence. His tactical abilities are all the freer for being unrestrained by excessive concern for consistency or even – in some circumstances – governing principle.

This is, unmistakably, a handy quality in business. But in politics, it becomes complicated.

The Tourang affair is the stand-out example, from Turnbull's career in business, of how far Turnbull is prepared to go to prove a point. And echoes of Turnbull's business style do reverberate in his approach to politics.

In the unblinking pursuit of Fairfax, one can easily spot the seeds of Turnbull's hostile 2004 take-over of the seat of Wentworth, where he ousted the Liberal incumbent, Peter King. In both circumstances, he used a combination of lateral thinking, charm, brutality and astute legal manoeuvring to extract results.

In the main, and with the exception of his convictions about tax reform, the values with which Turnbull is identified are soft values – that is to say, they concern enveloping themes rather than hard reforms. Like the duke of the Italian Renaissance, he is a libertarian in the classic sense, for all that these views may co-exist with a savage talent for warfare.

Here we encounter the most significant dissimilarity between John Howard and Malcolm Turnbull. Howard, as a politician, was an unprepossessing physical presence who was fiercely memorable for his convictions and what he did about them. Turnbull, on the other hand, is memorable for himself – for the person that he is, for his powerful character traits – more than for his convictions, which are of a much broader inclination than Howard's specific policy obsessions.

*

To the Liberal Party of John Howard, Turnbull is like a handsome stranger who turns up on a cruise boat. He's charming, witty, erudite and happy to buy the drinks. So why, oh why, do they hang back?

It can't be a 'new money' thing. The Liberal Party does not have the same sensitivity to this as does the British Conservative Party, where it was once disparagingly said of Margaret Thatcher's challenger Michael Heseltine that he 'bought his own furniture'.

It's more a 'new membership' thing. The Liberal Party is like a gentlemen's club. Anyone can join, and be treated politely. But after a few years, when you notice you're not getting anywhere, it might occur to you that you are not quite the ticket. To some in the Liberal Party, Turnbull is not quite the ticket. Perhaps it is the manner in which he seized Wentworth. Most definitely it has to do with Turnbull's tin ear for the unwritten codes of the Liberal Party.

'Malcolm doesn't always realise that in the Liberal Party, when somebody raises an eyebrow at you, it actually means something', laughs one Liberal warhorse, a supporter of Turnbull.

As a result, Turnbull often commits howlers, such as the time he was addressing colleagues and pointed out the curious habit Kevin Rudd has of mentioning him – Turnbull – all the time. 'Neville Wran, whom I regard as a great political strategist, told me he made it a practice never to mention his opponents by name', Turnbull told the meeting. Or the time – again at a party meeting – when he mused aloud on his suspicion Paul Keating was coaching Rudd and Wayne Swan behind the scenes. 'I rang Keating, and I said to him: "You're helping them, aren't you?"' Turnbull told his flock.

Now, in front of any other crowd, neither of these remarks would seem exceptional, let alone exceptionable. But Liberal MPs are a sensitive lot, and the effect was like a meeting of Orangemen hearing their preacher make a breezy reference to having phoned the Pope the other day.

Alexander Downer, who is definitely a creature of the Liberal Party, is quick to defend Turnbull from critics who believe his lack of flight-hours in the party prevents him from leading it effectively.

'It's sort of patronising, that view. I mean, what is the argument here? That he can't learn? Sure, he came into the Liberal Party and into power not knowing as much as people who had been there for twenty years, like me or John Howard or Peter Costello. But people aren't actually born to understand the Liberal Party. You have to learn.'

June 2009

A SHAPE-SHIFTER IN THE LODGE

The Wharf Revue, playing at the Sydney Theatre Company, depicts Kevin Rudd as Harry Potter – an earnest, nerdy boy-wizard with a delicately placed scar and a weakness for phantasmal buzzwords. The visuals are perfect.

But a better Potter analogy might have been with the Animagi – wizards with the power to change shape at will, depending on circumstances.

In his extraordinary ability to mould himself to the changing demands of world events and popular opinion, Kevin Rudd – in nearly two years as prime minister – has established a personal tradition to rival the classic shape-shifters of mythology and folklore.

In Ovid's *Metamorphoses*, the supreme Greek god Zeus changes form relentlessly. He's a thunderbolt one moment, a swan the next. His chameleonic tendencies also mainly concern seduction; Zeus was a swan when he overcame Leda and a bull in ravishing Europa, while poor old Danae got knocked up after Zeus appeared to her as a shower of gold.

One hesitates to make an immediate comparison with the prime minister, whose own manifestations before his subjects are not even faintly priapic, familiar as the shower of gold might sound.

But he is a shape shifter, all the same.

When orthodoxy demanded it, he was an economic conservative. When global financial exigencies encouraged it, he became a big spender. In the past month, we have witnessed manifestations in which the PM is by turns a hardline border protectionist and a humane friend to refugees. A public proponent of the 'calm, methodical' approach to policy debate, who last Friday night capped off a week of such measured exhortations with a foaming, quasi-Biblical attack on climate-change sceptics, whom he accused of conspiring to 'destroy our children's future'. A leader who was able to trumpet, on Thursday, his 'vast ... comprehensive micro-economic reform agenda', having smartly abandoned one element of it, the mooted abolition of parallel import restrictions in the publishing industry, just twenty-four hours earlier.

Depending on his audience, Rudd the daggy dad can morph seamlessly into the cold, ruthless administrator, and thence into the devout Christian. Footy scarves cause him to break out into a hive of Ockerisms; the merest flash of Australian Defence Force camouflage in an audience is sufficient to roughen his vowels and elicit the occasional expletive. The blueness of the language will escalate commensurate with the extent to which the soldiers are armed. 'You guys really know your shit', he enthused to a heat-packing posse of Australian troops in Kandahar last December.

But seed the audience with enough think-tankers, or anyone who works for the EC or the IMF or any acronymic international outfit beginning with the letters 'UN-', and you've bought yourself tickets to a jargon fight. He was a knockout in April last year in a room with the European Commission president, Jose Barroso.

'There has to be a greater synergy between, let's call it our policy leadership in this, which has been focused so much, legitimately, on targets and global architecture, almost reverse-engineered back to the means by which you can quickly deliver outcomes, and on the demand side in our economy we're looking at potential advances in terms of 20 to 25 per cent range if you do this across the board.'

After nearly two years of Rudd as prime minister, close observers find themselves in an unusual position; the more we see of him, the less we know about him for sure.

Should this be surprising in modern politics, where the news cycle is so anarchic that politicians are obliged to pitch mixed messages to fractured audiences? Perhaps the PM's chimeric tendencies are especially noticeable because of the stolid predictability of his predecessor, who was almost comically changeless, his views and predilections unmistakable through more than a decade of shifting circumstance.

Tony Blair, another contemporary shape-shifter of the broad left, used to talk defensively about his 'irreducible core'. What is at the irreducible core of Kevin Rudd? It depends who you ask, and when you ask.

Rudd is a creature of strange contradictions. His election campaign was self-consciously anchored in economic conservatism but his incumbency has been most memorable for its old-style Labor spending.

A hysterically popular PM for whom colleagues do not, in private, pretend to anything more than the most dutiful courtesies, he is feared in some quarters, marvelled at in most, but rarely warmly extolled by the nomadic hordes that gather in Canberra. He does not have mates in politics, or comrades for whom he would willingly spill blood. Not his own, anyway.

For all the intrigue of politics, and the sinewy networks of historical allegiance, power, and human obligation that usually bind Labor leaders in place, Rudd's political equation is startlingly simple; he is powerful inside his party because he is popular outside it, and that's about it.

In this sense, Rudd is unusually dependent on the polls for his continued wellbeing; doubly so, if you like. It's not just that the fortunes of his government are buoyed by strong approval ratings; it's also that his internal power is entirely dependent on them.

'He's sensitive to the need to retain high ratings', says one colleague. 'If he doesn't, he doesn't have a lot of friends around, to be frank.'

This doesn't appear to bother Rudd, who regularly affronts colleagues with his indifference to their tribal instincts. Colleagues were prepared, in general terms, for a leader who didn't dole out jobs to Labor boys. But to bite their lips as Rudd selects prominent retiring Liberals for public office? It's testing the friendship.

Paul Keating is not constrained by any notion of caucus solidarity. Of Peter Costello's appointment to the Future Fund a fortnight ago, he piercingly articulated the ill-feeling. 'The prime minister's goody-two-shoes approach of appointing former opponents of the Labor Party to important public jobs is no substitute for thoughtful and mature reflection as to the public requirement of those positions', he declared. 'It is also disloyal to all those members of the Labor caucus in the Keating government and those members of the Beazley, Crean and Latham Oppositions who stood and fought Costello.'

Wayne Swan, whose hide is riddled with scars from Costello's invective over the years, managed a weak smile. 'Kevin is a goody-two-shoes', he told ABC TV's *Insiders* last weekend. 'And that's a good thing!'

After two years in government, Rudd's colleagues are as much in the dark about his true motives and beliefs as anyone else.

Rudd's path through the federal party has been unusually linear. He entered Parliament in 1998, made it to the front bench as foreign-affairs spokesman three years later, and remained in that post until he became leader in December 2006.

Contemporaries like Swan, Stephen Smith, Lindsay Tanner, Jenny Macklin and even Julia Gillard spent years in Opposition jobbing around in a series of different portfolios, allowing colleagues to get a feel for their views on domestic policy matters.

To his comrades, however, Rudd is something of a blank slate. Recently Rudd's rhetoric parted company with his conduct, leaving none the wiser. How do you reconcile the 'tough but humane' public formulation of Labor's border-protection approach to the handling of the *Oceanic Viking*, which hasn't been either?

The affair prompted a couple of breaches in Labor's wall of discipline around its inscrutable leader, mainly by pro-refugee Labor figures who can't understand why the PM won't make a withdrawal from his public goodwill bank to introduce a higher-minded tone.

'It's weird', says one MP. 'Yes, he doesn't use the extraordinary amount of petrol he has in the tank to drive things, like change the dynamics of the refugee issue. But I don't know if anyone actually knows what he really believes on this stuff. Is he pursuing the tough line because it's the popular thing to say, or because he really holds the view that queue jumping is bad news?'

Says a minister, when asked to opine on Rudd's political core: 'I think his values are good. Values related to disadvantage and getting a good education for kids from disadvantaged families. And the homeless; he hasn't wavered in his commitment there, and I think he would like to think to himself when he eventually gives it away that he's made a difference there.'

Apart from a shared ministerial observation about Rudd's genuine concern for the homeless, there is little consensus among senior colleagues about the public policy for which the PM would be prepared to die in a ditch.

A shape-shifter without, and a shape-shifter within.

You get the sense that the whole thing holds together partially because of the sincere relief Labor's Opposition-scarred senior operatives feel at being in government, and partially because Rudd's continuing popularity has them so flummoxed, that they don't want to jinx anything by making trouble.

The last prime minister to achieve anything like this sustained public popularity was Bob Hawke. Like Rudd, Hawke was prepared to confront his party's sacred cows, but the two leaders could not possibly have had a more different approach to the management of colleagues.

Hawke's cabinet ministers were given their heads, while Rudd's are tightly controlled and even – in the case of some major decisions – bypassed entirely by the four-member Strategic Priorities and Budget Committee, a leak-proof high synod comprising Rudd, Gillard, Swan and Tanner.

A constant complaint – private enterprise and public sector alike – is that the concentration of power around Rudd constantly log-jams cabinet-level decision making. Some supplicants await Rudd's departures overseas to approach the government, reckoning their chances of speedy processing are much better with Rudd's deputy Julia Gillard.

Hawke declined to comment directly on Rudd management for this article. But he offered the general observation that prime ministers have 'a moral obligation to get the best out of your material'.

Hawke also is of the view that significant reforms must be accompanied by clear and honest explanations from leaders, for the benefit of voters and colleagues. 'Knowledge is the ally of good policy making, and ignorance and prejudice and fear are the enemies', he said.

14 November 2009

OH, WHAT A LOVELY CRISIS: RUDDBOT YEAR 2

DROP THE BALL, GO FOR THE JUGULAR

If any doubt remained about how Kevin Rudd is planning to play Malcolm Turnbull this year, it has now evaporated.

There's to be none of this 'play the ball, not the man' nonsense. With steely deliberation, the PM kicked the ball to the sideline yesterday and went straight for the squirrel grip.

'Mr Turnbull represents a radical, right-wing, free-market approach to the economy where governments shouldn't intervene, that has spectacularly failed', the PM advised reporters, in his first press conference of the 2009 summer parliamentary session.

Turnbull as a radical right-winger? If you listened carefully, you might just have heard the distant sound of the Liberal neo-cons choking on their baby-seal kebabs. Turnbull? That pinot noir-sipping, Henson-owning, gay rights-supporting Maltese terrier collector?

Mr Rudd delivered his lines with his now-customary air of tough competence. But inside, he must have been high-fiving himself at the sheer, exhilarating cheek of his tactic. It was a beautiful piece of manoeuvring.

The PM's job going into the press conference was to make the dolorous announcement that the nation has unfortunately mislaid $115 billion on his watch. A sticky task for any leader, let alone one who made so much of his fiscal prudence just fifteen short months ago. But attack is the best form of defence, as the PM so agilely demonstrated.

By the end of the press conference, a casual observer might have developed the impression that not only had Mr Turnbull caused the global economic crisis, but that he was actually proud of it, and would cackle with satisfaction as hundreds of thousands of Australians lost their jobs.

(Mr Rudd, on the other hand, is here to help. Witness the scenes at his Canberra church on Sunday; when an aged parishioner succumbed to the heat in a neighbouring pew, a pair of Samaritans positioned themselves to bear him from the stuffy church. Mr Rudd carried the man's left ankle, with an air of tough competence.)

Gone is Mr Rudd's old approach to the adversary, which during the

Brendan Nelson era was to purse his lips and insist primly that it was not his place to comment on the Liberal leadership. He has always despised Mr Turnbull in private; now the PM has decided to make it public.

But Mr Turnbull is a substantial enemy. At 3.15 p.m. yesterday, the rapacious face of right-wing extreme capitalism staged his own press conference, also at Parliament House. He seemed smilingly unfazed by the more hysterical of Mr Rudd's accusations (which is probably to be expected from a person who has been called much, much worse by Kerry Packer), and responded urbanely that Mr Rudd himself was a 'born-again socialist' with 'bizarre' views on financial regulation.

As we battle through this year, burning furniture for warmth and composing satisfying meals out of oatmeal and golden syrup, one of the lonely consolations is going to be the free-to-air drama of Rudd v Turnbull.

3 February 2009

TARZAN TURNBULL SWINGS INTO A JUNGLE FULL OF TROUBLE

The second and larger of the Rudd government's stimulus announcements was an eye-popping $42-billion disgorgement of public funds, to be spent on cash handouts, school and transport projects and the installation of free insulation in a rash of Australian homes. The Coalition, after much discussion, decided to oppose the measure.

It was a reasonably quiet morning in the parliamentary jungle yesterday.

Until Tarzan arrived, that is.

Swinging through the trees, Tarzan Turnbull alighted before the dispatch box and, giving his chest a vigorous, if figurative, thump, performed his most dazzling feat of machismo yet.

Clad only in the briefest of policy loincloths, Tarzan plans to stand between mum-and-dad Australia and $42 billion of free money, pink batts and school libraries.

'We do not support a further round of cash handouts. That is an unpopular thing to say, and I understand that', he declaimed. 'But it's the right thing to say and I think most Australians will recognise in their hearts that it is the right thing to say.'

Commentators gasped. Ladies fainted. The weak of heart covered their eyes.

Needless to say, not everyone shares his optimism about what most Australians will recognise in their hearts. 'Whatever else you think of Malcolm, he's certainly got a pair', marvelled one *Herald* blog contributor yesterday. 'They're going to be flattened like a pile of possum roadkill by the stampede of punters towards Big Kev's fistful of dollars. But he won't have died wondering.'

Indeed, debate raged around Parliament House yesterday about the political implications of Tarzan's actions.

Was he committing political suicide? Was this an incredibly beady-eyed act of political cynicism designed to allow Tarzan to dance all over Kevin Rudd's grave when the $42-billion package – passed ultimately through the Senate by a haggard and much-chewed coalition of Xenophons, Browns and Fieldings – turns out to be useless?

Realistically, though, most of the Coalition's troops really do think the Government's $42 billion is too much. They're against it, and now they've said they're against it. At least they can be credited with standing by their beliefs.

One suspects, too, that Tarzan is more comfortable with grand gestures than he is with the pettifogging process of parliamentary compromise. Not for him the humiliating business of brawling over tax breaks line by line. He intends to have an argument and he intends to have it on a grand scale.

For all his contemptuous invocation of Gough Whitlam this week, there is a touch of 'crash-through or crash' about Tarzan's entire approach. But he clearly felt the better for it – after looking positively peaky on Tuesday, as he scrambled about trying to avoid giving an opinion on the government's announcement, Tarzan looked yesterday as though he had recovered his balance.

His colleagues quickly caught the crazy-brave spirit.

'When somebody holds a gun to your head, maybe it's a bit silly, but I say – "Well mate, pull the trigger"', offered Joe Hockey, always a man for frankness in a crisis.

The prime minister won't hesitate to pull the trigger, either. The genius of his $42-billion gambit is that it is a sophisticated 'Vote Yes, Or the Puppy Gets It' device. Anyone voting against it will need to explain to forlorn local kiddies why they don't get a school library, or to sad-eyed single parents why $950 won't be coming their way after all.

Tough times for Tarzan.

5 February 2009

FORGIVE OUR LEADERS – THEY'RE HAVING A LOVELY, LOVELY CRISIS

State and territory leaders gathered in Canberra, eyes shining, to hear all about the prime minister's plans to shower them with federal moolah.

Whew – they signed it.

Obviously, there was always a bit of anxiety about whether all those premiers would ever agree to that $42 billion worth of free stuff. But they did – and did you ever see a happier little bunch of Vegemites?

In the old days, the premiers' conference tended to be a heavily orchestrated display of flounce-out. Yesterday, it resembled nothing so much as an episode of *Supermarket Sweep*, as the state and territory leaders zoomed about joyfully, piling their trolleys high with federally funded loot.

Schools, roads, railway wigwags – there was a lot on offer, and they gobbled it up. Even the lonely Liberal premier, Western Australia's Colin Barnett, had to make a visible effort to look sheepish as he joined the scramble for the Rudd billions. There was much excited talk of partnerships, roll-outs and 'shovel-ready projects'.

There are to be staged deliveries and a whole network of co-ordinators-general linking hands across this wide broke land. Kevin Rudd held court passionately and unintelligibly for several minutes on the details of the administration structure. It seems that after a spot of light benchmarking, most of these projects are in fact shovel ready.

In his enthusiasm for the $14.7 billion he is spending on school buildings, the prime minister announced – all in the space of a single sentence – that he would be rolling his sleeves up, cracking heads *and* knocking skulls in the weeks ahead. Those poor children!

The Victorian premier, John Brumby, was especially ebullient. He declared many of his projects to be 'site procured, community consulted and ready to go'.

'We haven't had such good news … since the last COAG meeting', he grinned.

The South Australian premier, Mike Rann, was also very enthusiastic, and proudly announced plans to stage his own summit of school principals and administrators.

Ten minutes of this carry-on is enough to bring on distinct feelings of violent shovel readiness in the average observer, but we have to forgive these state and territory leaders. They are having a lovely, lovely, crisis.

There was near silence when the nine leaders signed their nine copies of the agreement. After some initial confusion, it was agreed that each leader should sign the agreement in front of him or her, then pass it to the leader on their immediate right for further inscription.

At the far end of the road sat Councillor Geoff Lake, a charming-looking adolescent who was there representing local government. Cr Lake didn't get either a pen or an agreement, so he simply busied himself handing the completed sheets to an attendant, like a helpful diner clearing his own table.

And the prime minister saw what he had created, and he found it to be good.

6 February 2009

FEARLESS SENATOR UNLEASHES THE PINK BATTS OUT OF HELL

South Australian senator Nick Xenophon announced that he, too, would vote against the stimulus package. Along with the Coalition's 'no' votes, Senator Xenophon's demurral was enough to scuttle the bill. Don't panic, though. In the end, the government threw in enough money for the Murray River that Senator Xenophon finally agreed.

There was a sense of inevitability about the government's $42-billion stimulus bill this week.

With the continent scorched at one end and sodden at the other, and that other nameless, hulking economic threat gaining ground on us fast, it seemed likely that the general sense of urgency and crisis would speed up the government's legislation through the Senate. Even some members of the Coalition, which decided last week to oppose the thing in its entirety, were privately working on the assumption that it would pass nonetheless.

But Nick Xenophon, the wily Greek from South Australia, is a creature of surprise. Unlike his crossbench colleague Steve Fielding, Xenophon doesn't get too bothered by people yelling at him.

In his old job, as official balance-of-power pain in the bum in the South Australian upper house, he once refused to sell off the state's power assets after a long and tortuous campaign of wheedling, sweet-talking, bullying and pleading from the Olsen government of the day.

You can safely assume that this bloke's already been yelled at pretty comprehensively. It doesn't work any more.

'I didn't come to Canberra to make friends', he said yesterday.

This, of course, is not quite true. What he means is that he didn't come to Canberra to make friends in Canberra. He came to Canberra to make friends in South Australia, which is fair enough.

Watching negotiations at this level of politics is a bit like watching chess. Everyone can see the moves, but there's significant dispute about what they mean. In Canberra yesterday the corridors teemed with tuppenny strategists giving the good oil on what this result signified.

It's a disaster for the government, which has been exposed as a bunch of lightweights who couldn't get a sure thing through the Senate.

It's a disaster for the Opposition, which has been exposed as a gang of heartless thugs who wouldn't give a single mum $950 if the world was about to end, or – alternatively – a gang of political opportunists who would gladly run the Australian economy into the ground just to regain government.

It's a disaster for Xenophon, who will return home this weekend to be beaten soundly by uninsulated South Australian constituents, using pink batts they have now been forced to buy themselves from Bunnings.

Is it possible that a single result could simultaneously be a disaster for everybody?

The other funny thing about negotiations at this level is how different they can be from what you'd picture. You'd assume that – given $42 billion on the table and a clock going *tick-tick-tick* – the government would be stalking its extra Senate votes day and night. You'd think that every dawn at the Xenophon household would bring a Treasury delegation with a basket of Danish pastries and a quick seminar on macroeconomic policy.

But Nick Xenophon spent most of yesterday sitting in his office wondering why the phone didn't ring.

At this level of negotiations, he who picks up the phone first is weakest.

It's that silly.

13 February 2009

SCREWED ... IN ANYONE'S LANGUAGE

Economists are the druids of this crisis. They are its witch doctors, with their frantic and confounding ululations, their spells and incantations.

What are they talking about? Can they possibly help? As with most unfortunate souls who turn to the occult, we are in too much trouble to discount the possibility. We seek signs everywhere.

The Reserve Bank has cut interest rates by a hundred basis points – great! They're doing something! That must be good! The Reserve Bank's doing nothing this month – great! That means they're not panicking! That must be good!

One of the problems that we face is that neither our prime minister nor our treasurer is much good at explaining things simply. Each of them has been hanging out with economists so long now that they talk like they went to kindergarten with Amartya Sen.

Take the national accounts on Wednesday. The release of these ABS figures for the December quarter showed that the economy shrank during the last three months of last year, instead of growing. This unleashed a fresh round of incantations from the witch doctors, many of whom predicted a fractional positive result.

One of the big changes, apart from an increase in the cost of imports, was a 1.8 per cent decrease in something called 'inventories', which means, in simple terms, that companies aren't buying as much stuff any more; they're using up the stuff they already have, instead.

Let's take a sample fictitious factory. Let's call it – I don't know – the Snuggly Bits pink batts plant. The story of last year's final quarter for this little factory is that Snuggly Bits, rather than buying new supplies of recycled glass to manufacture their glass-wool wares, started drawing down on their warehouse stocks of glass instead.

They're exercising caution over there at Snuggly Bits, just as you or I would. If sales are going to go down, they don't want to get stuck with a million tonnes of busted Bacardi Breezer bottles while consumers spend their money on bread and dripping rather than insulation. So the delivery of the December glass consignment was cancelled, and at Snuggly Bits the guys on the forklifts started making some inroads into the warehouse stockpile instead.

So the truck delivery company gave their driver a few less hours in December.

And the sandwich shop around the corner from Snuggly Bits, where the driver normally goes for a sandwich and a chocolate milk while the consignment's being unloaded, sold one less sandwich.

And so on.

The closest Kevin Rudd came to explaining all this was on Thursday night, when Kerry O'Brien asked him the meaning of the national accounts figures.

'Well, the first point, Kerry, is that you know growth numbers have been calculated since time immemorial, including both the non-farm and the farm sectors of the economy', the PM began. 'And going back some time we've had some periods of negative contribution to growth from the non-farm sector as well. So these things change over time. If you go to the actual elements of the national accounts themselves, there are strengths still, but there are weaknesses.

'And you asked specifically about weaknesses – the one which stands up out of those national accounts, of course, is the fact that there has been a recourse to inventories by firms, rather than bringing in new production into their warehouses for the purposes of on-selling to consumers.'

Oh, Kevin. Don't you just want to thump him sometimes?

The weird thing is that in missing the opportunity to explain these things more clearly (and honestly – could they possibly be less clear?), Rudd and Swan deprive themselves of brownie points. There is a pretty good and simple story here, if anyone in the government could pull their heads out of their proverbials long enough to tell it.

Let's return to Snuggly Bits.

'What we're doing', (Rudd and Swan might explain, if they could ever form a sentence without using the terms 'difflator', 'fiscal policy settings' or 'synchronised contractions') 'is using federal funds to buy insulation for Australian houses. This gets Snuggly Bits manufacturing more so they resume their glass deliveries, so that Joe the driver keeps his job and Cheryl in the sandwich shop keeps hers, too.

'And we're also spending federal money on building school performing-arts centres and railway crossings, so that businesses that make wig-wags and besser blocks and Little Orphan Annie costumes don't get left out, either.'

Instead, their first priority always seems to be the covering of those very same proverbials in which their heads are so irrevocably jammed. The treasurer spent his entire press conference on Wednesday repeating the same message in different ways and using a variety of props. The message was: 'Sure, we're screwed. But not as screwed as we could be. And not as screwed as Germany.'

In particular, Mr Swan seems to think his most important responsibility is to convince people that things would have been worse had he not decided to start throwing money around. And indeed, that may be his most pressing responsibility to himself and to marginal seat holders in the government. But his chief responsibility to Australian voters is to explain what's happening, and what he's doing about it.

Here, by way of contrast, is Barack Obama last year, when asked on *MTV News* why the credit crisis should matter to a twenty-year-old.

'If the credit markets collapse, what it means is banks aren't lending businesses money. Businesses then can't invest in plants and equipment, and make payroll, so they shut down. And that means the suppliers of those companies, they shut down. Over time, what happens is you get the whole economy coming to a standstill.

'That's what happened during the Great Depression. And at that time, it was just banks that were in charge of capital. Now you've got all different ways that money flows but the bottom line is, that if money freezes up, businesses can't do business, and you get an enormous contraction of an economy.

'And that, ultimately, will affect that twenty-year-old, because that twenty-year-old is going to be looking for a better job after he gets out of school. If our businesses aren't creating jobs, they're not creating tax revenues – now it's harder for government to finance that college education or to build that new university. So it has a ripple effect.'

Just because you hang out with witch doctors doesn't mean you have to speak in tongues.

7 March 2009

KEVIN BLOODY RUDD SAYS TO HECK WITH CONSEQUENCES

To Mr Kevin Rudd, of the Lodge, and Mr Wayne Swan, of Brisbane: A healthy new euphemism, born at 3.30 p.m. yesterday, in the House of Representatives. Also in attendance Ms J. Gillard, with Mr L. Tanner assisting. Thanks to all staff.

'We're in the midst of a jobs consequence flowing from the global financial crisis', announced Kevin Rudd yesterday, in response to incessant questions from the Opposition about why the job queues are growing despite repeated government applications of fiscal stimulus.

A 'jobs consequence'? That's one way of putting it. Maybe the PM should go back to swearing.

Malcolm Turnbull suffered something of a 'jobs consequence' yesterday too. Of course, his 'jobs consequence' was mainly just a consequence of the job he's in – leader of the Opposition, where the employment specifications actually include being beaten around the head by half your colleagues, often publicly. In a properly re-regulated employment market, it would probably be outlawed, like bear-baiting or child labour. But Julia Gillard, who is often to be heard voicing her concern about ordinary Aussies forced to work in intolerable conditions, is nonetheless more than happy to see conditions in one very specific Australian job get worse and worse.

Yesterday, she was overjoyed to hear that Malcolm Turnbull had spent an uncomfortable morning presiding over a three-hour barkfest with his colleagues concerning what they were all to do about the industrial relations legislation.

'You're hopeless! You're a joke!' she carolled, practically before question time had even started.

The Coalition's party meeting was the main event yesterday; even the government seemed to rush through its regular Tuesday caucus meeting, the sooner to be in a position to enjoy the extended, Wagnerian difficulties of its rivals. Many on the Labor side can clearly recall the times when their own meetings resembled modern pentathlons of hatred, so to see it happening to someone else really does give their spirits a little lift.

The Coalition's meeting, with all its shrieking and rending of garments, went for so long that the standard post-match briefing for journalists was abandoned, and it was Turnbull himself who burst forth into the Canberra sunshine – minutes before question time – to give an account of what had been decided.

You've got to hand it to him. Turnbull talked talentedly and at breakneck speed about the bits of the government's bill to which his colleagues take exception, leaving precious little time for questions. His party would present amendments, he said, but the Opposition leader equivocated slightly on the question of whether they were do-or-die affairs.

'We will insist on the amendments we are proposing, yes, but we may be able to agree on alternatives to those amendments with the independent senators or perhaps with the government.'

The Opposition has also agreed that the government's definition of a small business as one with fewer than fifteen employees is wrong. That's not to say that they've come up with a better one. That's tomorrow's barney.

11 March 2009

WARNING: THIS BLOKE YAKS FOR AUSTRALIA

To listen to a parliamentary answer by Kevin Rudd is to enlist in a gruelling physical challenge.

At first, your correspondent was embarrassed about her inability to maintain attention all the way through to the end of even some of the shorter answers. But after yesterday's question time, in which the PM reached a personal best of thirteen whole minutes, it became clear there is a mystical power to the man's speech patterns.

At the thirty-second mark, the listener is feeling confident. There are a few 'early and decisives', the odd reference to the 'core facts' about something-or-other, but nothing to raise a sweat.

By the ninety-second mark, it's an effort. We're forging further and further away from the question. Ordinary landmarks disappear. The PM begins to introduce a few special effects – a column of ABS statistics, or the night thoughts of some long-dead Nobel laureate. Then he might go for a quick whip round the GDPs of some selected OECD countries.

Kevin Rudd is the Phil Spector of political oratory – his technique is 'Wall of Sound', with massive overdubbing of economic statistics.

By the second-minute mark, the human brain begins to wander, in search of the banal comforts of home. Have we run out of Vegemite? When is the cat due at the vet? Through the neural crack jemmied open by these uninvited thoughts, dozens of others rudely crowd. Legions of unwritten letters, unpaid bills, unwatered plants and unthanked great aunts jostle for attention, and suddenly Mr Rudd and his statistics are completely gone.

With an effort, the listener snaps back to attention, only to hear him take a long breath and say: 'Secondly ...'

It's the oddest thing; it's not that the sentences aren't sentences, or that they don't make sense grammatically. It's just that they attempt so little. Facts and figures flow remorselessly, interspersed with quotations from analysts or International Monetary Fund personages.

Mr Rudd's first answer yesterday lasted six minutes, but it seemed an eternity. When he fell silent, Brett Raguse (ALP, Forde), managed to struggle to his feet. 'My question is to the prime minister. Will the prime minister update the house on recent updates to the global economic outlook and ... ?'

What? Was the man mad?

'Flee!' your correspondent wanted to gasp, but was overcome. Mr Rudd resumed his position at the dispatch box.

Thirteen more minutes followed, interrupted by feeble cries to the speaker from a stricken Opposition at minutes six, eight, nine and eleven-and-a-half.

'This is verbal anaesthetic!' protested the Liberal frontbencher Tony Smith. Later, someone asked about bananas.

I wish I could tell you what the answer was.

12 March 2009

MPS GET THE BANDS BACK TOGETHER

Oh, to be young again. The environment minister, Peter Garrett, set aside his briefs for an evening on Thursday and shrieked out – largely unrehearsed – a goodly selection of his old hits at the National Convention Centre in Canberra.

'When the Generals Talk (You Better Listen to Him)' was an anti-totalitarian anthem of its time when first released in 1984. Sung twenty-five years later by a Commonwealth minister, just a sniper shot from the Defence Department headquarters (whose generals are engaged in open warfare with Garrett's own government), the song takes on a slightly surreal blush.

But at least Garrett is getting to have some fun for once. He was not the only one this week.

Peter Costello, as part of his 'Who, me?' leadership campaign, stepped into the House of Representatives on Thursday morning to make a contribution to the debate on voluntary student unionism. For the former treasurer, this was the equivalent of getting the band back together. If there is anything that unites Liberals – anything that can get them to suspend their petty hatreds and rivalries, open a bottle of cheap wine and get a bit tiddly while reliving the battles of the past – voluntary student unionism is it.

In 2005 the Howard government managed to get just enough votes to abolish the practice of levying compulsory student union membership fees in Australian universities. The Rudd government is now trying to reintroduce them, albeit under the guise of a 'student services' fee.

What did these fees pay for? It depends on who you ask. A Liberal MP will tell you that these fees represented the direct milking of money from decent, Howard-loving commerce students to finance the sex lives of university Marxists in the politics faculty. A Labor MP will tell you that they went towards childcare, career guidance and reasonably priced sausage rolls.

Both are probably gilding the lily a bit.

But the main usefulness of the debate, which reopened in the House of Representatives this week, is to make our MPs feel young again.*

When the speaker calls on the *Higher Education Amendment (Student Services, Amenities and Other Measures) Bill 2009*, you can see their shoulders straightening, their features softening in fond reverie. For a moment you can imagine what some of them might have looked like with hair.

For the Libs, this debate is an opportunity to relive the guerrilla days of campus life in the 1970s and '80s, when they fought bravely against the left-wing hordes, joined the debating club, defiantly wore ties to lectures and comforted themselves that at least they would get jobs. For the Labor hacks, who once again find themselves in the majority, it is a chance to taunt their old adversaries.

'I think they are just sore because the Liberal Party never succeeded on campus', offered Anna Burke, a Victorian Labor MP, this week.

And it's a chance to drag out all those old student newspapers, in search of embarrassing photographs and unfortunate public statements. Costello, who was a student warrior at Monash University in the latter part of the 1970s, saw active service; he was beaten up by left-wingers in 1977, and his mainstream newspaper debut was to be photographed in his jarmies, recuperating in his single bed at his parents' house.

In adulthood Costello continues to disapprove of student unions.

'By and large they were run by a small minority of students with a very left-wing outlook on life', he told the chamber on Thursday. 'The student unions were dominated by various communist sub-factions and anarchist groups, many of the leaders of which are now members of the Labor Party, having moderated in their old age.'

However, Labor's research experts have dug up a few reminders that Costello's views on compulsory student fees were not always so firm. One 1978 article, written by the fully recovered young Costello for the Monash student newspaper *Lot's Wife*, opines: 'The fact that some people object to the way in which some public funds are spent does not mean that they are therefore exempted from paying taxes.' This clipping tends to be carried around triumphantly on the tip of a spear by the Labor hordes.

Another young pup, Tony Abbott – then Student Representative Council president at Sydney University – also turned his mind to compulsory union fees in 1978. He was rather less equivocal, as you might imagine. The archives of *Honi Soit* contain a fabulous 1978 article penned by a young and passionate People Skills, in which he memorably advocates the destruction of his own organisation. 'Apart from the legal aid service, and the faculty grants and loans, which are administered separately from the SRC's other activities, the SRC's spending has achieved nothing beyond soothing the edges and obsessions of a few left-wing fanatics', he wrote. 'The useful work of the SRC has not involved the spending of any money at all. Late this term I shall seek to end compulsory subsidisation of the SRC. I will keep you informed of further developments.'

Heroic, audacious, quasi-suicidal; it's pure People Skills and a joy to read.

The finance minister, Lindsay Tanner, has fond memories of his university training ground. A contemporary of Costello's, he edited the University of Melbourne's student paper in 1977. 'We participated in epic struggles over issues like apartheid and East Timor, and saw ourselves as players in virtually every issue going, no matter where', he told his alma mater's magazine *Voice* in an interview for its current issue. 'We fought enormous battles within the student body around Middle East issues.'

Many of those student warriors are now in Parliament. For example, Tony Abbott's old Sydney Uni job was taken up in 1983 by Belinda Neal, the same year as the Australian Union of Students came under the leadership of one Julia Eileen Gillard. Two years later the student presidency at Sydney passed to Joe Hockey.

These days on campus the skirmishes are all a bit thinner on the ground. During Thursday's debate only one example of contemporary Marxist feather-bedding was cited, and it was a thin one at that. The student union at the Royal Melbourne Institute of Technology has affiliated with the community radio station 3CR and produces, on Saturdays, a half-hour program called *Blazing Textbooks*, which seeks to present an 'anti-capitalist perspective on current issues in education'.

'*Blazing Textbooks* first scorched the airwaves in December 2007 with a feature on the complexity of teaching issues of sexual assault', the union's website records, with a hint of immodesty.

Presenters would no doubt be surprised to learn that their little radio show was mentioned by no less than three Coalition MPs on Thursday, and that they are now viewed as the last surviving stronghold of university Marxism.

* *The exception to this is the prime minister, Kevin Rudd. He has no need to revisit his youth, because he spent it reading Hansard.*

14 March 2009

POLLIE FOLLIES IN HOUSE OF ILL FAME

It was as if an unseen hand seized control of the political script yesterday. A hand, perhaps, belonging to a rogue headline editor from London's *Sun* newspaper.

Politicians on both sides behaved as if they were in a contest to generate the splashiest tabloid headline. Wayne Swan got things moving at a press conference on plans to restrict executive severance pay. 'Haircut for Fat Cats, Sez Swan!'

Beauty, Wayne. But before the treasurer could repair to the Pen and Pint for a gazillion celebratory beers, Malcolm Turnbull had something to say. Would the PM advise how many criminals would get the '$900 cash-splash cheque?' the Opposition leader inquired sweetly in question time. 'Will the prime minister advise the House how burdening our children with Rudd debt to give borrowed money to crims rather than supporting struggling small business and self-funded retirees fits within his moral compass?'

Now it is true that any person currently incarcerated will receive cash if he or she filed a tax return lately. This is likely to be the case for a minority of prisoners, and in any event – as the PM explained – the tax bonus eligibility rules for pensioners are exactly the same as they were under Howard. Nevertheless, Mr Turnbull had his headline. 'PM Gives Tots' Savings to Crims!'

Joe Hockey then asked if pets inheriting fortunes from batty owners would get the bonus. 'Guinea Pig Trousers Tax Bonus! Pix!'

Mr Rudd, annoyed, snapped that he was not going to be lectured by a party that presided over 'the biggest corruption scandal in Australia's history … the wheat for weapons scandal'. 'PM in Shock Corruption Outburst!'

The government opened up another front: alcopops, and Turnbull's opposition to taxing them more.

'The Liberal Party, once calling itself the party for family values, has now become the party for binge drinking', thundered the PM.

'Turnbull in Teen Binge Shame!'

On one level, you do have to salute the PM. Anyone who can moralise about binge drinking while still holding authorship of modern politics' most celebrated episode of boozy excess deserves our awe, if not respect.

But one shocking episode remained. A Senate vote was called on alcopops, and to everyone's amazement, Labor looked to have won. What? It turned out the Coalition senator Nigel Scullion had missed the vote. Senator Scullion is best known for a fabulous 1998 night out in which, while drinking in a Russian nightspot with a group of Icelandic whalers, he was stripped to his undies and handcuffed to a pole.

Within minutes, Parliament was buzzing with the rumour that he had been stuck in a stairwell with Natasha Stott Despoja. Sadly, she nixed the rumour, ruining a perfect headline:

'Senator Pantsdown Russian to Vote, Snapped with Mystery Blonde!'

19 March 2009

IT'S HEAPS SERIOUS: KEVIN WENT MENTAL

It was now nearly a year since the Rudd government announced (by means of splashy weekend headline, followed by the federal budget) its intention to increase the excise on pre-mixed alcoholic drinks, known variously as 'alcopops' and 'ready-to-drinks'. But the Senate was still squabbling over the legislation.

Parents, teachers, academics and social theorists are scratching their heads. What are we going to do about our little darlings? I mean, you still love them and everything. But the secret drinking, the headstrong stubbornness, the self-centredness, the affected moral outrage, the prolonged fits of sulking – well, sometimes you just want to clonk their heads together.

I speak, of course, of this nation's federal parliamentarians. The House of Representatives and the Senate this week have resounded with dire analyses of teen behaviour, but at no point has any of the protagonists noticed something quite obvious about their own conduct …

*

The Alcopops Diaries by A. Backbencher
Okay, so the shit, like, totally hit the fan this week.

Remember a year ago when Kevin went all mental about binge drinking?

He rang up all the newspapers one day and said, 'I've got this big story for you but it's like, totally secret.'

And so all the newspapers went like, 'Yeah, OK', and then Kevin got all these public servants in and they spent all day making up this new announcement. Kevin rang all the newspapers that night and he was like, 'Set your face to stunned!' It was a new tax on Bacardi Breezers and stuff. All the parents were like, 'Excellent!' and it was cool because Kevin got all this extra money, too.

Some people reckoned it was because the newspapers were about to write this mean story about Kevin's girlfriend, Thérèse, but I don't know. I mean it's hard to say for sure.

So Brendan, he was running the Liberals at the time, remember? He was so cool he not only got his ear pierced like, AGES ago but also he has five guitars (totally sick) and rides a motorbike.

Anyway, he just said, 'You know, NO WAY is anyone paying any more for Breezers, and anyway it's not even just teenagers who drink them, you know, it's bogans, too, so the whole thing is just, like, so unfair.' Plus, he reckoned it was totally going to make inflation worse.

So Kevin and Nicola were just like, 'Whatever.'

I mean, they had to get the tax approved by Parliament within a year, but a year is a long time, right? And then all this stuff happened with the world financial crisis and everything, and it was fully random, like businesses going broke and banks going broke and that cool black guy in the United States getting elected and Kevin was like really busy and stuff. And then all of a sudden it was this week and the tax thing had to, like go through Parliament and stuff or the whole thing would be totally screwed and Kevin would have to give the money back even though he's like, already totally spent it on insulation and everything.

And it's heaps of money too, nearly $300 million.

So anyway, I forgot to say that Brendan got kicked out of the group, so now everyone's hanging around with Malcolm, and Malcolm still reckons the new tax sucks even though he's not so much talking about the bogans any more.

Or the inflation either, 'cause it turns out the inflation thing was, like, bogus and anyway Malcolm is always giving Kevin and Wayne a hard time about how they totally over-reacted on the inflation thing last year so he can't really talk about inflation either now, if you know what I mean.

So Malcolm's just against it 'cause he kind of just is, and he reckons Kevin and Nicola are just in it for the money anyway, and he reckons they are total losers.

Nicola reckons Malcolm is an apologist for binge drinking and a lickspittle to the significant distillers of this nation, or something (Nicola's really smart, but a hell dobber). She reckons it's Malcolm's fault that kids are getting pissed. It's sort of weird, because it's not like Nicola's spending, like, all the money on stopping kids drinking or anything, but she's really mad at Malcolm so they had this big fight.

So then there's also this nerd guy, Steve Fielding, and he's like 'Drinking sucks!' and he reckons Nicola and Kevin should spend the money on stopping the alcohol companies from sponsoring sport.

And Nicola was like, 'Hell, no.'

And Steve was like, 'OK, I'm voting against your stupid bill then.'

And Nicola's like, 'Fine.'

And Steve's like, 'Good then, I will.' So Malcolm and Steve and everyone voted against it. Well actually, at first they voted on it and Nicola and Kevin won, and everyone was like 'Huh? They totally don't have the numbers', and then it turns out that Nigel Scullion, that Country Liberal guy from the Northern Territory, he didn't make it to the vote 'cause he was, like, stuck in a stairwell or something.

And then we were all pissing ourselves because remember when Nigel went on that trip to Russia in 1998 and he got, like handcuffed to a pole in this nightclub and they stripped him down to his undies and everything?

Nigel is hell funny.

Anyway, so they had the vote again, and this time Nicola and Kevin lost, 'cause Malcolm and Steve voted against it and Nigel turned up this time.

And Steve's in big trouble, because his family's like really strict and they are totally bummed out about drinking.

And he's walking around saying like, 'I totally showed 'em' and stuff, but everyone else is, like, 'Yeah, right Steve.'

And then Malcolm's like, 'Oh, shit. I don't wanna give all that money back to the distillers', so he reckons to Nicola that they can keep the $300 million but just not collect any extra tax from now on.

But Nicola's like, 'No way.'

She's like, 'I don't want the stupid money. It's going back to the distillers because you voted against the bill, OK? Serves you right, moron.'

And then in question time they went totally psycho and Kevin said Malcolm and everyone were 'the party of binge drinking', and everyone was pissing themselves 'cause remember when Kevin went to New York and sneaked into that, like, strip club and he got so wasted he couldn't even remember anything?

And then Jodie Campbell, you know from Tasmania, she asked Nicola this question about binge drinking and we were pissing ourselves again 'cause Jodie got in trouble with the cops the year before last when she blew over the limit in her car and everything.

So glad it's holidays next week.

21 March 2008

PM TAKES TOUGHING IT OUT TO BRUTISH EXTREMES

Until yesterday, the prime minister had been very insistent that his emissions trading scheme would be in apple-pie order and ready to go by next year. His tone – immediately recognisable to any renovator who has ever stood numbly in the rubble of their bathroom and listened to the builder's blithe assurances that it will all be finished by Friday – was one of defiant optimism, daring the listener to disagree.

The start date of 2010 was originally chosen, it seems pretty clear, mainly for the fact that it was a year earlier than the date chosen by John Howard for his emissions trading scheme, and not because there was anything especially feasible about it. The announcement yesterday, in that sense, was unsurprising. What was surprising was the bold attempt to portray the inevitable backdown as some sort of toughening.

'These changes today are all about strengthening the carbon pollution reduction scheme', insisted Penny Wong.

Mercilessly, the prime minister spelled out the details of the tough new measures.

First, there would be a year's delay. Ouch! As if that alone weren't brutal enough, big polluters would be forced to accept more money from the government. And they would be obliged to pay a carbon price that has been remorselessly lowered to ten dollars a tonne by rapacious Rudd.

'Bring on … the comfy chair!' you almost expected the PM to pronounce, as he detailed his fluffy instruments of torture.

Rudd hates to be wrong. He clings to even arbitrary decisions with intense stubbornness. How else would you explain his handling of Peter Garrett, when instead of simply removing Garrett from the environment portfolio he went to all the trouble and expense of removing most of the environment portfolio from Garrett instead?

The announcement yesterday stuck just that little bit more annoyingly in the prime ministerial craw because it was exactly what the Opposition leader, Malcolm Turnbull, has been calling for. No wonder the prime minister had to butch it up a bit with talk of toughness.

He has increased the government's hypothetical upper limit for carbon emissions reduction, in a stunning display of hypothetical brute force. As is now customary for big announcements, Rudd appeared yesterday flanked by two other ministers. Their job was principally to look supportive while avoiding being physically struck by the PM, whose hand gestures at junctures of great national significance tend to be lavish and unpredictable.

In office the prime minister has displayed a strong preference for the 'dead spider' gesture, which has the palm facing skywards with fingers and thumbs in a relaxed half-curl, as if thoughtfully cupping a large grapefruit. Yesterday, however, 'dead spider' was revised noticeably; the half-cupped hand was repeatedly thrust palm first towards the camera, at various levels, to emphasise each point. Each thrust coincided with a brisk wrist rotation, creating the effect that our leader was trying a series of giant, imaginary doorknobs. As if looking for the one marked 'Exit'.

5 May 2009

QUESTIONS FROM A PADDED ROOM

Talk of an early election has resumed. And Malcolm Turnbull has no doubt about what's driving it.

'It is fear', the Opposition leader declared yesterday, somewhat boldly, at the National Press Club. 'Having made such a terrible hash of the economy, having run up so much debt, having wasted so much money, having demonstrated his financial recklessness again and again, I could well understand why he would want to run to an early election. He knows that the penny is dropping. He knows that the scales have fallen from all of our eyes.'

The penny may be dropping for Kevin Rudd, but it's not dropping into Malcolm Turnbull's pocket. The Newspoll published last Tuesday showed Rudd slumping three points in the 'preferred prime minister' stakes, from 67 per cent to 64 per cent. But Turnbull remained firmly on

19 per cent; the 3 per cent who have stopped thinking Rudd is the best available PM have switched their support to 'Jedi Knight', or 'the Scottish lady from *Britain's Got Talent*', or some other eye-catching, unnamed and no doubt ineligible figure who isn't Malcolm Turnbull.

It may well be true that the PM is afraid of becoming less popular. Kevin Rudd loves being loved nearly as much as he loves settling in between the fragrant, rustling sheets of a freshly commissioned white paper, which is a lot. But things will have to get a lot worse before Mr 64 Per Cent develops a genuine fear of Mr 19 Per Cent, and that's Turnbull's difficulty at present.

As opposition leaders go, Malcolm Turnbull is not especially accident-prone or foolish. He doesn't sniff chairs or make unsolicited remarks about mail-order brides or accidentally congratulate Karl Rove on his Silver Logie. You can watch him on TV without having to peek through your fingers or seriously consider a mercy call to Exit International.

Many of the points he makes are reasonable. Yesterday at the Press Club, he gave a speech that was resoundingly adequate. He asked why it was that Kevin Rudd is yet to make a hard decision. Which is a fair enough question. He asked how long it's going to take Australia to pay off all this debt. Which is a fair enough question. He asked why it was that the government is allowed to spend $43 billion on a broadband network that seems to have been roughed out on the back of one of Stephen Conroy's discarded footy-tips forms. Which is also a fair enough question.

But as far as the published polls are concerned, the Opposition leader might as well be screaming into a padded room.

7 May 2009

BRAG NOW, PAY LATER – IT'S JUST HOT AIR

OK. This climate change debate has now officially disappeared up its own fundament.

Consider this: Kevin Rudd and Penny Wong are now completely committed to forcing emissions trading legislation through Parliament as soon as possible. The legislation itself won't do anything, seeing as it will set the start date of any actual emissions trading scheme back beyond the next election. In passing the legislation, the government can harvest all the political kudos for having kept its promise to introduce an emissions trading scheme, while putting off the fuss and bother of actually having one.

It's a nifty idea, isn't it? Kind of like legislative lay-by. Legislate now and receive twenty-four months interest-free!

As a practice, 'brag now, pay later' is not entirely new. Successive governments have experimented, for example, with the art of back-loading promises into distant budgetary years. Many's the punter who's marvelled at a government minister's election-eve announcement that promises $10 billion on something-or-other 'over four years', only to look at the fine print and discover that 'over four years' means 'nothing this year, ten dollars the following year, fifty dollars the year after that, and the remaining $9,999,999,960 to be paid in year four, by which time my rabble of a government will be a distant memory and I will be seeking solace in the cushiony bosom of my superannuation'.

But the emissions trading scheme sets a whole new standard.

The Ruddbot and his Wongbot are investing deeply in symbolism, at the expense of progress. After all, symbolism has worked in the past for the Labor crowd; you can understand why they're having trouble abandoning it now.

The pair of them seem also to have pulled off a magnificent meta-swifty on the green lobby. In return for the business-friendly concessions in their revised emissions trading scheme (more money for big polluters, lower carbon price, free neck rubs for everyone at Rio Tinto), the green crowd has been thrown the assurance that if things go well at the Copenhagen summit this year, the government might commit to 25 per cent emissions cuts by 2020.

It takes considerable skill to execute a successful trade of something real for something pretend. But effectively, the deal Kevin Rudd has pitched to the green lobby goes something like this:

KR: OK, funsters. Here's the new situation. Things are getting tougher, so I'm gunna need those sandals, that hemp shirt, your bike and those fun hacky sack balls. All three of 'em, thanks.

Greenies: Huh? What? Damn! Et cetera.

KR: Wait a minute there, dudesters. Calm your farm. You're not gunna lose out. In return for all that stuff, I might be able to get you the Obama puppy, depending on whether the two little girls are willing to give it up.

Greenies: No way! Excellent! Isn't that a Portuguese water dog? They rock! Et cetera.

The truth is that climate-change policy in this country has always been arse-up, no matter who's in power. To sign legislation to reduce emissions without actually reducing any emissions, as Kevin Rudd is doing, seems weird, sure. But is it any weirder than containing emissions while steadfastly refusing to sign legislation to contain emissions? That's what John Howard did, year after year. Remember?

When the Kyoto Protocol was signed in 1997, Australia's delegate to that memorable conference – the Howard government's then education minister, Robert Hill – pranced home to great acclaim for the permissive deal he had secured for Australia, in which we were permitted to increase our carbon emissions by 8 per cent over 1990 levels by 2012.

John Howard was especially pleased; giving Hill a scratch behind the ears, he described the outcome as a 'stunning diplomatic success' and a 'first-class outcome for Australia'. It wasn't until later on that Howard – having listened to the coal industry and chewed the fat a little with his Texan friend, Mr Bush – started to see the Kyoto deal as a flawed agreement that would cost Australian jobs.

So he decided not to ratify it. But he did promise to honour Australia's undertakings to contain greenhouse emissions nonetheless. So you ended up with a very strange situation whereby the Howard government complied with Kyoto but refused to capitalise on the political advantages of doing so. This cleared the way for Kevin Rudd to win the election, so that he could legislate an emissions trading scheme but not actually reduce any emissions.

Anyone looking for a simple answer on where Australia stands on the climate-change issue could be forgiven for feeling very confused at this point. The government that only a year ago was advocating the necessity of tough and timely decision-making on carbon emission reduction has pulled back because the whole thing turned out to be quite tough.

You can almost hear the Rudd cheer squad now. 'What do we want? TOUGH DECISIONS! When do we want them? WHEN IT'S EASIER!'

And Malcolm Turnbull, who was one of the Howard ministers who tried unsuccessfully to get his old boss to take a more digestible line on Kyoto, isn't providing much by way of useful clarity these days. Poor old Turnbull. It's been a trying week for him, all round. Fair dinkum, he must be the only Opposition leader in the developed world dealing with a retail trade mini-boom and a spike in employment.

How he must yearn for England, the land of his forebears, with its deserted high streets and its bitter armies of unemployed; where the Labour prime minister, Gordon Brown, has just whacked the top tax rate up by 10p in the pound and seems certain to be run out of town on a pointy stick just as soon as voters get a chance.

But Malcolm Turnbull is not in England. He's in Australia, where Kevin Rudd has just acceded to the two key Turnbull demands he's been making on the emissions trading scheme: delay it and make it nicer for business. Having secured this victory, Turnbull – who does not want to vote for the scheme – is now obliged to rely instead on his objection that the government is not sufficiently interested in biochar, or the burying of small charcoal pellets in arable land.

Turnbull has recommended that the Productivity Commission – that collective of master reinvestigators – stage an inquiry into emissions trading.

A new inquiry? Ordinarily, that would sound like a Rudd idea.

But not in this crazy, mixed-up age.

9 May 2009

BETRAYED BY A MOMENT OF PASSION

In Australia, politics – and almost everything else – was briefly obscured by the revelation that a group of NRL players, including the Nine Network's Footy Show *personality Matthew Johns, had been investigated over a group-sex incident. The ABC's* Four Corners *reported that group sex, known as 'bunning', was a common practice. Meanwhile, in Britain, a corruption scandal involving the expense claims of dozens of MPs crippled the Parliament.*

What a strange week. One of the most significant budgets in living memory and yet the news was dominated by the NRL scandal. How intriguing it is to watch an insulated community, whose members have been behaving a certain way in private for many years, struggle with the realisation that most people view that behaviour as deplorable.

Funnily enough, the British press this week has been occupied with exactly the same phenomenon. In Britain, politicians of all stripes have been caught up in a catastrophic expenses scandal. Scores of MPs, it turns out, have been stinging the public purse for everything from having the moat cleaned to doing up the beach house.

At Westminster, the atmosphere is rife with tears and cheques, as politicians publicly repent of their avarice and deliver stricken personal apologies to the cameras. In their eyes, you can see something similar to what we saw this week from Matthew Johns: desperate remorse, tinged with bafflement.

'But everybody was doing it', you can almost hear them wail to themselves, although of course they are too well briefed to claim that excuse in public.

One group was guilty of scamming, the other of 'bunning'. (Dear God. What must this affair be doing for the Bunnings hardware chain? Perhaps we can expect a cheeky new ad series targeting the broad-minded League gent: 'Secretly enjoy checking out your mate's hardware? Come to Bunnings.') But the behaviour pattern is rivetingly similar.

The psychology of groups; always a fertile area. In a quiet way, the psychology of individuals was worth watching this week in Canberra, too.

Politics is full of carefully calibrated emotion. There are times at which politicians publicly smother their anger and annoyance. Think Kevin Rudd on Thursday, as he clapped on a hard hat and grinned for the cameras, holding a shovel with Nathan Rees, a man on whom he would almost certainly prefer to use the shovel in quite a different way.

And there are times at which politicians amplify their anger. Think the Ruddbot's recent press conference on people smuggling, his human-speech simulator going at warp speed to come up with vocabulary of sufficient outrage. The result was a sort of quasi-human gargle of wrath: 'They represent the absolute scum of the earth … they should rot in jail and, in my own view, rot in hell …'

What is more interesting is the less carefully scrutinised moments, when politicians take the bait and show their genuine vexation. It can be very revelatory of what they really care about.

There was a lot of abuse hurled at Kevin Rudd and Wayne Swan this week; they were accused of everything from wimpiness to fiscal treason. But I saw each of them betray genuine exasperation only once.

For Wayne Swan, it was at the Press Club lunch, when it was put to him that his budget had betrayed single parents, the unemployed and – in the course of a second question – working Australians, who will now face a retirement age of sixty-seven.

Swan bristled and delivered a heated defence of his own credentials.

'I've spent my whole life in politics squarely focused on what we must do to ensure that all Australians have dignity in employment and access, to back that up, with access to affordable health and education and housing', he shot back. 'Now I move around the community and there are people in my community who have lost their jobs, and the personal experience that comes with that, the impact upon the family, the impact upon local communities and the impact ultimately upon the social and economic life of the nation, of rising unemployment, is something that goes to the very core of why I'm in politics.'

The redistributive elements of this budget tell you a lot about Wayne Swan's passions; so does his annoyance at the Press Club. He can stand being called a surplus-raider, a chicken and a dunce. But he draws the line at the criticism that he doesn't care about the unemployed.

What makes Kevin Rudd mad? Apart from in-flight sandwiches, that is?

Well, his little moment of tetchiness came during Thursday's question time, when the Opposition foreign-affairs spokeswoman, Julie Bishop, asked this question: 'At a time when the government is plunging this nation into record debt, why should tens of millions of dollars of additional taxpayers' money be spent on a vote-buying spree in Africa and Latin America to support the prime minister's personal ambition of a temporary seat on the United Nations Security Committee? Are Australians paying for his job application as UN Secretary-General?'

When the prime minister gets cross in Parliament, he doesn't shout – he gets a flat, sarcastic tone instead. In reply to Bishop, he made a sneering reference to her 'track record of originality in all things', then referred to one of her colleagues as 'the member for Xenophobia'.

Then he lashed the lot of them with a long and impassioned and not quite relevant justification of Australia's support for the International Monetary Fund, closing with an invocation of 'the spirit of Bretton Woods going back to 1944', which for Kevin Rudd is a pretty big card to play.

Rudd is a huge fan of Bretton Woods, the postwar summit that established the beginnings of world financial regulation. Others might dream of time-travelling back to Woodstock to leap about in a chemical haze watching Jimi Hendrix torch his guitar, but you can be pretty certain that Rudd would rather visit Bretton Woods, New Hampshire, in 1944 to watch John Maynard Keynes electrify the crowd with his B-side classic, 'Single World Currency'.

Kevin Rudd really is passionate about world diplomacy. This is not to suggest he doesn't care about his other responsibilities; it's just that you can tell this stuff is his favourite bit of the job. After watching him for some years now, I would judge that the issues for which Kevin Rudd feels real passion are: international relations, homelessness and the welfare of children.

Does he really want to be secretary-general of the United Nations?

Well, of course he does, in the same way that I want to be head cheese-taster at King Island; it would be the ultimate reward for a lifetime of unstinting dedication to the subject area. Whether there is a folder marked '760 United Nations Plaza or Bust!' in the Rudd career portfolio remains to be seen. But his passion betrays him.

16 May 2009

HARD HAT AND A HEAD FOR FIGURES

Something is happening to the stimulus package.

Remember that $43-billion behemoth? The one that squeezed through the Senate by inches back in February, opposed by the Coalition but rescued by a motley band of crossbench senators? Back then, the stimulus package was just an unthinkably large chunk of money, a joke sum. Now it has blossomed into hundreds of thousands of building projects across the nation, which is why Kevin Rudd has rarely been seen without a hard hat lately.

The prime minister is also equipped with large, laminated photographs of many of these building sites, and a long, long list of the projects under way in each electorate. Each of them, of course, opposed by the Coalition.

This gives the PM a fiendishly comprehensive humiliation kit for use against just about any Opposition MP. All an Opposition MP needs to do these days is heckle the Ruddbot – yell something about his fondness for hard hats, or wonder aloud about whether the entire global financial crisis has been an elaborate cover for the prime minister to disguise his real hair.

When this happens, you can see him stiffen. His dalek gaze swivels mercilessly to fix on the offender; within seconds, the prime minister's hard disk surrenders the relevant information from the stimulus database, and he recites a list of playgrounds, solar panels, shade cloths and so on that the government is building in that very member's electorate. If the Opposition MP has been foolish enough to attend the launch ceremony for a local swing set or a drinking fountain, the Ruddbot and his ministers will doubtless have an incriminating photo on hand. Several National Party MPs were reduced to rubble yesterday by this means.

Then Christopher Pyne and Wilson Tuckey threw themselves into the fray and were swiftly oxidised with twin blasts from the Ruddbot, who mercilessly outlined $35 million of schools spending in Pyne's electorate and $37 million in Tuckey's.

'Which of these schools would he prefer not to have upgraded?' he asked caustically of the beet-faced Tuckey. 'I am surprised! He is normally so quick to his feet.'

The prime minister was having so much fun that when Bronwyn Bishop rose to intervene, he made a little joke.

'Given that she is wearing her own high-visibility vest today, [the member for Mackellar] is obviously entering into the spirit of the occasion', he jibed.

(To call Mrs Bishop's jacket 'canary yellow' would be unjust to canaries. Even at the ethically shadowy extremes of avian genetic engineering, plumage of this hue is unknown.)

The prime minister's levity and his use of props has spawned an outbreak of copycat offences. Large posters reading 'Labor's debt bomb' were handed out across the Coalition's back bench. The Liberal MP Don Randall stole out of the chamber and returned with a bright yellow hard hat, which he wasn't quite brave enough to put on his head. Ministers lined up with their own photos, to crow.

The stimulus package may have been expensive, but you get the feeling the Government is getting the full $43 billion worth of fun out of it.

27 May 2007

TURNBULL GETS BIG BICKIES WITH HIS MORNING TEA

Politics is a cruel game. You can be having a perfectly OK day of it when suddenly, out of nowhere, an anvil drops on your head.

Take Malcolm Turnbull yesterday, for example.

There he was, pinching himself at having somehow got out of his party's climate-change jam with hide intact, when – CLANG! – the *BRW Rich List* arrived, with its happy news that Malcolm Turnbull has just got richer, and is now worth $178 million.

The first sign of trouble arrived in the morning when the Opposition leader strode along a parliamentary corridor to attend the Parliament House chapter of Australia's Biggest Morning Tea. As he approached, flanked by wife Lucy and a media adviser, Mr Turnbull perceived the sinister shape of Laurie Oakes, lying in ambush next to the alcove in which the morning tea was scheduled to occur.

Finding Laurie Oakes waiting for you at a minor event is a deeply unnerving thing for any politician. It's like coming home to find a cop car outside, lights flashing; there is a chance that everything will work out OK, but not a big chance.

Mr Turnbull is one of nature's optimists. 'Hello, Laurie!' he began brightly.

'Congratulations', Oakes responded, before commencing the full workover, which involved some questions about how the Opposition leader could argue for rich people to keep their private health insurance rebate when he was so copiously well-off himself.

Mr Turnbull first disputed *BRW*'s estimate of his wealth (an interesting conundrum. Either he's right, or there's $100 million or so down the back of the couch that he's forgotten about). Then, a light sweat breaking out across his generous forehead, he mentioned that Kevin Rudd and Thérèse Rein were rich, too. Every time he stopped talking, Oakes administered another question.

So the Opposition leader began a skilful Filibuster of Fear, in which he explored at great length the historical antecedents and legislative purpose of the 30 per cent private health insurance rebate. This took several minutes. When he had finished, the cameras were still there. So Senator Bill Heffernan (net worth: four-fifths of bugger-all plus several kelpies) leapt to his defence.

'That's a political bullshit ambush', he blustered. 'When a bloke with that success wants to make a contribution, you want to pull him apart.'

Senator Heffernan has a point; the Turnbulls made their money themselves, and give a good chunk of it away every year. But the Opposition leader knows his millions present him with a perception problem; why else would he keep reminding us that he grew up in a flat?

Mr Rudd knows conspicuous wealth is troublesome, too; that's why he is careful with his shots at Mr Turnbull, lest the spotlight be turned on his own family's net worth (about $50 million according to *BRW*, now that you ask).

Think of it, if I can offend Sol Trujillo further with some classic Australian racism, as a $228-million Mexican stand-off.

28 May 2009

LIBERAL FIGHT CLUB DOWN FOR THE COUNT

Extraordinary scenes unfolded in the Coalition's regular Tuesday morning meeting.

After Alby Schultz took a wild lunge at his Liberal colleague Chris Pearce yesterday, it took about four seconds for everyone in Parliament House to hear about it. The news spread out through staff, journalists, Labor politicians, baristas, security guards, and by 11 o'clock even children in the parliamentary childcare centre were discussing the ramifications of the scuffle over their rusks.

Why is this?

Well, it turns out that the first rule of Coalition Fight Club is that you talk about Coalition Fight Club. To anyone who will listen.

Like many opposition parties, the Liberals leak like a sieve, and so we have a moment-by-moment breakdown of yesterday's action. As second-hand voyeurs we can gasp as Schultz (a former meatworker) lunges for the throat of Pearce (a talented pianist, whose ivory-tickling phalanges were mercifully undamaged in the attack). Hearts in mouth, we can marvel at the bravery of the former coppers Jason Wood (La Trobe, Victoria) and Stephen Parry (Senator for Tasmania), as they intervene to separate the pair. And we can chuckle along with the absurdity of Wilson Tuckey's sage observation to the room after it was all over: 'There's a lesson in why you should keep your mouth shut.'

The Coalition is a fractious place to be at the moment. Schultz is convinced that the National Party wants to steal his seat; hence his angry denunciation of the Nats in the meeting yesterday, which preceded his angry storm-out, which prompted Pearce to call out sardonically 'Have a nice day', which caused Schultz to wheel around and attempt to throttle Pearce, and so on.

Between the Libs and the Nats, there is plenty of tension, even before the fundamental disagreement on the whole idea of an emissions trading scheme, a notion Barnaby Joyce described on Monday as coming 'direct from the manic monkey café of inner-suburbia nirvana-ville'. Ever wondered what a manic monkey café looks like? A bit like the Liberal Party meeting yesterday.

The permeability of the group's Chinese walls has become a matter of strategic concern. 'In the interests of not having it leaked, I am now not going to say what I was going to say', Sussan Ley (Farrer, NSW) said to her colleagues, then sat down. After the scuffle it was decided that mobile phones should be banned from the Coalition's group sessions. A sound precaution, given a Liberal happy-slapping scandal cannot be far away.

In question time the government took every opportunity to comment on the match of the day.

The prime minister cackled about the 'Heavyweight from Hume' and the 'Lightweight from Aston', while the manager of Opposition business, Chris Pyne, sniped from the wings. Hoping to clean things up, the speaker asked Pyne to withdraw his remarks.

'On behalf of my team, I withdraw "nasty ner" and "bitch"', he obliged. There, much better.

3 June 2009

WEETBIX KIDS PLAN CEREAL-LED RECOVERY

The national accounts figures came in. A wafer-thin margin of positive growth in the Australian economy meant that Australia had, unlike so many of its Western contemporaries, avoided a technical recession.

It's always funny to watch pleased politicians trying not to look too pleased. And it was a big ask for Kevin Rudd and Wayne Swan to compose themselves before yesterday's press conference trumpeting – I mean soberly greeting – the news that the Australian economy has narrowly avoided recession.

Can you imagine the sheer human effort it took that pair not to simply fall into each other's arms, sobbing tears of pure joy, or form a two-nerd conga line and make their way around the Blue Room in an ebullient display of high kicks?

Really, the pair of them should just have quietly found a couple of farmers and kissed them from head to foot, seeing as this miraculous economic result owes more to the increased exports of cereal crops than it does to the combined brilliance of the PM and his treasurer. But politics is politics; a win is a win, and Mr Rudd's triumph is no less significant for being built on sorghum.

The great man himself concentrated on not looking smug. When invited to express a view about whether the other leading industrialised nations could do worse than emulate Australia's GFC-fighting techniques, Mr Rudd denied himself the indulgence.

'We're never in the business of providing public lectures to anybody else', he said, provoking one trusts gales of laughter from the ranks of people on the face of this earth who have ever met Mr Rudd.

Malcolm Turnbull and Joe Hockey, on the other hand, were two disappointed men trying not to look disappointed. They pointed out that the major influencing elements to the comparative strength of the economy were situated firmly in the non-Rudd sector, but knew they were beaten.

In question time, Mr Rudd continued with Operation Modesty.

Even a moment of bosom-swelling national pride and resolve like this one could not induce the prime minister to deliver a lyrical piece of prose.

For England, Blake summoned the timeless vow: *I will not cease from mental fight; Nor shall my sword sleep in my hand.* For Australia, Rudd summoned this: 'Our strategy is to build the economy up, and we will continue to implement that strategy.' One could almost picture his grateful public roaring assent: 'Oh implement it, implement it, great conqueror! Implement it again!'

Inside the House, his reception was predictably divided.

'Sit down, you mad pixie', one Opposition MP called out.

But Mr Rudd did not mind; he was having a lovely day, and all the catcalls in the world cannot unsettle a man who knows that his economic growth is the strongest in the OECD, that his debt is the lowest, and that his chief of staff is even now drawing him a bath of warm asses' milk in the private office.

In the end, the prime minister poured all that forbidden triumphalism into the only area of Australian life in which rampant smugness is still allowed: sport.

'Go the Maroons!' he chirped, after seeking special indulgence from the speaker to make some footy-related remarks.

4 June 2009

IS KEVIN THE NEW BARRY MCKENZIE?

Every now and again, a phrase of Kevin Rudd's is so odd that it becomes a national talking point. 'Detailed programmatic specificity', a phrase that he invented during a press conference with Germany's Angela Merkel, is one example. Here's the story of another …

Even machines aren't perfect. And when the Ruddbot, on Tuesday, developed a mild glitch in his cranial colloquialism receptor, the malfunction was immediately apparent.

'Fair shake of the sauce bottle! Fair shake of the sauce bottle!' he quacked at his puzzled human interlocutor, David Speers of Sky News.

It sounded well, sort of nearly there, but garbled, like one of those phrases that you feed into Babelfish to translate into German and then back into English again.

Incidentally, if you do that with the Ruddbot's phrase, you get 'appropriate vibration of the sosseflaschele'. Try it in Mandarin and you get 'sauce bottle's fair play'. Or Russian: 'The valid agitation of the bottle of the sauce.' If you take the Russianised version and translate that into Korean, and then back into English, you get 'the restlessness which the bottle of source is effective'. And so on.

Kevin Rudd has mangled innocent phrases before. To the prime minister, the entire English language constitutes a killing field, and none can ever be sure where he might strike next.

So why did this one cause such a fuss? Mainly, it prompted questions about authenticity. Half the time, our prime minister sounds as though he has just swallowed a training manual. The other half, he sounds like he's reading out an old script from *Kingswood Country.* How can those two Rudds be reconcilable?

Show me a tight-shot sequence of the prime minister talking, and I'll be able to make a pretty good guess about who he's addressing. If he's swearing, it's probably Australian troops. If he's talking about cuppas and bikkies and brekkers and Brisvegas, odds on it's *Sunrise.*

If it's 'creative middle-power diplomacy', he is definitely overseas.

'Can I just say, you know, if you're making a speech at the United Nations or whatever, you're going to speak in a particular way', the PM told Kochie on *Sunrise* yesterday morning, before dissolving into a quick-fire exchange of 'strike me pinks' and 'strewths'.

'If you're talking with an Australian, what's wrong with Australian English?'

Well, yes. But we are not used to seeing our prime ministers change tack so nakedly. Take John Howard, for example; you always had the feeling that Howard would look and sound exactly the same even in the most extraordinary of circumstances, whether called upon to address a group of transgender fisherpeople in Alaska or abducted by aliens. You'd still get that wooden little lecture about Australia being a country built on mateship, and so on.

Every political leader has something that drives their adversaries mad. For the Howard haters, it was Howard's jut-jawed intransigence on matters dear to their hearts, his stubborn refusal to issue a national apology, et cetera. There was something about that stubbornness, that quiet conviction that he was right, that proved uniquely infuriating to those who disagreed with him.

There really isn't a settled public band of Rudd haters yet. Maybe because he hasn't done anything divisive enough to alienate any distinct groups. After a year and a half of the Howard prime ministership, who was upset? Lots of people: gun owners, universities, the Friends of the ABC, Indigenous Australia, you name it. After a year and a half of Kevin Rudd, there isn't anything like that spread of the disenchanted.

Alcopop drinkers? Fifty-three-year-olds who in 2023 will become the first generation of Australian workers to work all the way through to their 67th birthdays? Families on $151,000 who were kind of counting on the Baby Bonus? It's very piecemeal, this potential network of Rudd haters.

Often, the Rudd government seems like an outfit that governs with its potential detractors in mind, not its natural friends. Oddly enough, the only broad group that the Rudd government seems intent on antagonising is the very group that got it elected in the first place: the union movement. Curiouser and curiouser.

For all his dominance, Kevin Rudd seems strangely timorous of giving offence. His earnest search for terms of extreme disparagement for people smugglers, arsonists and Gordon Ramsay, and his eager deployment of matey Australianisms, all bespeak a cry for acceptance. 'Like me. Please, like me!' is what it sounds like. Odd, seeing as Astralians already plainly like Kevin Rudd. They elected him, after all, and continue to support him warmly, according to all available formal indicators. How is it that a prime minister who is, according to most accounts, more than prepared to antagonise people he does know, be so ginger about annoying the hordes of people he doesn't know?

What this all means, for the time being, is that the real, frothing Rudd haters are mainly confined to the ranks of the Coalition. And within the ranks of the Coalition, this week's outburst of Rudd ockerisms engendered pure, white-hot, impotent rage. Tony Abbott could not conceal his disgust. Rudd's words were 'the kind of dated slang we got from Barry McKenzie films', he sniped.

If Howard haters were driven mad by the stubbornness of his conviction, Rudd haters are driven mad by the sight of the Ruddbot getting away with murder. People like Tony Abbott, for example, think Kevin Rudd is an insufferable, smug, know-it-all, sucky, phoney, smartarse show-off. And what's the only thing that's more annoying than an insufferable, smug, know-it-all, sucky, phoney, smartarse show-off? Easy – a lucky, insufferable, smug, know-it-all, sucky, phoney, smartarse show-off.

The hard edge to the Coalition's hatred of Kevin Rudd is that they believe he is living off their hard work in government, spending their surplus on buying the votes he needs to keep them out of office. Lucky because Australia's circumstances have allowed him to escape the worst ravages of the global recession. Lucky because the 'hard decisions' in this crisis involved spending a gazillion dollars on election-proofing his parliamentary margin.

On top of all this, the prime minister's blithe ockerisms drive the Rudd haters into special paroxysms of rage.

Who is the real Kevin Rudd? The polylingual pointyhead or *Sunrise*'s chief dag? History suggests that the former incarnation is probably the more authentic one. But the Australian people voted for *Sunrise* Kevin. It's no wonder he gets dragged out for a walk every now and again.

13 June 2009

POODLE'S BARK IS WORSE THAN HIS BITE

Question time opened yesterday on a fascinating moment of mutual bravado. The Opposition, having successfully firebombed the government's

'Ruddbank' legislation in the Senate overnight, ploughed confidently into a series of questions to the PM about his hare-brained plan to get into public finance. They think they are on a winner with this one.

The government, meanwhile, arranged for a series of Dorothy Dix questions about how the selfish Opposition could possibly be so insensitive as to oppose something which would safeguard Australian jobs. They think they are on a winner.

Both sides cannot be right.

The clinch was broken when the Opposition moved on to Julia Gillard and what the shadow education spokesman, Christopher Pyne, has optimistically dubbed the 'schools stimulus debacle'. In Mr Pyne's opinion, Ms Gillard is a bogan control freak who is constantly forcing school libraries upon schools who really wanted arts centres and giving them $2.5 million when $900,000 would probably do. He would like Ms Gillard to refer the whole scheme to the auditor-general.

In Ms Gillard's opinion, however, Mr Pyne is a snotty-nosed little whinger who could take a long walk off a short jetty, for all she cares.

Mr Pyne calls Ms Gillard 'Kath'. Her scrapy vowels remind him of Fountain Lakes's first lady.

Ms Gillard calls Mr Pyne 'Poodle', for his flawless grooming and tendency to yap.

Like an actress who invariably falls in love with her leading man, Ms Gillard often seems to develop complex psychological relationships with the Coalition frontbenchers she shadows or is shadowed by. The love–hate thing she developed with Tony Abbott, for instance, is even now still in evidence.

Mr Abbott is forever flinging besotted little verbal bouquets in her direction, like last week's declaration that she would make a brilliant prime minister (a pronouncement which did not delight Mr Pyne, who is flat out convincing a reluctant nation that La Gillardine is not much good at her current job).

Mr Pyne's practice is to ask Ms Gillard questions, then accompany her answer with a highly audible commentary of his own. As Ms Gillard yesterday discussed the Stradbroke Primary School in Mr Pyne's own electorate, whose principal Cathie Wilson has declared that her pupils are 'thrilled' with their slice of school stimulus dough, Mr Pyne niggled away loudly, sending his colleagues into fits of giggles.

'Did you break her femur? Did you snip her Achilles tendon? Poor old Cathie. Was she blindfolded and gagged? Stop waterboarding Cathie, Julia', and so on.

Ms Gillard then read out some rave reviews from another school in Mr Pyne's electorate, Burnside Primary.

'If the member for Sturt had the guts to go to Burnside Primary …' she said, eliciting an immediate squeal of outrage from her tormentor.

'I WENT to Burnside Primary!' Mr Pyne protested piercingly. 'It was my SCHOOL!'

And for a moment of crystal clarity, we saw exactly what he would have been like there.

18 June 2009

SHOCK: CAR SALESMAN GIVES PM A REFERENCE

The beginning of the end for Malcolm Turnbull came with the saga of Kevin Rudd's ute. Mr Rudd was supplied with a free ute by a car dealer in his electorate. Later, when the government gave thought to a scheme to bolster vehicle financing during the global financial crisis, the very same car dealer sought assistance. The public servant administering the scheme, Godwin Grech, told a Senate inquiry that he had received direct instructions in an email from the PM's office to give special attention to the dealer in question. It all looked like a bullseye for the Opposition, and for Malcolm Turnbull, already exultant at the departure of Peter Costello – finally! – from politics. But Mr Grech himself was then exposed as a fraudster.

There are times when stories are orchestrated by Oppositions, or juiced up by journalists, or even gussied up by governments. But the story of the ute is now officially a rogue elephant, lumbering crazed and out of control, and threatening the life of its handlers.

Malcolm Turnbull's confidence was supreme on Friday as he called resonantly for the resignation of the prime minister and the treasurer. A week already memorable for the bloodless departure of his major internal enemy was made gloriously replete by the evidence of Godwin Grech, the Treasury official with the Dickensian name and the handy memory for emails.

But as yesterday unfolded, triumph succumbed to the oldest wrecker in the book – events. And the smile faded from Turnbull's face. Australian Federal Police located the email, and pronounced it a fake. Grech is now assisting them with their inquiries.

What was that audible hiss? The wind escaping from Turnbull's sails? Or the colossal intake of oxygen required for Kevin Rudd's masterful performance of puffed-up outrage on any evening news service that would put him to air?

The departure of Peter Costello has, in a strange way, laid bare the utter enmity between these two men. As Rudd entered the chamber yesterday, he fixed Turnbull with a stare of such acid loathing that one feared for the enamel on Turnbull's bared teeth. Neither will give the other quarter, and the PM took line honours yesterday.

The pity for Turnbull is that there is a perfectly pursuable case against Wayne Swan, whose initial, modest account of the government efforts made to accommodate car dealer John Grant now appears, in hindsight and with greater knowledge, inadequate. It's a reasonable prosecution for the Opposition. And if it wasn't for the Gothic drama of *Godwin Grech and the Incredible Exploding Email*, playing over on cable, maybe more people would be tuning in. But the case against Swan is procedural, rather than literal.

After all, when you strip away the sizzle from this sausage, when you get to the matters which are as the prime minister actually put it yesterday 'core and foundational', the real-world corruption equation against the government is kind of thin. Prime Minister receives rusty ute from Queensland car dealer, who in return gets diddly-squat.

The technical point on which the Opposition is probably right turns on something far more cerebral: whether Grant got a warmer degree of hand-holding and nicer biscuits in the waiting room than his professional brethren, and whether Wayne Swan misled the Parliament on this point.

The chief of the Motor Trades Association, Michael Delaney, insists Grant got no special favours. Delaney's remarks were repeated with enthusiasm about a gazillion times by both the prime minister and the treasurer, which tended to confirm suspicions about what this episode has done for the trustworthiness of politicians in general.

It is understood to be the first time a prime minister has sought a character reference from a car salesman.

23 June 2009

BLACK KNIGHT COPS IT OVER SEARCH FOR HOLEY GRAIL

Different people celebrate victory in different ways. Formula one drivers tip champagne all over their heads. Football players smother each other in hugs. And Kevin Rudd, when he's riding high on a week of political triumph, indulges himself by putting on a PowerPoint presentation.

That's what he did yesterday when he faced his colleagues at the regular caucus meeting, after the bizarre and turbulent fizzing cocktail of events that was Monday. Such was his excitement about the previous day's vanquishing of Malcolm Turnbull that Rudd allowed himself twenty minutes and many, many transparencies, dealing with bank-bond issuances, household consumption, employment patterns calculated with and without the effects of the stimulus package and so on.

A comparison of major country credit spreads showed Australia's position to be very competitive, he explained to his comrades, as their congratulatory cries died upon their lips. Call this 'nerd hubris', I guess.

The real and nasty political attack came later, in question time, when every Labor minister who stood in response to a Dorothy Dixer did so in order to aim a new kick at the cods of the Opposition leader, from a different direction.

'Will the minister outline the importance of maintaining integrity in e-communication and what lessons can be learned from National E-Security Awareness Week?' asked David Bradbury (Labor, Lindsay), very sweetly, of Anthony Albanese.

This allowed Albanese to deliver a scathing lecture on the fickleness of emails and why Opposition leaders would be best to avoid using them as a basis for demanding the resignation of, say, prime ministers.

'Will the minister advise the house of allegations regarding misuse of public resources?' elicited a skilful rant from Lindsay Tanner about how the Opposition should hand over its computers to the Australian Federal Police.

'My question is to the minister for agriculture, fisheries and forestry', piped Nick Champion (Labor, Wakefield). 'What are the likely seasonal outlooks ahead, and what policy options have been supported in the past?'

This gave Tony Burke an opportunity to remind the house of the time Malcolm Turnbull, as minister for the environment, approved a $10-million grant for an experimental rain-making company operated by one of his party fund-raisers.

You get the idea.

And through it all, Malcolm Turnbull himself punched on in his pursuit of the treasurer, ignoring the hail of blows from the government with all the nonchalance of Monty Python's Black Knight.

'Tis but a scratch! I've had worse!' you half-expected him to yell. 'It's only a flesh wound!'

Turnbull's resilience is impressive; he even made a spirited attempt to blame the treasurer for the very existence of the bogus email, which takes some serious cojones.

But the beaky spectre of Godwin Grech haunted the chamber with a gloomy persistence. Grech's house was pelted with eggs overnight. A forensic team is understood to be attending the scene. Should they prove to be quail eggs, or Fabergé, the Opposition leader will have some extremely serious questions to answer.

24 June 2009

SPELLS, CURSES AND A DOLLOP OF GOBLIN GRECH

'This isn't a bad dream that will just go away. It is a nightmare, and it will never go away.'

These are the words with which the prime minister, Kevin Rudd, greeted his deadly enemy, Malcolm Turnbull, yesterday.

Is it just me, or is this week in politics turning into a bad version of a Harry Potter novel? And it's not just the intriguing, goblinesque figure of Godwin Grech that's creating this impression. It's the mystical, good-versus-evil quality to the parliamentary debate.

If you believe the Opposition, Malcolm Turnbull is the pure knight battling the dark storm troopers of the evil Rudd overlord, whose illicit trade of influence in return for ageing Mazda Bravo utility vehicles keeps his oppressed people silent under an iron boot.

If you believe the government, Malcolm himself is the reckless, vain necromancer whose mythical offences against cats stand as a bleak prophecy of his intentions vis-à-vis the human occupants of this fair land.

And so on.

Spells and curses were hurled indiscriminately yesterday, and bizarre rituals practised.

'I move that so much of standing orders be suspended as would prevent the leader of the Opposition from moving that this house condemn the treasurer', bellowed Turnbull, who remains defiant despite being pounded to a bloody pulp every time he gets to his feet on matters ute-related.

'I move that the speaker no longer be heard!' was the response from Anthony Albanese, a boy wizard who warred extensively with the Ruddlord at Hogwarts, but has since joined forces with him and these days is as loyal as an owl.

'The noes have it! No, the ayes have it! Is a division required? Lock the doors!'

These incantations brought question time to a halt several times, as 149 MPs solemnly trooped back and forth across the chamber like druids crossing a stone circle on the winter solstice.

Even He Who Must Not Be Named got a look-in.

'I could have sworn I was witnessing the ghost of Mark Latham!' said Albanese, as he reviewed Turnbull's bellicose morning interview with Kieran Gilbert of Sky News. 'It was all there: the jaw jutting out, all the fake aggression, all the machismo, all the "We're going well"! We used to hear it.'

Given that most Labor MPs cannot articulate the two words of their former leader's name without crossing themselves and spitting, it's unusual to hear He Who Must Not Be Named even mentioned in the chamber, let alone invoked in this manner. This tells us something about how confident the government is feeling at the moment. After all, as insults go, 'You're just as crazy as the nut bar we wanted to install at the Lodge' carries some fairly obvious tactical risks.

As the rest of Australia looks on and scratches its head, these warring wizards seem determined to zap happily away at each other, untroubled by Muggle concerns. Except for Albanese, of course, who will no doubt find life difficult when he wakes this morning to find that he has been turned into a newt.

25 June 2009

WHERE THE RUDDY HELL WERE YOU, MALCOLM?

After the horror of the Grech saga, Mr Turnbull entered a period of deep introspection. The prime minister, on the other hand, was virtually uncontainable.

Grave fears had been held, until yesterday, for the welfare of the Opposition leader. After a defiant performance on Sunday's *Meet the Press*, Malcolm Turnbull disappeared from our screens. Monday, with its trio of horrible polls, came and went without further sight of him.

'Follow Malcolm on Facebook! Flickr! Myspace! YouTube! Twitter!' his website enjoins visitors. But Mr Turnbull had abandoned his usual cyber haunts; on Facebook this week, he has been faceless. He has Flickrd out. MySpace might as well be called Outer Space for the amount of attention it has received from the member for Wentworth since the celebrated backfiring of the ute last week. Even his dogs haven't blogged since May.

Once a Malcolm stronghold, Twitter has now become an arena for unrestrained prime ministerial triumphalism from the Ruddbot, who is still fielding cyber high-fives for his Sunday night appearance on *Rove Live*.

'Go Ruddy!!! Btw u r the koolest PM eva no otha PM has eva been this kool!!' enthused Twitterer joycee97, one of hundreds who dropped the PM a line on Monday.

Once briefed by his handlers that this remark was positive, a clearly emboldened Mr Rudd moved in to capitalise on his enemy's disappearance by keeping Twitter fans rakishly apprised of his every move.

'Cabinet meeting in Logan. Popped in to see Amber & Geoff at Kingston Fare Bakery who sent me a tweet. Picked up cake for Swanny's birthday', he Twittered on Tuesday, adding 'Don't tell Swanny about the birthday cake. He is not on Twitter so won't know about the surprise!' This message, like many on Mr Rudd's Twitter page, was his own work.

But where was Malcolm? Was it true that he was living under the surface of Lake Burley Griffin, with pals Eric Abetz and Godwin Grech, and breathing through a straw? God forbid that he was hiking through the Appalachians.

Yesterday, the nation's fears were set at rest. It turns out Mr Turnbull has been in Afghanistan. Obscured from view by that forgiving modern cloak of invisibility, the national-security media embargo, he has spent the past few days visiting a country that must seem blessedly safe and serene compared with his own ideological homeland.

'Afghanistan has a stark beauty of its own, but it is in these picturesque ranges of the Hindu Kush and in the green Baluchi and Mirabad valleys where the dangers of improvised explosive devices and other insurgent attacks are at their worst', he mused in a press statement issued yesterday.

The statement was issued after Mr Turnbull and his companions, shadow defence minister David Johnston and Deputy Opposition Leader Julie Bishop, had left Afghan air space. As they flew home, one imagines they gave some serious thought to how they would cope in the new security environment of their destination.

Light Kevlar vests, chinos and helmets are all very well in Afghanistan, but to be a Liberal leader in Australia just now requires something a little more heavy-duty.

2 July 2009

THE BRUTAL, THRIVING INDUSTRY THAT IS THE MODERN GARRETT HUNT

Peter Garrett, the environment minister, announced that he had approved Australia's fourth uranium mine. As a former anti-uranium activist, he immediately faced a certain degree of opprobrium.

It's hard not to feel sorry for this giant, iconic mammal. So trusting! So vulnerable! So easily harpooned!

If you listen closely, the traces of the threatened behemoth's famous eerie song are still audible. But the hunters care nothing, as they draw alongside with their cruel barbs. It's like shooting fish in a barrel, and the hunters have no mercy.

I write, of course, of the brutal, thriving industry that is the modern Garrett hunt.

Was ever a politician easier to skewer? Most practitioners of politics have some sort of youthful exuberance from which they quietly distance themselves over time; Brendan Nelson's long membership of the Labor Party, for example, or Malcolm Turnbull's political apprenticeship at the knee of the anti-Semitic former NSW premier Jack Lang.

But how many of them leave us a whole discography to trawl

through? How many of them occupy portfolios which bring them into daily and heartbreaking hand-to-hand combat with their former selves in the manner that Peter Garrett's job does? This bloke's job is beginning to look like a reality TV show, in which the contestant is forced to consume ever more grotesque dishes, all the while maintaining an expression of determined enjoyment.

'Peter Garrett: Every Show a Sellout!' goes the most biting of the sledges. But there's another way of looking at all this. And that is that Garrett is proving extremely resolute in his adherence to the decision he announced in June 2004, which was that he was going to join the Labor Party.

Labor has a binding caucus system, which means that once you're in, you are at the mercy of the group majority, which effectively means, in contemporary Labor terms, the benevolent dictatorship of a bespectacled bloke from Nambour, who has the significant game advantage of sleeping only three hours a night.

All of the Labor candidates are subject to this rule. But for some, the sacrifices are greater than others. And for superstar candidates, who come to politics with an existing set of beliefs, passions and publicly stated convictions, handing all that in at the door is necessarily much harder. It's a brutalising process, and for some people – think Cheryl Kernot – the loss of independence is too much to bear.

How many of us would sacrifice the easy delights of widespread adulation, the companionship that comes with associating exclusively with people who agree with you, and the luxury of speaking from the moral high ground? How many of us would trade that for the grub and muck of actual change, the hard and often dispiriting slog of working within the system? Politics is awful, a lot of the time. It's full of debilitating compromise and settlements that are a pale shadow of what you'd really like to do.

His announcement this week that he had approved Australia's fourth uranium mine is probably the most devastating punch that Pete Garrett, environment minister, has yet landed on Pete Garrett, rockstar activist. The mine would have gone ahead whomever was environment minister – Labor's three-mine policy was revoked in 2007 by the party's national conference, over the vocal objections of Garrett, then shadow minister for the environment.

Garrett could have resigned when the will of cabinet inevitably endorsed the conference's decision. People have resigned for much, much less. And resignation would have been the signal that Garrett has finally had enough; that he couldn't bear any further insult to Rockstar Pete.

But he didn't resign, which tells us that the environment minister still thinks he is more use in there beavering away at the conditions on approval for a fourth uranium mine than he is protesting outside the proposed site, whatever the unattractive personal ramifications for his own already battered image. It's not very glamorous, but it is a rather spectacular variation on conviction politics.

Politics is about outsourcing, after all, isn't it? We have politicians because we need people, for practical reasons, who will take decisions on our collective behalf.

We reserve the right to shellack them personally, of course, and to rubbish them for making the compromises that our very democracy forces upon them. We want other people to make the compromises – that's the point. And Garrett has made them, without a word of protest. On one construction, it's a personal hypocrisy. On another, it's the most earnest surrender of ego to the democratic process that this government has seen.

Has it been worth it? Only Garrett can know the answer to that question. But there is another function to the environment minister's discomfiture on the nuclear issue. It obscures a much greater lapse on Labor's part, which is the failure to engage in a rational debate about nuclear power in this country.

The Howard government's nuclear review, headed by the former Telstra boss Ziggy Switkowski, reported that one-third of Australia's energy needs could be supplied by twenty-five nuclear power stations, commissioned and built by the year 2050.

Labor did not hesitate; it commenced the most opportunistic public campaign of opposition imaginable, ignoring the report's conditionalities and its long lead-time and spruiking 'Mr Howard's twenty-five nuclear reactors, coming to an electorate near you'. Local electorate material advised marginal-seat voters that seeing as John Howard hadn't specified exactly where the associated 'nuclear waste dumps' were going to go, they might as well go on and assume that a home Chernobyl was heading for the nature strip. Pretty potent stuff; when it comes to political fruit in this country, it doesn't hang much lower than 'nuclear reactor coming your way'.

As a result, Kevin Rudd is just as hidebound by his own past words and pronouncements as Peter Garrett is. The only difference is that the PM is showing no signs of recanting, even in the face of the growing energy crisis.

Here's what the environmental activist Tim Flannery wrote in 1996: 'Before we make up our minds on how we respond to the prime minister's call for debate on nuclear power, let's think through where our response might lead. An angry rebuttal of nuclear power could mire our nation in a heated but not very enlightened argument that will take the focus off the real issue climate change for years.'

Sounds kind of prescient, doesn't it?

Malcolm Turnbull believes that nuclear power is a real option for Australia, but he doesn't see any use at all in pursuing it without some kind of bipartisan open-mindedness, and he is right. And Labor's refusal to contemplate the issue is looking more and more like stubbornness. We are quite happy to flog our uranium to others for peaceful purposes, after all.

Many of the reservations about nuclear power, including the cost, need to be reconsidered in light of what we have learned about the real cost of fossil fuels. And the prime minister is only too prepared to remind us that the consequences of failing to cut our carbon emissions are gothic in the extreme; death by sunstroke or beriberi, catastrophic weather events and the disappearance of the Great Barrier Reef. If climate change is indeed the greatest challenge of our time, is it really appropriate to be ignoring one feasible and low-carbon – albeit contentious – solution? Is the government serious enough about all of this to risk its own political hide?

Not at the moment, it seems, although there are ministers who will readily concede in private that nuclear should be part of the debate.

Why should Australia martyr itself for world energy purposes by consenting to store nuclear waste in the vast and peaceful expanses of our largely deserted continent, the nuclear opponents ask. Well, the sacrifice of Australian business interests towards an ambitious world effort to cut carbon emissions has the distinct whiff of martyrdom about it, and that doesn't seem to bother the Ruddbot and his followers.

What would it mean for the Rudd government now to allow a sensible revisitation of the nuclear issue? A strong degree of political discomfort, certainly; accusations of backflipping, of course, and considerable loss of skin from the prime ministerial hide.

It's a lot to ask. But they're asking it of Peter Garrett.

18 July 2009

A BUCK THAT HAS A LOT OF GROUND TO COVER

The middle of 2009 had come, and was well on the way to going, and still there was no sign of Kevin Rudd's promised plebiscite on a federal take-over of the hospital system. 'The buck stops with me', he had promised as Opposition leader.

The buck's still going to stop with Kevin. Just not yet.

It's got a lot of ground to cover before it comes to rest, that old buck.

And it's already had a busy two years. It's been up hill and down dale.

When this whole thing began – with Kevin 07 two years ago, as a weary nation eyed its ageing prime minister and toyed with the idea of turfing him in favour of the nerdy young challenger – there wasn't much doubt about where the buck belonged. It belonged with the old guy – with John Howard who, as Kevin told us, had neglected the task of reform for far too long.

And it spent some time surfing, cursing and beating up on Bernie Banton with Tony Abbott, too, the last of the Howard health ministers and the one who was obliged to buy that little hospital in Tasmania, just to make Howard's point.

'I'm committed to ending the buck-passing on health between Canberra and the states', Kevin 07 told voters in a TV advertisement on health, to the reassuring accompaniment of an acoustic guitar. 'I'll work co-operatively with the states to get our hospitals fixed, but in the end, the buck will stop with me.'

When Kevin 07 was elected, though – that's when the buck started on its giddy travels. And it's kept some low company, let me tell you.

It's hung out with Nathan and the rest of the premiers out the back of COAG, cadging cigarettes from passers-by, seriously on the grift for stimulus money from the feds.

It's hung around the emergency room at Royal North Shore Hospital for hours on end among the drunks and chronics, among the barking babies and sad-eyed mothers, triaged to the end of the queue by strung-out staff.

Don't get me wrong: the buck's had a bit of fancy, too. It's spent some time in Point Piper with the Turnbulls, taking a rest poolside and enjoying some canapés while Kevin zooms around getting his plebiscite in order. It's been back to the Howards' place for a quick sherry, too, a couple of times in the past twenty months or so.

But there was a violent and unexpected mugging late last year, and the buck was unexpectedly taken hostage by a giant brute of a foreigner: the global financial crisis, which still has the poor bugger in its grasp.

Kevin hasn't given up on the buck.

It's still going to stop with him in the end, he said yesterday – all that's left to do is a quick round of public consultation, a deep but temporary direct engagement with industry stakeholders, one more premiers' conference, then another one and then we'll have made it to the drawing board stage for a plebiscite, depending on global conditions.

Beaten, exhausted, drunk and sporting a strange unexplained tattoo, the buck might then find its way home to Kevin's.

It's already been a hell of a buck's night.

And the night is yet young.

28 July 2009

BATTLELINES DRAWN EARLY FOR PEOPLE SKILLS

A much-refreshed Tony Abbott reappeared, bearing a new book.

As Tony 'People Skills' Abbott delivered his latest progeny, a bouncing baby bio-manifesto, his nearest and dearest gathered round.

His father, his sister, his priest, his celibacy consultant, a collection of friends from the Liberal Party, his publisher ... Anyone on that list catch your attention at all?

Yes, that's right. One of the many individuals thanked yesterday at the launch of Abbott's book *Battlelines* was a lady called Josephine Ul, who – according to People Skills himself – was his 'celibacy adviser' in the year he spent doing pastoral work as a trainee priest in the Emu Plains parish in 1987.

One hesitates to question the professional qualifications of Ul, even in the light of Abbott's widely documented wanderings off the path of celibacy. But it is probably for the best that Ul has subsequently changed careers and now is happily ensconced in a managerial role at Myer.

You never forget your first job, though, do you?

'As you can imagine, Tony was a very fit, athletic, gorgeous man – intelligent, funny – some of the girls were quite infatuated', she recalls. 'He was mindful of his position in the parish. He didn't want to let Father Hannon down.'

Ul, who was the parish co-ordinator at the time, took on a counselling role, talking the young seminarian down when he needed it.

'I didn't have a 100 per cent success rate', she acknowledges. 'There were one or two lapses. He didn't ever get caught but there were some close encounters.'

In the end, the student proved the master's equal; Abbott went on to have three daughters, and Ul to have three sons, for whose adolescence she now believes her early experience with Abbott to have been 'good training'. Early in his career, Abbott described himself as being the 'ideological love-child of John Howard and Bronwyn Bishop'. Many were surprised by this pronouncement – not least Howard and Bishop, who have never really liked each other in that way. But both ideological parents joined Abbott after his launch yesterday for a congratulatory lunch at Lucio's.

The launch of *Battlelines* at The Wharf restaurant formalises People Skills's unofficial revival campaign, in which the shadow family and community affairs minister emerges from an eighteen-month funk after the 2007 election loss. Abbott has been reborn stronger and fitter, with a few surprising new functions: a strong belief in paid maternity leave, for instance, and an admiration for Malcolm Turnbull, which he expresses at every opportunity.

Turnbull himself, who was absent from the launch, managed to make it to lunch after a morning spent debonairly parrying questions about the latest Newspoll, which has him at sickening lows in the preferred prime minister stakes.

Abbott, Howard, Turnbull and Bishop? Now there's a lunching foursome you wouldn't ordinarily expect to see. Better call the celibacy adviser.

29 July 2009

PASSION BYPASS AS MEN IN SUITS RULE

The Labor Party gathered in Sydney for its national conference.

The Ruddbot Revolution is complete.

Labor's national conference has successfully eliminated the all-too-human mess and fuss which were its reliable attendants in the past. Instead, an eerie calm reigns; the triumph of android over hominid.

Kevin Rudd left the conference about 11 a.m. yesterday and will not return until tomorrow, but his dominance of the event cannot be threatened by anything so trifling as his physical absence. Wandering through the Sydney Convention Centre on the opening day was like stumbling into an international conference of loss-adjusters. The conference hall itself has been stripped of all triumphalist gewgaws, the central platform – with its bare lectern – a model of thrift.

As delegates prepared to greet their leader, there were no throbbing theme tunes, and none of the usual uplifting video packages. 'By the order of Conference, no banners, placards or signs will be allowed into the conference hall or other conference areas', the delegates' guide decreed.

The entire venue has been swept for any trace of extravagance or excess. Everything was stripped-down, pared-back, deliberately drab – except treacherous Darling Harbour, which sparkled expensively in the late July sunshine, presumably because no one on the Rudd advance team had managed to find the dimmer switch. Typical Sydney; it never was very good at austerity measures.

By the time the Great Helmsbot arrived on the conference floor, accompanied by Julia Gillard, the delegates had been so comprehensively drilled to resist any demonstrations of triumphalism or hubris that nobody even knew whether it was OK to applaud. After an awkward silence, one headstrong fool started clapping. His comrades followed gratefully, and the crowd ended up on its feet in a nervous ovation.

Too much? The Helmsbot smiled magnanimously – indulgence! Relief flooded the room.

The prime minister's speech contained some gifts and trinkets for delegates as reward for their discipline: there was a highly stylised attack on neo-liberalism for the Trots, and 50,000 new 'green jobs, green traineeships and green apprenticeships' to mollify the greenies and unionists.

Poor Mark Arbib, the employment minister, later confessed to Sky News that he wasn't exactly sure where or what these jobs would be; his faulty connection to the Ruddbot matrix was one of the few public irregularities of the day.

The Ruddbot's language was, as ever, faintly ungraspable. He lauded the proud Labor conferences of the past, and their passionate resolutions calling for a national apology, for the abolition of Work Choices and humane treatment of refugees. 'Those resolutions represented the consistency of our purpose! The conviction of our resolve!'

It sounded all right, until you realise that many of the Rudd phrases can be rearranged almost infinitely and still make sense, such is their boilerplate blandness. Try this, for example: 'Those convictions represented the purpose of our resolve! The resolution of our consistency!'

See? It works fine like that, and means just as little. The Ruddbot's fond musings about the impassioned conference battles of the past were consigned firmly to the historical part of his speech; disciples were implicitly but unmistakably invited to conclude that there was no need for that sort of carry-on today. Refugee policy, industrial relations, Indigenous affairs: Labor prefers to reserve these wrenching arguments for the Opposition years, when they are pointless.

A team of scrutineers, headed by the finance minister, Lindsay Tanner, vetted conference motions and amendments lest they contain anything interesting. Delegates voted predictably.

And the Ruddbot saw everything that he had made, and, behold, it was very good.

31 July 2009

FAREWELL DR MAYBE, HUMAN SPONGE

Brendan Nelson announced his retirement from politics.

One of my favourite anecdotes about parties in opposition comes from Labor's Crean era, that turbulent period during which the federal ALP chewed unhappily at itself in a mire of self-loathing.

Crean was under challenge from Kim Beazley, and the numbers were close. Geoff Buckland, a nondescript South Australian senator, was judged by the Crean forces to be a waverer and a negotiator was duly dispatched to see if he couldn't be won over.

'Mate', the Creanite numbers man began, 'to be honest, I dunno if we can promise you a spot on the front bench. But how would you like to be deputy Opposition whip in the Senate?'

There was a sad little pause, before Buckland replied plaintively: 'But … I am the deputy whip in the Senate!'

Opposition is a state of mind; usually a scrappy, nasty, venal state of mind. Whatever the stripe of the party involved, the outward signs of Opposition Syndrome are easy to spot. Backbenchers swarm forth from the woodwork, brandishing strange views on which they privately feel they have been silenced for far too long.

All sorts of mad berks turn out to be nursing leadership ambitions. New heroes emerge, are hoisted onto flimsy pedestals and strewn lavishly with magazine profiles and much talk of 'fresh starts', but are soon toppled, their corpses dragged through the streets in front of their sad-eyed spouses. Those with vestiges of influence hunker together in the dust and trade furiously.

It's dreadful to watch grown adults going through it, this Opposition Syndrome; it seems a dreadful indignity, like late-onset adolescence or something. The amazing thing is that in some circumstances – rare, but compelling – some parties can manage to achieve the Opposition state of mind while actually in government.

Witness the NSW government, where all the elements of a real midwinter opposition – ceaseless backbiting, unsightly self-promotion, a horrid preoccupation with the filthy scraps of defeat and an almost total oblivion to the needs of the voting public – flourish, despite the fact that this group of people is in power. It's quite an achievement, this, matched only at present by the spectacular disintegration of Gordon Brown's Labour government in Britain.

Opposition Syndrome is a seemingly inevitable part of the political cycle; like a catastrophic bushfire, it appears to obliterate all in its path but often presages the miracle of new life. And like all catastrophic events, Opposition Syndrome creates martyrs. These are people who throw themselves into the path of the horror, knowing their own situation to be pretty much hopeless. History records them mercilessly as dupes, fools and flops. But they are absolutely invaluable to the process.

Think of Simon Crean, the memory of whose period in the leadership still occasions eye-rolling and bitter laughter among some of his former subjects. Crean's Pyrrhic battles against the forces of Labor's factional and union power structure were hard to watch; the subject matter was archaic and the public effect violent and messy. But the breakdown of the factional system that the Crean and Latham periods initiated now serves as the wellspring of Kevin Rudd's authority.

How else could Rudd have managed so breezily to announce, early in his leadership of the ALP, that the job of selecting a front bench – a privilege hoarded for decades by snarling factional heads – would now be his and his alone? In the sacrificial ashes of Saint Simon, we find the seeds of King Kevin. Time will tell whether this is a good thing.

This week was marked by the resignation of another Opposition martyr: Brendan Nelson, former Liberal leader, street name Dr Maybe. The famously diabolical former editor of Britain's *Sun* newspaper, Kelvin MacKenzie, once became enraged by one of his news editors, Stuart Higgins, who never seemed to rise to the bait of MacKenzie's taunts and tantrums.

In desperate revenge upon his subordinate, MacKenzie splashed a picture of Higgins all over page five, with the text: 'Ring Higgy the Human Sponge! He'll Soak It Up! ... He LOVES loudmouths. Can't LIVE without a tongue-lashing. A week without being called a wally – or worse – is a week wasted in his books. So pick up the phone and fume!'

Thoughtfully, MacKenzie printed Higgins's direct line, and the poor man spent several days fielding riotously abusive calls from complete strangers, according to Peter Chippindale and Chris Horrie's brilliant 1990 biography of the *Sun*, *Stick It Up Your Punter*.

There was something of Higgy the Human Sponge about Brendan Nelson during his short period in the Liberal leadership. He soaked up the grief and bewilderment of the 2007 election's Coalition survivors, and soothed them as they got long-held grievances off their chests. He agreed warmly with those who felt that the 2007 defeat was a stern message to the Coalition to dispense with certain of its longest-held policy obsessions. Equally, he nodded sympathetically to those who felt that this, of all times, was not the moment to panic and abandon key Liberal values. To the external observer, this was a confusing phenomenon, and Nelson's mawkish line in oratory further contributed to a constant flow of gags at the good doctor's expense, including some from your current correspondent.

In April last year, the indefatigably upbeat Nelson was asked by the radio host Mike Carlton how his mum dealt with all the headlines and criticism.

'I just say, "Don't worry, Mum! We're going all right",' chirped Nelson in response.

'No, he's not, Mum', growled the *Herald*'s recently retired Alan Ramsey with crushing finality. 'When even old farts like me start to feel sorry for him, you have to accept your son has no chance of surviving, let alone winning. None at all.'

But like Higgy the Human Sponge, and like Labor's Simon Crean, Nelson rose every day, put on a smile and absorbed the criticism.

'Not all of you guys have always been friendly to me in the media', Nelson said on Tuesday as he announced his decision to vacate the safe seat of Bradfield as soon as possible. 'Send this down to Canberra, will you? But I've got to say that I thank all of you for the respect that you've shown toward me. I don't think any of you have ever received an abusive phone call from me. I might have thought about it but I've never done it. I think what goes around comes around. See you later.'

Planted at the end there is a reminder that even nice guys occasionally allow themselves a sly dig; that one was for Malcolm Turnbull, whose personally delivered rants are becoming a talking point among journalists and colleagues.

Turnbull doesn't have too much sympathy for his predecessor, and that's the usual way of things. But Nelson absorbed some of the pain that otherwise would have been his, and that is worth something.

29 August 2009

MR 70 PER CENT HAS VOTERS IN THE PALM OF HIS HAND

Something funny happens to Kevin Rudd when a fresh opinion poll comes in, confirming that he's just north of chocolate eclairs in the popularity stakes.

He becomes more animated. It's as if the adulation from his people is actually flowing through to his motor neurons and bringing the prime ministerial limbs to new and exultant life.

The PM's repertoire of gestures is always worth watching, but yesterday – crowned Mr 70 Per Cent by the *Herald*/Nielsen poll – he was especially transfixing. The old favourites were there, of course. Like 'Dead Spider', in which the hand is held palm upward, fingers and thumb limply curled, and bounced up and down in emphasis of a point. 'Glasses Still There?' – in which the prime minister's right thumb and forefinger fly up to grasp and steady the right lens of his specs – is likewise a classic.

But as he thundered through an impassioned speech marking the first birthday of the global financial crisis, he added some new and daring moves. After 'Glasses Still There?' he added – while verbally dismissing the Opposition's approach to the whole economic situation – a furtive flick of the index finger at waist level, a gesture we'll call 'Bidding for Erotic Drawings At Sotheby's'. This flowed beautifully into 'Fake Finger Count', a common Rudd gesture, which he uses to alert the listener to a new dot-point in his harangue. Interestingly, the number of fingers held up rarely bears any relation to the order number of the point he is actually making; for example, three fingers might signal his second point, but it's just as apt to herald his eighteenth.

This is something that infuriates the other side particularly, as was clear yesterday from manager of Opposition business Chris Pyne's regular and emotional appeals to the speaker as the PM entered his tenth minute at the dispatch box.

Other moves emerged, including 'Cupping the Breasts of an Invisible Peasant Girl', a rare and heartfelt gesture of British origin, first recorded last century by the *Guardian* sketchwriter Simon Hoggart.

As the PM turned up his rhetoric, they came thick and fast: 'Winning at Checkers' (thumb and forefinger grasp an invisible checkers piece and leapfrog it forward, emphasising each jump with a new economic statistic), and its distant but more ambitious cousin, 'Trying To Catch Evasive Frog With Upturned Pint Glass'.

The Opposition, plucky as ever, threw everything it had at the government despite this bewildering visual barrage. First it threw Mr Pyne, who is turning into a handy projectile. Then in desperation the shadow treasurer, Joe Hockey, committed what, to the faithful in the Cult of Kevinology, must rank as one of its gravest blasphemies; he quoted Kochie against the government. Mr Hockey read aloud from an article co-written by the *Sunrise* host and his wife, Libby, in which the pair express the view that the stimulus spending should be phased back. Mr Rudd coldly ignored this insolence, but the speaker of the House soon found grounds to toss the shadow treasurer out.

15 September 2009

OH BOY, JULIE AND JULIA TURN UP THE HEAT

The Liberal Party is having woman trouble.

It all started yesterday morning with the *Herald*'s report that Coalition chicks were not getting their fair share of questions at question time. The government, with its rash of senior sheilas, made preparations to administer some high-level taunting. And Opposition MPs went to the barricades to defend their feminist record.

Each did it in his or her own way, of course.

Tony Abbott, re-entering the chamber at 2.40 p.m. after a 24-hour suspension, blew a lavish kiss to a surprised Jenny Macklin, minister for families.

Wilson Tuckey continued his one-man commentary on women in the workplace, a loose series of mutterings tentatively entitled: 'They Just Want a Job on the Weekends When Dad's Home To Look After the Kids.'

To be fair on the Libs, they have been trying. Malcolm Turnbull launched the 'Engaging Women' campaign to reach out to Liberal-minded ladies, although this enterprise had an early setback; the chap retained to handle the PR had to be sacked in June after 'engaging women' rather too directly at the Press Gallery Ball by means of a liquored-up, indiscriminate funbag-grabbing spree.

The minister for the status of women, Tanya Plibersek, started things off yesterday with a reading from the 'Women and the Liberal Party' page on the Libs' website, which referred to the Liberal Party as 'he government' throughout; slightly out of date, then.

All of a sudden, something snapped. Julie Bishop, deputy Liberal leader, stalked to the dispatch box and delivered 'Blue Steel', the most withering look in her considerable inventory. The manager of Opposition business, Christopher Pyne, moved 'that the speaker no longer be heard', and bedlam ensued as Ms Plibersek observed that it wasn't just that women weren't allowed to ask questions in the Libs – now they weren't allowed to answer them, either.

Twenty minutes later, the Opposition called a similar motion to silence Julia Gillard. Suddenly, there were Liberal chicks everywhere. The justice and customs spokeswoman, Sussan Ley, was allowed to ask her third question for the year, and she shuttled busily back and forth from her place in the frontbench cheap seats to the dispatch box.

At one point Ley, busy making a point of order at the dispatch box, was actually tag-teamed by Julie Bishop, who rose with a second, cumulative point of order, while Ley retreated to wait patiently behind her in a complicated feminist parliamentary formation, known in the trade as the Ley/Lady/Ley.

Ms Bishop was very fired-up; triumphantly, she produced some Hansard transcript of Paul Keating describing the increased participation of women in the workforce as 'something of which we should be ashamed'. This turned out to be Hansard from Keating's maiden speech in 1969, at which time – by way of context – the White Australia Policy was also still in place.

The government benches collapsed in hysterics. Really, it's amazing Ms Bishop could speak at all, with such a big mouthful of baited hook.

16 September 2009

QUESTIONABLE LOGIC ALL ROUND

It's kind of ironic that the Coalition started this week fighting tiredly once more on that well-worn battleground, Work Choices.

Why ironic? Well, because these days the conservative side of politics in this country resembles nothing so much as a crumbly old trade union. You know: one of those post-amalgamation affairs where a new leadership, resplendent in up-to-the-minute ties and eager to forge ahead, is incessantly reviled by its long-standing members – the horny-handed sons of toil – for being sell-outs.

The characters are so easy to spot. There's Malcolm Turnbull – he's the schmick new general secretary, keen to modernise. He is anxious to discard the shibboleths of the past and is openly suspected of having an ego. He is unforgettably wealthy. He owns a Kindle and he Twitters.

Ranged against him are the forces of tradition – the remnants of the pre-amalgamation landscape. There's Barnaby Joyce, the colourful young spokesman for what was – in grander days – the Federated Union of Cockies, Banana Benders and Small Arms Bearers, now in graceful decline.

Young Joyce knows what he is doing. He's giving his members a show, his periodic threats to tear up his own card a reminder to them that their interests have not disappeared entirely into the forests of Wentworth.

There's Wilson Tuckey, senior honorary assistant secretary of the defunct Mad Old Codgers branch. An inveterate clanger-dropper and bottom-pincher, Tuckey is something of a museum piece and tolerated only because he annoys the enemy just as much as he annoys the comrades.

'The only problem with Work Choices was the name', Tuckey told the cameras this week, demonstrating the iron grasp on logic that is the special stamp of the Mad Old Codger.

The leading industrial issue in Capital Hill's busy workplace this week was question time. In threatened industrial organisations, it is not at all uncommon to select, as a major campaign issue, something that about 0.02 per cent of the general population gives a toss about.

And for the oppressed ranks of the downtrodden (i.e., the Opposition) the protest was this: 'Why should we participate in question time, when the government never answers our questions, when Kevin Rudd goes on and on for hours without saying anything, and when everyone to the north of the speaker's chair is so unbearably smug that we can't even stand to look at them?'

Complaints about question time are very common among those not currently enjoying political power. When she was the manager of Opposition business, Julia Gillard was very drawn to the idea of a four-minute limit on ministerial answers. Life, however, is a learning process and these days La Gillardine is beginning to appreciate the latent beauty of a system that allows her unlimited time to torment her enemies.

Early in the week, Tony 'People Skills' Abbott was ready to go over the top. People Skills is from the militant wing. He is the Dean Mighell of the conservative movement – he even shares that famed Electrical Trades Union firebrand's fondness for scatological metaphor.

Mighell said of John Howard at the last election that he was a 'skid-mark on the bedsheet of Australian politics'. Comrade Abbott said of La Gillardine last week that she had worn a 'shit-eating grin' as the malfunctions of her grand primary-school building plans were laid bare.

No prizes for guessing where People Skills stood this week, as the industrial dispute over question time intensified. He favoured wildcat strike action. On Monday, People Skills was ejected from the chamber after an impromptu 'run-through' in which he interposed himself physically between the chamber cameras and La Gillardine, temporarily cutting off the life-giving supply of publicity to the education revolution's haughty high priestess.

On Tuesday, he was interviewed extensively, warning the government that 'if they don't lift their game the Parliament will become unworkable, there's no doubt about that'.

Rumours of a boycott gathered currency.

But in the manner of most bold acts of defiance proposed to divided rabbles, the strike idea dribbled away to nothing over the course of the morning.

The grumbling ranks of the dispossessed turned up to work at 2 p.m as usual. And as is customary in paralysed industrial outfits, the firebrands worked out their frustrations by moving a series of pointless procedural motions instead. 'I move that the speaker no longer be heard!' was their battle cry.

Of course, owing to a certain electoral event in November 2007, the Coalition is now unable to win a vote on the floor of the House of Representatives, so these spills tended to be as dully predictable as democratic elections in Iran. But they made the comrades feel better.

In any event, another complication was afoot in the form of Brendan Nelson, the exiled former general secretary and honorary lightning-rod for the Amalgamated Climate-Change Deniers sub-faction, which has historic links with the Cockies, Banana Benders and Small Arms Bearers and moreover can generally count on the Codgers for tactical support, as long as it's before dinner.

Dr Nelson, who has resigned his prime north-shore branch secretaryship and is jumping ship, used his last authorised stop-work meeting on Tuesday morning to issue a war cry to the comrades on climate change. 'Never give in to the bosses!' he cried (or words to that effect).

Dr Nelson's words were a direct challenge to his successor, who wants nothing more than a negotiated settlement with the enemy on this of all matters. So when the time came on Wednesday evening for Dr Nelson to deliver his final speech to the House of Representatives, the atmosphere was tense. What would he say, this departing warhorse of the resistance?

In the end, Dr Nelson listened to his better angels and delivered a moist, heaving speech full of wisdom and benevolence.

Malcolm Turnbull, hearing it, was so overcome with relief that his response threatened to outdo Dr Nelson for treacliness, and his rush to the bleachers to pump his predecessor's hand afterwards was reminiscent of Pat Cash's victory climb through the stands at Wimbledon in 1987.

But Dr Nelson, unlike the vanquished Lendl, was playing a long game. The comrades were as stunned as everyone else to learn, the following day, that their do-or-die hero had actually cut a deal to accept the quid of the bosses, and was Brussels-bound to represent both Kevin Rudd and his despised emissions trading scheme.

Dark days for the movement, indeed.

19 September 2009

FAKE-WRESTLING RIVALS BOX ONE ANOTHER'S EARS

In late 2009, the rate of asylum-seeker boat arrivals was on the increase. Mr Rudd, who had abolished some elements of John Howard's immigration policy, including temporary protection visas, was anxious nonetheless not to be seen as soft on border protection. He pioneered the term 'tough but humane' and used it wherever he could. The Opposition, meanwhile, which had not opposed the abolition of its earlier policy, was equally anxious to portray the PM as a pushover.

'You should go back to eating earwax', remarked Malcolm Turnbull pleasantly to his opponent the prime minister, towards the end of yesterday's wing-ding about refugee policy.

And he had a point; we all might as well have been consuming aural sediment for all the sense this silly, mutually fraudulent exchange is making. Yesterday, witnesses in the House of Representatives chamber were treated to a stagey, bizarre mock-argument between two men who agree with each other.

Kevin Rudd has humanised the immigration process for asylum seekers by easing detention requirements and abolishing the issuance of temporary protection visas. Neither of these changes was opposed by the Coalition. Largely, they've reached consensus on this stuff. And yet they bellow and strut and accuse each other of deep moral turpitude … why?

It's an entirely confected argument, staged for entirely political reasons. Rudd likes to portray his policies as tougher than they really are because, like most Labor MPs who were around in 2001, he clearly remembers the Atomic Wedgie that he and his colleagues copped back then over immigration. His buttocks now flinch reflexively every time the subject comes up, which is why he keeps saying things like, 'I make no apologies for my staring-eyed, extremist, hardline, definitely not soft or anything ideas about illegal immigrants.' And why he persists with describing his policy approach as 'humane toughness', a deeply

Ruddesque contradiction in terms that fits well with his Scores policy (responsible drunkenness) and his fiscal policy (conservative recklessness).

Turnbull portrays the prime minister's approach as softer than it really is. Not because he disagrees with it, and not because he isn't sympathetic to asylum seekers, but because if the argument isn't about boat people then it will be about climate change. And no matter how miserable it might be to be aboard a leaky boat fleeing persecution, death, pestilence and the extermination of loved ones, that sort of thing still looks kind of like a picnic compared to being Malcolm Turnbull in a room full of National Party hardliners who don't see why their cows shouldn't be able to break wind as much as they like.

So confused are these two men about the ideological plumage they have donned for the purposes of this fake fight that at several points yesterday, they got their roles arse-about. Merciless Malcolm, amid a torrent of reproach for Kid-Glove Kevin for his namby-pamby softness, at one point asked for an assurance that nothing nasty would happen to the most recent boat arrivals when they ship off to Indonesia for processing. Wrong glove puppet, Sir!

And Ruthless Rudd took his gimlet eye off the ball for a bit when he delivered a foaming denunciation of Wilson Tuckey for his extremist views about boats carrying terrorists.

The honourable exception to all of this buffoonery was the foreign minister, Stephen Smith, who took advantage of a quiet moment to explain, in quiet and measured tones and without resort to imprecation of any kind, exactly how Australian authorities had handled recent boat arrivals and why.

He'll never last in this joint.

23 October 2009

LEFT FOR DEAD LIKE A DUTTON CHOP

Peter Dutton, the shadow minister for health and one of the new breed of Liberal frontbenchers carving out an existence post-Howard, got into a horrible spot of bother when he tried to abandon his Queensland seat of Dickson for the Gold Coast seat of McPherson, which was being vacated by his retiring colleague Margaret May. Dickson, always marginal, had been rendered even less winnable by a federal redistribution. The Liberal–National Party preselectors of McPherson, however, turned out to be extremely tough on border protection and told him to go home.

Certain ancient and enduring themes occupied the minds of our representatives under the Canberra Coat Hanger this week. The seasonal plague of bogong moths – the fat, calorific insects that invade Parliament House in spring, creating cholesterol problems for the currawongs and a deep and uncharacteristic fear, in senators, of opening their mouths – lent an appropriately Old Testament air to the proceedings as the following knotty ethical questions were considered:

1. Can it possibly be considered humane to send an asylum seeker back to his homeland, if to do so risks significant chance of death or serious injury?
2. What if that person is judged to be of particular social value? Does this factor alone excuse an otherwise egregious act of queue-jumping?

These question were considered, primarily, in the case of *The People of Dickson v Peter Dutton, Liberal MP.*

It's an all-too-familiar parable.

A talented young man finds that his homeland has become unbearable. Advancing hordes from the north and south have changed the political balance of power there, and where he once was representative of a narrow political majority, he now finds himself the member of an oppressed minority, with all the anxiety that such status entails.

In his homeland he is persecuted with unkind flyers by his well-funded political enemies. He seems certain to lose his job. The future appears bleak. After consultation with his family, he decides to embark on a risky mission: a voyage to the friendlier climes of Australia's Gold Coast, and its safe Liberal seat of McPherson. Here he could pursue in comfort the career he has chosen; his children would grow up knowing ease and confidence; and his wife would have access to unlimited pairs of three-quarter-length white trousers, if she is into that sort of thing.

As I say, it's a risky plan; there is no guarantee his asylum claim will be accepted. The Gold Coast, while sunny and welcoming in appearance, nurses a deep suspicion of outsiders.

This might seem surprising, given that the Gold Coast is itself a migrant community, heavily peopled by international thrill-seekers and Melburnians who were prepared to put up with rugby league if it meant the end of chilblains, but that's the way it so often goes with these things. Migrants love migrating, but sometimes they want to shut the doors behind them.

As is frequently the case with the high-profile asylum seeker, the young man's case becomes something of a cause célèbre. Former prime ministers and premiers intercede on his behalf. Influential journalists argue that a young, vibrant country should do its best to help such a man of promise and that, if this man is left behind, it will constitute a failure of heart and courage on the part of his party colleagues.

In the space of two weeks the young man – previously viewed as a competent and promising frontbencher – finds himself draped with the heavy robes of martyrdom. His supporters talk of a glittering future – perhaps even the prime ministership! Comparisons are made with John F. Kennedy.

The young man experiences the pleasurable thrill of hearing his own political eulogy without yet having actually succumbed. Life suddenly seems rich with possibility.

But darker whispers abound. The fact that the young man has been embraced by Sydney politicians and the elite media does not help him in the Sunshine State. He is not assisted, either, by his own past remarks about Gold Coast blow-ins.

With a particular jut-jawed doggedness, the Gold Coast preselectors reject the young man's plea for clemency, opting instead to favour a pleasant if anonymous local. The fact that the young man is deserving, they feel, is not their concern. He is an interloper, and they will decide who comes to the electorate of McPherson and – most particularly – the circumstances under which they come.

What are they, they argue – the fairy godmothers for the world's stricken? If Dutton is so talented, let him be talented on his own turf.

The young man now is obliged to return to his homeland and near-certain political peril, to which he can now add the ignominy of having tried unsuccessfully to escape.

For a week or two, he considers his future. Appeals to the Coalition's higher authorities are considered and abandoned. Recourse to the United Nations is not possible; the rules are in place for a reason and must be observed.

And on Tuesday this week, with the pale dignity peculiar to the doomed, he emerges to face his fate. He will return to his homeland, and what seems like certain death. With all the composure of Sidney Carton, he steps into the tumbril, vowing to fight until the end.

Presumably, his former colleagues who in 2007 succumbed to the brutal scourge of the marauding Ruddites watch all this with interest from beyond the political grave. Did they resent the idea that Dutton might be offered the chance at salvation that was denied them?

Because that's the problem with refugee policy, isn't it? Who to choose? For every promising young man we read about, there are many more who didn't get the column inches. Somehow, it's easier to read about the 300,000 in Sri Lankan camps than it is to witness the one nine-year-old Tamil girl as she sobs into the cameras. Every time a face emerges from the amorphous mass of the dispossessed, a person who stops being a statistic just long enough for us to register a family, a story, a pair of eyes into which it is impossible to look at length, the true dreadfulness of the equation becomes apparent.

It seems so simple to help the ones that we can see; satisfying, too. But, in so doing, what a ghastly game of dice we create for those left behind: the slim chance that, by wagering your children's lives on a perilous boat voyage, you might ultimately save them.

This central question is so upsetting that it is no wonder the political debate skitters off to ancillary matters, like whether Wilson Tuckey is a beastly old throwback who should be stripped of his preselection, or whether Kevin Rudd is an insufferable faux-moralist fraud.

24 October 2009

PM MAKES NO APOLOGIES FOR BEING UNAPOLOGETIC

It was the previous prime minister, John Winston Howard, who became famous for not being able to apologise. Whole books have been written, and endless conversations had, about that individual's utter intransigence in the face of the S-word.

Kevin Rudd, the all-conquering angel of contrition, seemed to put all that to bed with his national apology, delivered with due solemnity on 13 February, 2008. But since then he has become increasingly, even defiantly unrepentant. About all sorts of things, in fact.

In May this year, he declared himself an 'unapologetic optimist about this region's future'. By July, he was also an 'unapologetic supporter of the United States'. In September, he refused point-blank to apologise for calling a delegation of colleagues 'fuckers' when they asked him not to cut their electorate printing allowances.

'I made my point of view absolutely clear; that is, that these entitlements needed to be cut back and I make no apology for either the content of my conversation or the robustness with which I expressed my views', the prime minister insisted, when questioned about the incident.

Perhaps emboldened by his own example, he then reminded the Australian public that he and his government had 'unapologetically taken early, strong, decisive action through our national Building for Recovery Plan'. And anyone who in the past ten days has been knocking the top off a cold one every time the prime minister describes his own immigration policy as 'unapologetically tough' would by now be too plastered to read this column.

Here's the trick, for any L-plate politician just picking up the knack of the non-apology apology. First, you take a principle or proposition of which the listener is odds-on to approve. Caring for puppies, let's say. Then you profess to uphold that principle 'unapologetically': 'I am an unapologetic supporter of puppies.'

This first endears you to the listener, and affirms their own views.

But the use of the term 'unapologetically' does something else, too. It implicitly suggests that the listener is part – along with you – of a small but courageous minority.

It says: 'To those who hate and revile puppies, let them today understand that this government will – fearlessly and without thought of political fashion or fortune – fight for the rights of puppies everywhere, especially the ones who are so teensy that the back legs fall over every now and again.'

By the time you are finished, you and your listener are brothers-in-arms, visionaries swimming bravely against the tide of a brutal orthodoxy. All because you have promised to be unapologetic about holding a perfectly unexceptionable view. Take the above-mentioned examples, in which our own PM has refused to apologise – in turn – for his optimism, his courage, his decisiveness, and his support for Australia's largest military ally.

What makes the past week an exceptional performance – almost deserving of a special Not Sorry Day – is that the prime minister has now mastered the art of unapologetically endorsing two conflicting concepts at once. In the space of a single answer in question time, Mr Rudd described his immigration policy as 'unapologetically tough' and 'unapologetically humane'.

That, ladies and gentlemen, is champagne unrepentance.

27 October 2009

GROUND CONTROL TO RUDD: WHO THE HELL IS RUNNING THE SHIP?

Into this snowstorm of rhetoric sailed the Oceanic Viking. *An Australian naval vessel, the* Oceanic Viking *had intervened at the request of the Indonesian authorities to rescue seventy-eight asylum seekers whose vessel foundered in Indonesian waters on its way to Australia. Having rescued the seventy-eight at Indonesia's request, the Australian government was determined that they should be Indonesia's problem. But Indonesian port authorities would not let the group land. So for more than a month, the* Oceanic Viking *bobbed about while in Canberra, the situation grew more farcical by the day.*

Who's steering this boat? After a third day of Coalition questioning on this matter, the answer remains resolutely unclear.

All week, the Opposition has wanted to know just exactly who, within the Australian government and its lavish archipelago of departments, authorities and administered agencies, is the smouldering genius responsible for deciding where the *Oceanic Viking* sails with its load of seventy-eight asylum seekers.

And all week, the prime minister has experimented with increasingly novel ways of not saying. On Monday, he declared that the decision-making on the matter of the *Oceanic Viking* had 'obviously occurred in the government, but by which agencies within the government and by which officers, I am unaware'.

On Tuesday, the PM flapped his wrist vaguely in the direction of the question, observing jadedly that 'the precise sequence of events concerning the handling of this particular vessel I cannot recall in absolute detail; they were complex diplomatic negotiations ... I imagine it was an operational matter'.

There exists in the realm of human knowledge a detail in which the Australian prime minister is not interested? Hmm. If you believe that, I've got a bridge I'd like to sell you.

Yesterday, as Malcolm Turnbull and Sharman Stone continued their impudent campaign for an actual answer to this question, Rudd seemed to crack a little, giving away some valuable clues as to who was in control of the *Oceanic Viking* and the nomadic souls who currently call her home.

In his first answer, the prime minister reluctantly disclosed that the negotiations with the Indonesians had been carried out by 'relevant officials'. Later, he narrowed it down to 'men and women'.

Men and women! Having thus successfully eliminated the Australian public sector's eunuchs and hermaphrodites, the Opposition hit a brick wall. Taunt and entreat as they might, they could elicit no further detail.

Do not suppose for a moment, by the way, that the prime minister took any of this sustained Opposition impertinence lying down. He punished everyone in the chamber with an oratorical guitar solo that was so paralysing in its tedium – incorporating his detailed thoughts on the topic of urban planning as a complex riff against the bass line of an all-points warning on coastal inundation, punctuated with the occasional trill on productive capacity in the economy – that the weaker and frailer of the chamber's MPs dropped like flies.

He also read aloud from the United Nations Convention on the Law of the Sea.

Julia Gillard, who has developed asbestos ears and can easily handle even the highest-grade Rudd oratory, was nonetheless chastened by the reference to coastal inundation; she hastily declared that she had been presented with a hand-painted pair of gumboots by an adoring delegation from the Penguin Primary School, in coastal Tasmania. The gumboots should give her a few extra years, at projected rates of sea-level rise.

Whether the *Oceanic Viking* finds a home within that time remains anyone's guess.

29 October 2009

GRACIOUS RUDD TURNS GRUBBY

One of the most gracious things I have ever seen Kevin Rudd do happened on February 13 last year, at 10 minutes to 10. Brendan Nelson, the then leader of the Liberal Party, had just completed his reply to the prime minister's formal speech of national apology to the Aboriginal children removed from their families by former governments.

It had been a typical Nelson speech in many ways: passionate, heartfelt, yet unsettlingly at odds with itself.

It endorsed the apology but implicitly questioned the validity of the exercise, and its bald recitation of contemporary evils done to Aboriginal children by their own families and communities, including one case of a four-year-old child raped in its bath, seemed awkwardly out of step with the tenor of the day and cannot have been anything but distressing for the legions of schoolchildren watching the event on TV.

Inside the chamber, a susurrus of dismay rustled through the ranks of the Aboriginal leaders gathered there.

Outside, the knee-jerk game of protest was much quicker under way, and crowd members began booing, and turning their backs on the giant screens.

And Kevin Rudd, spotting what was about to happen, threw away his choreography notes for the ceremony and did something rather extraordinary.

Due to accept the gift of a coolamon from the Aboriginal delegation on behalf of the Parliament, the prime minister detoured past Dr Nelson's seat and collected him, too, grasping him by the arm, deftly defusing the ill-feeling in the chamber and binding the Liberal leader into a lasting image of unity on that significant national day.

It was only Mr Rudd's second sitting day as prime minister, and it was a powerful thing to see: a leader rescuing an adversary from a spot of bother, for no other reason than that the greater good seemed to warrant it. Mr Rudd's approval ratings climbed to a vertiginous 70 per cent.

Nearly two years have passed since that day.

The prime minister's popularity is still unseasonably high.

Parliament is caught in the fangs of another debate, on another emotional, divisive, difficult issue, one which also involves dark echoes of the past for both sides of politics.

But the prime minister we see is a different man.

Having snarled himself somewhat in his own net of tough rhetoric, he spent much of this week in question time lashing out at his opponents, often in unnecessarily caustic and personal terms.

'Thank you, Mr Speaker. We have that man of constant principle, the member for Berowra, who has always maintained a consistency of line when it comes to asylum seekers over years past', went one of his snipes at Philip Ruddock.

The Australian unearthed a particularly nasty little Opposition memo endorsing the strategy of dirt-digging, and Mr Rudd went on to cite that memo at every opportunity, questioning the bona fides of just about any Coalition MP who rose to quiz him.

In reply to reasonably straightforward questions from the Opposition frontbenchers Julie Bishop and Sharman Stone on the government's plans for the *Oceanic Viking*, he threw in sarcastic asides about their credibility and their reputations.

And when asked on Thursday about the national secretary of the Australian Workers Union, Paul Howes, and his criticism of the government's handling of the asylum seeker issue, the prime minister dismissed the unionist with a cold contempt: 'It does not surprise me what the given individual might be saying in any public policy debate on any given day. He has a habit of expressing his views in his own way.'

Decoded: The fellow's a windbag. I don't care what he thinks.

Now, Mr Rudd is a politician.

And there is an abundance of points to score here, not least of which is that the Opposition, which is long on cries of outrage and accusations that the prime minister has muffed his 'Indonesian solution', is very short on ideas about how it would do things differently.

The prime minister's feelings for those opposite are such that he cannot contain them; he cannot forgive what he sees as the brutal manipulation of voter sentiment that in 2001 damaged the country and laid waste to morale in the ranks of his own party.

The prime minister is perfectly entitled to score points.

It's just that this whole debate would be healthier, pleasanter, more useful and altogether less depressing if he didn't.

After nearly two years of Kevin Rudd, prime minister, we know this about him: he is capable of magnanimity and great generosity of spirit, especially when things are going well.

But when the pressure mounts, he has a tendency to cattiness, and it's not a very inspiring look.

'The immaturity in political debate in Australia sometimes makes me sick', is what Mr Howes actually said.

'There are politicians in both the Liberal and Labor parties who are exploiting the issue of race to whip up fear in the community.

'[Mr Rudd] has the unanimous loyalty of his caucus. He has an almost non-existent Opposition. He is in a unique position to change the debate. Changing the way Australia deals with race would be pretty special – that's Labor hero stuff.'

Mr Rudd has spent the past week in studied nonchalance about the details of the *Oceanic Viking*'s movements, first claiming he couldn't recall all the details of the negotiations with the Indonesians and then vaguely attributing the management of the situation to 'officials'.

The truth is, however, that somebody has to be in charge.

And being in charge doesn't just mean deciding where a boat full of asylum seekers will sail.

Being in charge also means being responsible for the tenor and shape of an argument, and seeing that – in the spiral of politics, where there is always precedent and justification enough to be found for bad behaviour – there must be a point at which a strong leader cuts his losses for the greater good.

As long as the argument against bipartisanship is 'But there's nothing bipartisan about my enemies', then we'll never have it, not on any issue, and especially not on this one.

If we could recover the Kevin Rudd of February last year, with his outstretched hand and his quick ability to see how a fractured political situation could, with goodwill, be mended to build a part of something greater, we might all have some hope for a better week next week.

31 October 2009

ALL TOO HUMAN: THE REBIRTH OF PEOPLE SKILLS

I AM THE BOSS – OF THE MOST UNRULY RABBLE EVER

After a year of turbulence, it was climate change that accounted for Malcolm Turnbull in the end. Strongly of the view that Australia needed to commit itself to a robust scheme of carbon emissions reduction, Mr Turnbull committed his own party to negotiations with the Government on how it might pass a version of Mr Rudd's Carbon Pollution Reduction Scheme. But the Coalition was anything but united on this front. An increasingly vocal group of climate-change sceptics, whose ranks featured politicians ranging from WA hell-raiser Wilson Tuckey to Senate leader Nick Minchin, opposed the notion of any deal that would allow the legislation to pass. When Mr Turnbull presented the compromise model to his party room, there was heated disagreement. Mr Turnbull quickly pronounced the matter resolved – in his favour. Bedlam broke out.

It was a landmark Turnbull victory: electric, anarchic and quite possibly Pyrrhic.

'I am the leader', he reminded attendees at his late media conference last night, five times, with a brilliant smile.

And so he is: the leader of what must, after yesterday, rank as the most incredible rabble recently to grace these parliamentary corridors. Even the Labor Party, in the depth of its despairing Opposition years, never quite achieved the exuberant madness of yesterday's performance by the federal Coalition.

Entering the Coalition's party room for the leader's victory media conference, one was surprised not to see the walls spattered with gore, such were the scenes that took place there during the day. Turnbull staffers twittered about straightening the flags behind the lectern.

And when Turnbull himself entered, it was with the air of a freshly released game-show host, all megawatt grin, with his lovely assistant Julie beaming at his side.

Honestly – it was too, too strange.

'I'm not interested in Wilson Tuckey. Either in his correspondence, or in his comments to you', he responded royally, when asked about Tuckey's stated intention to call a leadership spill on Thursday. 'I'm the leader – right? And if people are unhappy with the leader, they can take any steps they deem appropriate.'

You have to hand it to the Liberal leader: no one bounces back from a near-death experience quite like he does. Maybe it's all the training he put in, fighting with Kerry Packer.

Because at 7.50 last night, Malcolm Turnbull looked gone for all money. His party was in uproar, its day-long meeting on the climate change legislation abandoned in circumstances of unspeakable tumult. Turnbull's whereabouts were unclear, but lavish rumours were abroad. The Liberal leader had thrown a tantrum and was being comforted by Joe Hockey. He had just popped out for a sandwich. No – he was about to be rolled in a leadership vote.

In the Canberra gloaming, all sorts of rich and exotic possibilities loomed. An Abbott–Bishop leadership team? Pleasingly reverent and nicely balanced in gender, geography and ideology. A Kevin Andrews leadership tilt? Shareholders in Grecian 2000 rubbed their hands in anticipation, and cartoonists dribbled at the thought of a Kevin '11 showdown.

The Coalition had, all day, been sliding from 'policy debate' mode inexorably into 'leadership challenge' mode. You could smell it developing as the day wore on: wild-eyed aides skidding about the corridors on mobile phones; the growing security presence ranged around the Coalition room's door; the energetic lobbying that continued before our very eyes when they took a break for question time; the way Malcolm Turnbull kept taking out and scribbling away at a scrap of paper on which were inscribed two careful columns of names.

But in the end, the petrol just wasn't in the tank. When the opportunity for a leadership challenge lay on the table, no one picked it up.

25 November 2009

PETTY OFFICERS, MAJOR BATTLE AND GENERAL CONFUSION

Kevin Andrews, who had been minister for immigration in the Howard government, put up his hand to challenge Mr Turnbull. A vote was staged on the question of whether the leadership should be declared vacant. It failed, narrowly.

Never, in the field of Liberal warfare, was so much energy expended to achieve so little.

As the dust settled yesterday, and the ack-ack faded from the surrounds of the Opposition party room, the veterans of the Allied Climate Resistance straggled from the ruined ramparts and reviewed their campaign.

And found that nothing had changed.

After two days of fierce open fighting, itself coming on the heels of a months-long underground guerilla campaign, the Resistance has fallen short.

Their adversary, General Turnbull, grins maddeningly in victory.

Despite all the harrumphing within the ranks of the Resistance about his callow lack of political judgment or experience on the battle field, he seems to have stitched them up pretty nicely this time.

He remains in power; the party he leads remains set on a path to vote for an emissions trading scheme, and there's nothing much the Resistance can do about it.

All the plotting, railing and screeching of the past two days has been expended for nought.

It's a difficult business, after all, trying to drum up a proper Resistance when there is nobody available who quite cuts the mustard to lead it.

Brigadier Colonel Kevin Andrews, with his neatly trimmed sable hair-helmet, was anxious for selection yesterday.

In the hour before the crucial vote – the time usually spent scurrying about promising officers' badges to likely converts – Brigadier Colonel

Andrews instead called a long press conference to explain his vision for the Liberal Party.

He listed 'freedom of the individual, support for the family and community that give meaning to people's lives', and 'human dignity and respect for all people'.

Pow!

That could have been a fatal blow for the general, who is on record as fervently supporting enslavement, depravity, family breakdown and the razing of popular bingo halls.

Brigadier Colonel Andrews, who counts among his achievements a strategic role in the Battle of Work Choices and the 30-Day Haneef War, shyly confessed yesterday to having the requisite 'people skills' to merit appointment to supreme leadership.

'I was successful in getting through the party room legislation that was unpopular', he reminisced.

Very true, but to the faint-hearted this might have sounded horribly like 'I have successfully sold you some lemons in the past. Here's your chance to buy the tree!'

And in any case, if the party were seriously in search of people skills, why would they accept second best?

The original People Skills, Lieutenant General Tony Abbott, remained zipped firmly into his pup tent yesterday, and refused to emerge for combat, as did the other fancied recipient of the field marshal's baton, Joe Hockey.

Both of these men, it must additionally be noted, emerged after the battle was over to apologise to the Australian people for the spectacle of the past few days.

The victorious General Turnbull, for his part, made a heroic attempt to appear humble, though no one would argue that this is his natural metier.

'Even someone as quiet and unassuming as myself can improve', he conceded.

26 November 2009

LOVE AND OTHER LIBERAL CATASTROPHES

Malcolm Turnbull's victory was to last only a matter of days. Driven to insurrection by the imminent prospect of the Coalition's 'Yes' vote on the government's emissions trading scheme, a host of Coalition frontbenchers decided to resign in protest. They included Tony Abbott, who earlier had encouraged his colleagues to vote for the government's scheme in order to clear the air. He had since, he now explained, had an epiphany on the subject. Something to do with driving around in South Australia and talking to Nick Minchin a lot. Mr Abbott became the hero of the Climate Resistance.

Oh, People Skills, People Skills.

What a marvellous creature you are.

Was there ever such an exotic as Tony Abbott? So joyously unpredictable, so boyishly impetuous – so passionate, yet so changeable?

It seems only a matter of moments ago that you were advocating that the Coalition close its eyes, think of John Howard, and pass the emissions trading legislation simply to get it out of the way. And now your colleagues having done exactly that (though not without considerable bloodshed), you declare yourself unable to bear it!

Having apologised to the Australian people on Wednesday for the extraordinary farce of the preceding forty-eight hours, you bounce back yesterday to initiate a return season! Having become a Malcolm Turnbull supporter at the most unfashionable of junctures, and – indeed – having delivered a paean to him on Tuesday before an audience of your colleagues, you reappear yesterday to smite him. What rough magic is at work here?

Yesterday looked – to all intents and purposes – like the end of the parliamentary year. Sure, the Senate is doomed to slog through until Monday to clear its backlog, but this was not the concern of Kevin Rudd, who has nipped off to Trinidad for the Commonwealth Heads of Government Meeting, and thence to Washington for a play date with his new best friend, the president of the United States.

By the time the Senate finally, haggardly signs his emissions trading legislation (probably in the actual blood of Nick Minchin) the prime minister will be moistly ensconced in the Obamas' hot tub, yukking it up with the other saviour of the universe, or romping photogenically with the White House puppy. There was an audible 'CLANG!' in the chamber yesterday when Mr Rudd carefully dropped Mr Obama's name, closely followed by an agonised groan from members opposite, and the sound of drawers scraping as Liberal MPs searched desperately for somewhere to throw up.

Can you imagine the photo opportunities? Can you imagine the Twitter opportunities?

'Yo – the Ruddster here. Just cooking up a mess of chilli dogs with the Bamster and Michelle, and rapping about climate change. Dig it! KRudd.'

Before he left, the prime minister delivered a valedictory speech in which he exhorted Parliament's combatants to love each other a little more. Love-starved Malcolm Turnbull eagerly took up the theme.

'Love is what makes us human', he soared in a moving aria of response to the PM. 'So often we do not love enough. So often we deny or suppress or set to one side our love for each other. Surely this is the time of year when we should be loving and generous to all people, but particularly to our families.'

It was a lovely duet between Mr Rudd and Mr Turnbull, who have been showing distinct signs of liking each other – on White Ribbon Day, for example, they were practically holding hands.

But Mr Turnbull's problems were all with the backing vocals; by sundown, there was a Jackson Five of defectors to ruin his weekend.

It is increasingly clear that the Opposition leader is looking for love in all the wrong places.

27 November 2009

DIVIDED LIBERALS LIMP TO DAY OF RECKONING

Malcolm Turnbull refused to die quietly. Tony Abbott confirmed that he would be a leadership challenger. Shadow treasurer Joe Hockey, having been tickled extensively behind the ears by Liberal kingmakers urging him to run as a consensus, eventually agreed to enter the race, only to find that there was very little consensus on offer. The vote was set for Tuesday morning, 1 December.

What would Robert Menzies make of this day? Three Catholics, fighting over the ruins of his Liberal Party. Late into last night, the meetings continued, the frantic hamster-wheel of negotiations, the tinselly deals struck one minute and renounced the next.

What is it about this party? Two-and-a-bit years ago, it was running the country. These days, it looks like a speeded-up vaudeville comedy routine, a sort of 'Who's on First?' patter in which transitory detail inevitably gives way to the comic effect of the whole.

Yesterday afternoon, Nick Minchin convened a meeting in Joe Hockey's office which was also attended by Tony Abbott, putative deputy candidate Peter Dutton and Opposition business manager Christopher Pyne. The purpose, hilariously enough, was to try to establish an approach to the emissions trading legislation that everybody could live with.

In the face of Mr Hockey's insistence that the matter be a conscience vote, Mr Abbott eventually lost his temper.

'So', he summarised bitterly. 'Malcolm Turnbull's for the ETS. I'm against the ETS. And Joe – nobody knows what the fuck you stand for.'

And so was lost the last possibility that the Liberal Party could use this morning's events to present a united front. As the day dawns in Canberra this morning, the Liberal Party has three candidates to lead it.

There's the leader it already has – Malcolm Turnbull, who is so determinedly wedded to his deal with the government that he would rather lose his leadership than give an inch. For years, his detractors have whispered that Mr Turnbull is not a creature of the Liberal Party. In recent days, he is more of a Louis XIV figure, whose '*Je suis l'état!*'

('I am the state!') fulfils the demand for strong leadership, but scares the bejesus out of foe and friend alike.

In the past twenty-four hours, talk inside the party has turned from whether Malcolm Turnbull can survive to what he will do after his defeat. Cause a by-election in Wentworth? Create a new party? Neither is likely, but the very fact of the speculation suggests that a group conclusion has been drawn about the regent's viability.

Then there's Tony Abbott – the great People Skills himself, whose defiance of political orthodoxy is beginning to rival Mr Turnbull's own. What other leadership candidate would have had the magnificence, on Sunday, to ignore not just one, and not even two, but three central tenets of the political picture opportunity?

'Don't wear silly hats' has been defied before.

'Don't wear budgie smugglers' has also been defied, though with tragic results for the former NSW Liberal leader Peter Debnam, whose photoshoot in the briefest of swimming costumes heralded his imminent failure at the polls in 2007.

'If you have an extremely hairy back, for God's sake keep your shirt on' is not so much an accepted political maxim as an article of common sense, but it is sage advice nonetheless.

And yet: there was People Skills on Sunday, prancing about in the shallows wearing naught but a scrap of lycra, a lifesaver's cap and a fascinatingly goatish pelt.

Three months ago, Mr Abbott was advocating a vote for the government's emissions trading scheme, just to get it out of the way. Last night, he vowed to stand against Joe Hockey because he could not countenance the prospect that any Liberal would vote for it, even as part of a conscience vote.

And finally, there's Joe Hockey, the reluctant candidate who was dragged to the contest by the siren promise that he would be the consensus candidate, and now finds, in the closing hours of the campaign, that he has become the compromise candidate instead.

This isn't a non-viable position for him to be in. It's just what Kevin Rudd would call non-optimal.

1 December 2009

THE MAD SPLENDOUR OF KING MALCOLM

Malcolm Turnbull was headed for defeat. But his last days were memorable, as Turnbull days tend to be. On the Sunday before the party's leadership vote, he gave an interview to the Nine Network's Laurie Oakes in which he left no doubt about his destructive powers.

'Turnbull was very vigorous in his representation of the naked madman; his crouchings and wild outbursts were, on the whole, well done and the danger of being comical was, for the most part, avoided.'

So reads the review, in Malcolm Turnbull's old school magazine, of his portrayal of poor mad Edgar in Shakespeare's *King Lear* – the critically acclaimed Sydney Grammar 1969 production, that is.

Mr Turnbull was fifteen years old.

There is something madly splendid about the grown-up Turnbull, this past weekend. Having absorbed the sort of assault that would utterly devastate most political leaders (the wholesale resignation of numerous colleagues, and public attacks from some of the most powerful members of his parliamentary team), he remained astonishingly blithe throughout.

On Friday, his ramparts hopelessly invaded, he lunched with senior figures from the *Australian* at Tabou, the News Limited tribal hang-out in Surry Hills. On Saturday, gone for all money, he repaired jauntily with a fleet of small dogs to a local park, there to stage a defiant press conference with his smiling family.

It is as if the condemned at an execution, having weathered a ten-minute fusillade of bullets from a bank of riflemen, had cheerily picked himself up and popped out for a sandwich. Colleagues are amazed. Why doesn't he die?

For years, they have been talking about his big head. Now the hushed chatter has turned decidedly southward, anatomically speaking, and you can't pick up the phone to a Lib without being reminded – whether proudly or with grudging respect – that whatever else you think of Malcolm, he's certainly got a pair.

In the past few days, he has refused to be bowed by the prospect of political humiliation or open insurrection, which demonstrates – as if it required further demonstration – that Malcolm Bligh Turnbull does not answer to the same gods as most of his colleagues do.

Watching Laurie Oakes' interview with Mr Turnbull yesterday was to watch a man carefully, deliberately and coolly securing bomb belts around every inch of his person. If Nick Minchin and co. succeed in bringing him down, they will not themselves escape injury; the Oakes interview is replete with quotable quotes that would provide perfect fodder for a Labor election campaign.

'We will end up becoming a fringe party of the far right', is just one example.

Kevin Rudd has been anxious to portray the Libs as a fringe party of the far right for two years now. That any Liberal-oriented person would vocalise this analysis on television is something of a fantasy come true for the Labor campaign. That the words would issue from the lips of the Liberal leader himself must seem, to those already crafting Labor's TV ads for the next campaign, like the sort of dream one normally only has after consuming too much cheese last thing at night.

Not that the moderate wing of the Liberal Party escaped attention in Mr Turnbull's interview; he threw a few good, solid loops of the bomb belt around Joe Hockey too, just to be sure.

'Joe Hockey has told me as recently as last night that I have his complete support', Mr Turnbull said. 'Joe is absolutely at one with me on the need to get this legislation passed.'

It's not simply that Malcolm Turnbull is prepared to engage in savage conflict. It's more than that; increasingly, it seems that he thrives on it. All year, he has seemed dull and muffled, as he struggled to placate the warring sides of his party and arrive, through a grim series of manoeuvrings and tactical dodges, to avoid the chasm that lies at the centre of this policy debate for the Liberal Party.

Now, out on his own, increasingly friendless and bristling with self-timed explosive devices, he's never seemed more alive.

30 November 2009

ALL ABOARD THE PEOPLE SKILLS WILD RIDE

The leadership ballot, to the surprise of many including Tony Abbott, installed Mr Abbott as the Liberal Party's leader. Climate change skeptics, exercise freaks and political cartoonists all over Australia nipped out for a bottle of something bubbly.

Snap on your Speedos. It is going to be that sort of an election.

After the most wild and disordered week imaginable in conservative politics, the Liberal Party has staggered forth, somewhat to its own surprise, having adopted Tony 'People Skills' Abbott as its federal parliamentary leader. The party has turfed Malcolm Turnbull and ignored the public's popular choice in Joe Hockey.

Having spent the past two years agonising over the best way to move on from John Howard, the Liberal Party has instead placed itself in the hands of the man who most faithfully represents Mr Howard's legacy in the land of the political living. And Mr Abbott himself, whose last federal election campaign was a tripping, cursing, roundhouse-punch-swinging triumph of political absurdity, now finds himself in charge of the next one.

It is great news for politics nerds.

Mr Abbott rarely minces his words; he is candid, provocative and a proper conservative who does not adjust his views to account for what he judges to be the fancy of his audience. His contempt for Kevin Rudd, whom he has termed a 'toxic bore', will make for thrilling political combat (his crush on Julia Gillard, one trusts, will respond to shock treatments administered discreetly by Liberal HQ's highly skilled re-education squad).

Mr Abbott's popular image is well-established – a political bruiser of the right wing, a muscular hardline Catholic with a tendency to let his religious views colour his political activities. This will be his first problem, especially among female voters.

In truth, People Skills has changed significantly in recent years. He entered a Trappist phase after the defeat of the Howard government; a long, dark funk from which he rarely emerged except to bemoan his new and straitened living conditions, or set forth gauntly on yet another 200-kilometre bike ride.

But he emerged from his long confinement with some fascinating new views – an enthusiastic new interest in paid maternity leave, for example, and a redoubled interest in Indigenous affairs, which for Mr Abbott means regular lengthy trips to Indigenous communities; he spent the last parliamentary break working as a teacher in Cape York.

He is far from being the single-dimensional biffer that some voters see. The question is: how quickly can he change his public image, especially in view of the fact that his policy position on the emissions trading scheme (ETS) might well dramatically truncate the period of time he has available before the next election?

Just like anyone who is interesting in politics, People Skills has a fabulous show-reel of howlers. His old claim to be the ideological love-child of Mr Howard and Bronwyn Bishop, for example. His rough treatment of the dying asbestosis victim Bernie Banton during the last election campaign. His burst of pub language around the same time: 'Shit happens, Tony', he told *Lateline* host Tony Jones when a biography of Mr Howard exposed new criticisms from Peter Costello.

'That's bullshit, Nicola, and you know it!' he snapped at his opposite number, Nicola Roxon, when she reproached him for showing up late for a pre-election Press Club debate.

Mr Abbott's new partnership is with deputy leader Julie Bishop, the Zsa Zsa Gabor of Australian politics whose dazzling smile at the lectern proclaimed her utter loyalty to her third political spouse in just over a year. Having been denied forever the leadership team of Abbott and Costello, the Australian conservative voting public at least have been thrown the bone of an Abbott and a Bishop.

The pair of them have a shared passion for exercise; both endorphin addicts, the Abbott and Bishop leadership duo does not have a spare ounce of body fat between them and – in a time of penury within the Liberal Party – might have something to offer by way of attracting corporate sponsorship.

1 December 2009

IT'S JOCK V NERD AT CANBERRA HIGH

Kevin Rudd now found himself facing the fourth Liberal adversary of his short career as Labor leader. Two by-elections, one in Brendan Nelson's old seat and one in Peter Costello's, were predicted to go badly for the Coalition but ended up being fairly benign. Despite legions of candidates from the Greens, the Sex Party and Family First, Liberal candidates won easily. Perhaps Mr Abbott did have people skills, after all?

Australian politics, after several years of explosive rearrangement, has now offered us for the next election one of the most classic high-school contests of all time: the Jock versus the Nerd.

The Nerd has spent the last two years taking control of the school finances, engaging in high-level liaison with student bodies in sister schools, and presenting regular, brain-numbing Powerpoint presentations about his complex scheme to save the planet.

The Jock has been fizzing and twitching away at the back of the class throughout much of this, and distracting himself with excessive dieting, recreational firefighting and regular 200-kilometre bike rides.

But all of this changed last week.

A schoolyard intrigue of epic chicanery has installed the Jock as official challenger for the role of head prefect. And he has wasted little time in declaring a pungent new challenge to the Nerd: 'I don't understand your dweeby old Powerpoint presentations, and what's more I bet I'm not the only one, egghead. Now: Watch me bite the head off this chicken!'

This weekend was the Jock's first tangle with the democratic process. True, the Nerd disdained to send a delegate to the orchestrated rumbles of Bradfield and Higgins, so you couldn't call them a fair test of the two principals' elemental appeal. Instead, the Jock's baptism of electoral fire in Bradfield and Higgins was at the hands of a ragged coalition of minority cultural sub-factions, including the Hippies, the Sluts and the Bible Club.

But widespread expectations were that the Jock would take a mauling at the weekend, and he didn't. In the politics of the schoolyard, perception is everything. Or, as the Jock put it the other night, 'One vote is a landslide'.

And the Jock's team-mates, roughly half of whom had been expecting grotesque humiliation at the weekend, are now preparing themselves for the possibility that this might not be a disaster after all.

Poor souls; they are as serially disappointed as St Kilda fans of late, but green shoots of optimism can appear in even the bleakest of landscapes. The Jock, whose rippling abs have distracted attention from his temporary absence of campaign manager or settled policy, has goosed the Nerd in all his soft spots. He's been rude about the Nerd's detailed programmatic specificities, and his fondness for overseas missions. He's suggested that planting trees could fix the environment faster than all the Nerd's international summits, and he's giving serious consideration to messing up all the book work.

The Nerd has replied loftily that the Jock doesn't know what he is talking about. But with national polls suggesting that up to 80 per cent of Australians, when questioned privately, don't know what the Nerd's talking about, whose side are they likely to be on?

All eyes are now on the Jock's next move, as he selects his team of prefects. He's already indicated that the Bush Basher, Barnaby Joyce, will be asked to rack his spitball-shooter for the time being and assume a position of frontbench responsibility. Privately, we know the Jock yearns to promote the School Bully, Bronwyn Bishop – but will he dare? Delicately minded types from the previous regime, including the Milk Monitor (Christopher Pyne) and Mr Congeniality (Joe Hockey), would take it very hard.

The Jock's deputy, the Prom Queen, having confessed last week to having laughed privately at her new leader's penchant for immodest swimwear, is unlikely to have much say in all of this. Like many of her colleagues, she is probably more than ready for a summer break.

7 December 2009

BARNABY'S SACRIFICE FOR THE GREATER GOOD

Thrillingly, Mr Abbott not only promoted Bronwyn Bishop, but he installed the National Party's blunderbuss Barnaby Joyce as shadow finance minister. It wasn't to last, but gosh it was fun.

Anyone who reckons there isn't a precedent for Barnaby Joyce is wrong. His name was Arthur Fadden.

He too was an accountant from Queensland, and a leading light in the Country Party. A pugnacious, charming and ribald character, he skated though the ranks of conservative disarray to become Australia's prime minister from 29 August 1941, until 7 October of the same year – Fadden joked Biblically at the time that he had 'reigned for forty days and forty nights'. Later, he served as treasurer in the second Menzies government; the last Country Party or National Party representative to hold that portfolio.

Yesterday, the new Liberal leader Tony Abbott broke with firm Coalition convention to give Mr Fadden's heir, Senator Barnaby Joyce of Queensland, a key economic portfolio – finance. The move amazed some Liberals; after all, the National Party is not a grouping that has traditionally screamed 'fiscal restraint'. But others viewed it as a strategic mission to teach Joyce a lesson.

'Barnaby may be a genius at retail politics', said one yesterday. 'But let's see how he is at making things work with a team.'

Senator Joyce himself describes his acceptance of a shadow cabinet position as a 'sacrifice for the greater purpose'.

'It's a cost of now having to present one view. But on the upside, we (the National Party) are in a pretty powerful position.'

The assumption is that Senator Joyce will be compelled by his shadow cabinet loyalties to quell his taste for expressing pungent views on everything that comes to mind. It doesn't seem to be working just yet.

In an interview with *The Drum*, Senator Joyce is unrepentant about his support for the government's national broadband network and plans to structurally separate Telstra – a topic on which he has differed from shadow cabinet in the past.

'The position on that is that cabinet doesn't have a position on that', he insists. 'Everything's changed. New cabinet, new position.' But he does offer that 'whatever cabinet comes up with, I'll abide by'.

He also wades into an attack on the government's preparedness to borrow foreign cash to fund its stimulus program.

'This is money that people want back. Most of them are from overseas. How much more money do you want to owe to these people? The biggest one being the Communist People's Republic of China. There comes a time when you stop calling your bank manager Bob, and you start calling him Mr Smith. You start calling him Mr Smith when you owe him far more money than you are comfortable with. Ultimately, you can get yourself into so much debt that your position becomes precarious.'

Senator Joyce says that he never voted for any element of the government's stimulus spending, and he wants people to remember that.

'Do you want me to build a school hall just to make people happy? How about you fly the flag of the country we borrowed the money from over it? Does the new school hall make your child any better at mathematics?'

Senator Joyce is gratified by the Fadden parallel.

'Artie was an accountant, I'm an accountant. I'm the only accountant in the Parliament. The trouble with politics is that it has a great potential to attract lawyers and no ability to attract accountants. I'm a very unusual accountant.'

But his political role models tend more toward 'Black' Jack McEwen and Joh Bjelke-Petersen.

'Bjelke-Petersen because, no matter how everyone ridiculed him, he left the place with money in the bank and he built things on the way through. He electrified central Queensland, built the dams and highways. Curtin and Chifley's efforts during the war were good. For capacity to bring stability, Menzies was good as a safe pair of hands. But I'm more interested in military history. Anything from Alexander the Great, and his military engagements through Asia Minor right off to

Northwest India. The campaigns of Carthage as conducted by Hannibal, right up to the Vietnam War.'

His latest reading has included a biography of Alexander the Great and – perhaps even more fittingly – John Keegan's *A History of Warfare*. In his office, a copy of Machiavelli's *The Prince* sits on the bookshelf behind him.

'It's great because it confirms all my worst fears', he says of the Italian bible of skulduggery. But he adds a caveat: had he lived to witness the past two weeks in the Liberal Party, 'Machiavelli would have been deeply disturbed.'

9 December 2009

RUDD'S YEAR OF LIVING B-MINUS

Barack Obama gave himself a 'solid B-plus' last week when invited by interviewer Oprah Winfrey to mark his own performance as president of the United States. It was what they call a broad-ranging interview, which also involved the first lady and covered domestic policy advances including the White House puppy's recently acquired ability to give high-fives. Mr Obama said he would upgrade his mark to A-minus if he were able to get his healthcare reforms through the US Senate – a result which now seems likely, given the news from the States overnight.

The US president thus concedes that success is a brutal measure in politics; all the hard work and goodwill in the world are meaningless if you cannot achieve the result you seek. Likewise, success will bring glory even if it is owed partially, or even substantially to the work of others.

This is also the story of Kevin Rudd's first term, of which two years have now flashed by. His greatest success – the extraordinary performance of the Australian economy under dreadful global conditions – is an outcome for which he makes the strongest case for an 'A' grade. And it is the accomplishment whose authorship is the most strongly contested, having been built on a strong existing base.

'My base', former treasurer Peter Costello would argue.

'No – my base!' would come the immediate rejoinder from Paul Keating.

This is what politics is like: it's a rare triumph that only claims one author. And it's a rare politician whose successes in public life are born of his or her own efforts alone.

But any prime minister who can display an economy in growth and an unemployment rate below 6 per cent, at the end of the calendar year we've had, is not a candidate for flunking. Results are results, and however jealously it is debated, he'll get his A.

The global financial crisis has given occupation and structure to the Rudd government's first term. Thanks to the crisis, the last two years have been a gratifyingly busy blur of hyperactivity on the part of the Rudd team. While global financial meltdown is hardly a phenomenon of which new governments would necessarily dream, it has had its compensations.

A magical efflorescence of hard-hat photo opportunities, for example. An electorate by electorate building program of schools and railway crossings; a snowstorm of cheques. In short, the financial crisis has given Kevin Rudd cover to be the kind of big-spending Labor prime minister he spent much of the 2007 campaign denying he would be.

And without the crisis – what would we have to discuss? How would the Rudd government of late 2009 match up to the promotional material circulated by its figurehead in 2007, when he was still but a twinkle in the Australian electorate's eye? Without the crisis, it's pretty thin gruel.

'The great moral challenge of our generation' – climate change – has provoked much by way of government process but little by way of formal advance. It has been the government's greatest failure. Two years of consultation, absorption and high-flying rhetoric have produced an emissions trading scheme that has only two more votes now than when this whole thing lurched off on its messy trajectory through the Australian political system. Those two votes – from the Liberal floor-crossers Sue Boyce and Judith Troeth – are welcomed by the government, but are about as useful as a pair of fluffy dice given that seven votes are needed to secure the passage of the bills, and two years of moral-challenge wrangling hasn't dislodged even a single Greens vote.

Robbed of a clear result from Copenhagen, the prime minister now flies back to Australia to rejoin a domestic debate that is made harder, not easier, by the weekend's events. The intransigence of China lends powerful ballast to the Coalition argument that if big polluters aren't prepared to commit themselves to enforceable emissions reductions, then neither should we.

For much of this year, the prime minister's public marketing campaign for his emissions trading scheme was occupied rather less with the detail of the scheme itself than it was with the proposition that the Coalition was an unsightly rabble of mad uncles and denialists who wouldn't care if the Great Barrier Reef boiled dry. Behind the scenes, compromise after compromise bleached the scheme of clear purpose, which won't make anything easier for a government now required to sell it on its own merits, on a near-deserted global stage. Even the government's climate guru, Ross Garnaut, finds the legislative response uninspiring.

Success is its own legitimator in politics, and it is very difficult to describe anything to do with the government's climate-change response as a success; given the dismal results, it's hard to award anything better than a C-minus here, despite the elbow grease applied by Penny Wong.

Given the new vogue for 'retail politics' as popularised by Tony Abbott and his heart-attack-inducing new finance spokesman Barnaby Joyce, it's worth a glance at the promotional gewgaws promised by Mr Rudd two years ago as part of his hard-sell routine, and where they are now.

Easing cost-of-living pressures on Australian working families? Fuel Watch and Grocery Watch ended up, unsurprisingly, on the rubbish tip – cheap gimmicky toys that succumbed quickly to the inevitable and were deemed not worthy of repair. These initiatives earn a 'D' for 'Disingenuous'.

The wafted promise of federal command over the strife-torn hospital system? This was a confident alarum from Opposition, but in government it has swiftly acquired a swarm of qualifying sentiments and is now comfortably marooned in a review process, anointed temporarily with extra dollars.

Which brings us to the Education Revolution.

The Education Revolution is another entity with much for which to thank the Global Financial Crisis. Without the GFC, after all, we would never have had the BER, or P21, both of which have given the DPM so much to talk about.* A crippling potential shortage of acronyms has been averted through application of extensive public funds, and by happy act of intervening crisis, the Education Revolution, which was in distinct danger of not being very revolutionary at all, at least has activity to report.

Julia Gillard, meanwhile, has a creditable preparedness to take on the Labor constituency and make enemies – something at which the Rudd government on the whole has proved surprisingly timid – on the matter of school performance assessment. Education earns a B.

What about the other promised Bs of the 2007 campaign – bipartisanship and an end to buck passing and blame shifting?

Well, there was a genuinely gracious moment early on during the national apology to displaced Aboriginal children, but since then bipartisanship has been pretty thin on the ground. And despite campaign assurances, the buck has at no point seemed at any danger of taking up permanent residence at the Lodge; this prime minister is as eager to point and blame and nag as all of his predecessors. Which is not especially surprising; just disappointing, as it always is.

Overall, I'd call the Rudd government's first term so far a B-minus: Student shows a strong work rate, but it's not always well-directed.

**BER stands for Building the Education Revolution. P21 means Primary Schools for the 21st Century. DPM is the Deputy Prime Minister.*

21 December 2009

DEMOCRACY THE WINNER WHEN KEVIN AND TONY GO TOE TO TOE

It's the uneasy political pause between Christmas and New Year's Day.

The prime minister, yet to make any prolonged public comment about his frustrating excursion to Copenhagen, popped up on Boxing Day for a quick stint in the MCG commentary box, then returned to seclusion with his papers. He's not on holidays, his office says; he's just working out of the spotlight.

His new opponent, Tony Abbott, is working from his northern beaches home and Manly office.

Both of them face a demanding February deadline.

The prime minister's is to tell Australians and the world what sort of national carbon emissions reductions he is prepared to offer in the context of a distinctly squirrelly post-Copenhagen global mood.

The Opposition leader's self-imposed February deadline is to come up with a plan that would cut Australia's emissions without the need for an emissions trading scheme or carbon tax. Both are fraught exercises, conducted – at this stage – in private.

The festive season feels like a lull before the battle that will be Australian politics in 2010, fought out between two adversaries who have not yet faced each other over the dispatch box. The suspense is palpable; how will these two tackle each other?

Even the weather isn't giving anything away. A long, hot, bushfire-plagued Christmas week might have given the prime minister the sort of apocalyptic backdrop he tends to favour when reminding voters of the need for decisive action on climate change. On the other hand, it might have provided Tony Abbott, a volunteer firefighter, with a series of politically restorative photo opportunities (stuck up a burning gully with his cinder-smudged heroic comrades) or yet another chance to be glimpsed with his shirt off.

But the weather, perhaps prudently in a period during which it is enjoying unprecedented political significance, has decided to run dead on the issue, offering a mild sort of Christmas blessedly clear of natural disaster.

For Christmas news we are obliged to comb through the possibilities of tax reform presented by the Henry Review, or listlessly argue about whether we should still be allowed to carry nail clippers aboard Qantas flights, given the near-bombing committed by a young man wearing explosive underpants on a Detroit-bound flight on Christmas Day.

There are some certainties, of course, the first being that Labor will seek to encourage the view that Tony Abbott is a Howard clone, determined to restore elements of Work Choices and to oppose outright the introduction of an emissions trading scheme. 'Don't Go Back!' warned the Labor ads that surfaced about fourteen seconds after Tony Abbott won the Liberal leadership ballot.

The bit about emissions trading, incidentally, is made all the odder by the fact that John Howard went to his political grave offering an emissions trading scheme not a million miles from the one Mr Rudd is now hawking. It is a fact conveniently ignored by both the 'Step Back in Time' Labor message-massagers and the creatures of principle within the Liberal Party who decided in November that they could not bear to be part of a political party which supported an ETS.

The other certainty is that Tony Abbott, given a choice on each and every issue to be aggressive or conciliatory toward his opponent, will be aggressive.

We already know what Mr Abbott thinks of Mr Rudd. A man who is himself plain-spoken to the point of recklessness, he is irritated beyond belief by the prime minister's fondness for diplo-babble, for the interminable bouts of jargon that so copiously infest both written and spoken communications from the Lodge.

'The guy is a toxic bore', he complained earnestly this year in a Sky News interview.

The most intriguing aspect to this political match-up is not that one protagonist is boring and one isn't (although that is certainly an obvious point to make, and Mr Abbott's swashbuckling candour, disdain for political convention and adventurous choice of frontbench render him virtually immune to accusations of tedium). The real difference is that one man thinks 'boring' is a problem, and the other doesn't.

Think about the recent parliamentary skirmishing about border protection, for example. For hour after hour in question time, as the *Oceanic Viking* blundered about with its load of Sri Lankan asylum seekers, the prime minister was at his paralysing best. Repeating his mantra about a 'tough, humane approach' to the management of our borders, Mr Rudd fudged at length about the exact terms of his dealings with the Indonesian government in an oratory style so viscous as almost to defy quotation.

This is the sort of thing that drives Mr Abbott wild. It didn't do much for some sections of Mr Rudd's natural constituency, either, where it was felt that the prime minister was missing an opportunity to speak clearly with a new language of compassion for those forced by circumstance to seek refuge on our shores.

'He has the unanimous loyalty of his caucus. He has an almost non-existent opposition. He is in a unique position to change the debate. Changing the way Australia deals with race would be pretty special – that's Labor hero stuff', lamented Paul Howes, the young national secretary of the Australian Workers' Union who was one of the few to vocalise these thoughts publicly.

Those of us in the media who are critics of Mr Rudd's impenetrable oratorical style puzzled anew about his inability to express himself clearly – assuming, in our self-centred fashion, that making himself clear in a way that also suited us would be his natural goal. But perhaps we were missing something.

Where did it leave him, in the end, this featureless filibuster? Well, it kept him off the television, for one thing. And if getting yourself on TV when you want to be on the TV is one political skill, then keeping yourself off it is quite another, and the asylum-seeker debate is one in which bitter historical experience has taught Labor that it is better to keep a low profile.

Mr Rudd has no difficulty in summoning plain speech when he wants to get on television; he might designate a group of people (arsonists, people smugglers, Gordon Ramsay) as 'scum of the earth', or 'low-lifes', or similar. But he is prepared to use his boringness as a protective device, which you could never imagine Mr Abbott doing.

The other major difference between this pair of leaders is that they have an entirely different approach to the business of offending people.

Mr Rudd offends people rarely, and when he does, it's calculated. His style, from the strong reliance on task forces and working parties and consultative processes right down to the fact that he can change his manner and language depending on the audience in front of which he finds himself, bespeaks an unwillingness to make enemies. His talk of tough humanity in the border protection area bespeaks his hopes of retaining the support both of those who want to hear about the toughness as well as those who are more interested in the humanity, to take one example. The exception is when he decides to make a popular enemy; the photographer Bill Henson, for instance, or the banks, or extremist union leaders.

The Opposition leader is, on past evidence, far less strategic. He tends to say what he thinks, in the hope that clarity and the democratic process will provide its own reward.

What will be fascinating to watch, as the new year begins, is whether the prime minister will alter anything about his style to defray the threat from a new and robust Liberal leader. Mr Rudd's chart-topping popularity continues, but he is by no means immune to paranoia, especially given his acute dependence on continued public popularity to retain his authority over his colleagues, who respect but do not love him. And there is little triumphalism in Labor ranks about Mr Abbott's elevation; he is viewed with caution and interest.

In Tony Abbott, Kevin Rudd finds the adversary most different from himself he has ever faced. It should be a good year for democracy.

30 December 2009

AFTERWORD: WHY I LIKE POLITICIANS

I like politicians.

There – I've said it.

You've got to be careful about saying that sort of thing out loud, especially in Sydney, where teams of voters driven mad by long hours in hot delayed buses and the prospect of having to wait until 2011 to eject the miserable NSW state government would happily punch your lights out for entertaining such a thought.

Lots of people will proudly confess to not knowing much about politics, but it's a rare member of the populace who doesn't know that they don't like politicians.

Disliking politicians is the easiest thing in the world to do. You won't get much opposition; smarmy, opportunistic, shonks, pocket-liners, full of bullshit, turn up once every three years, and so on.

Politicians are the first and last point of call when there is blame to be laid. Roof of your house fall in? Damn inadequate planning laws – where are the politicians when you need them? But ask anyone who's building a house about the damn nanny state and politicians with their interfering ways and red tape, and see what kind of rant you elicit. We can't stand them in our faces, and yet we despise them for laziness if we never see them.

On one hand, we want our politicians to be normal people; knock-about types who understand the importance of friends and family and would be happy to buy us a beer if we found ourselves next to them at a quiet moment. But on the other hand, we reserve the right to roll our eyes if our local MP takes his wife along on a business trip, or is given a bottle of wine by a friend.

Genetically convinced that our politicians are naturally corrupt, we search everywhere for flashes of confirmation.

Tony Abbott is presently 'under investigation', according to Perth's *Sunday Times* newspaper, for using his publicly funded travel allowance several months ago to travel to a town in rural Victoria to speak at a Liberal fundraiser at which copies of his book were also on sale.

Mr Abbott's defence is that he also conducted meetings in the town, qualifying the trip as electoral business. Asked on radio this week, he argued that plenty of Australians organised their business lives to fit in with their private lives. 'There are lots of people who think, well, you know, I'd like to go to my best mate's wedding, let's organise a couple of business trips on the Friday so I can go to my best mate's wedding on the Saturday', he said.

He's completely right, of course. He won't gain anything by spelling it out, and one flinches to hear him formalise it so baldly, but that's pretty much the Abbott way.

Don't forget that one of the most strange and memorable political episodes of the year began with a hard-line question about political influence-peddling. History will now record it as the Godwin Grech Affair, thanks to the intriguing, Harry Potter-esque figure at its heart, but the question that really launched the episode was: did the prime minister, in return for the permanent loan of a second-hand ute, either direct or implicitly allow special attention to be shown to a certain car dealer in the operation of a government scheme to assist car dealers?

The car dealer in question received nothing in the end, but the question still burned: had the PM accepted a rusty old bomb in return for the implicit prime ministerial undertaking that in other circumstances he might have got something? It's not exactly Watergate, is it? Although it might have been comforting for Joel Fitzgibbon, who had just lost his job as defence minister for accepting a free suit and some flights from a Chinese friend.

The basic wage for a backbench politician is $130,000 a year, or thereabouts. Electorate allowance adds another $30,000, which is designed to be spent on electorate donations, raffles, awards and so on. It's a good income. But the hourly rate works out to be rubbish.

And you or I would blanch at the sort of stuff local MPs are required to do. Imagine attending a school speech night for someone else's kids –

a dozen times. Or being professionally required to listen to the mad bleatings of people like you and me when we turn up to complain about our roof falling off, or the fact that we can't chop down a tree in our backyard.

Imagine having to trail around knocking at tens of thousands of doors, introducing youself with a perky 'Hello!' – yet knowing that at best, the person answering will suspect you of being a crawler or a home invader and at worst, you will end up with ankle lacerations from their territorial shih-tzu.

Meanwhile, your kids will grow up to despise you – if they recognise you at all. Mr Abbott – again, the master of disclosure – told us recently that his teenage daughter called him a 'lame, gay churchy loser'. This is why I like politicians.

I like the fact that they still do a job that is in many ways crummy, depressing, lonely and weird. I like the fact that the best of them still find time to believe in something.

Of all the politicians I've met in ten years of writing about federal politics, I would say that perhaps one in ten is there purely for reasons of ego, self-aggrandisement or self-enrichment. Many of them – particularly those who live through long periods in Opposition – pour their energies into creating alternative ideas about how the country could be improved, only to watch their work swept away by democratic vote, leaving them right back at the beginning to start again.

Can you imagine how devastating that would be? And yet they pick themselves up, time after time, and reapply themselves to the task – if they are lucky enough to keep their seats.

Given that most Australians are already predisposed to think them frauds and mountebanks, I particularly like politicians who are nevertheless prepared to stick their necks out and say things that are truthful even when they know that so doing will buy them extra criticism and contempt.

The greatest danger – the greatest corruption – of Australian politics does not lie in the spending of electorate allowances, or the taking of domestic flights to regional Victoria, or even the acceptance of second-hand vehicles. It is the culture by which we increasingly oblige our politicians to waffle – to deliver long tracts of platitudinous gumpf, rather than simply give us the unpleasant truths and let us come to terms with them and make our democratic decisions accordingly.

We in the media are extensively responsible for this; the dramatic shortening of the news cycle means that 'Politician X Commits Gaffe; Accidentally Says Something True But Embarrassing' is very much an easier story to write than the longer and more thoughtful version.

'I am going to say something that few people in public life will say, but most know is absolutely true: a vast aspect of our jobs today – outside of the really big decisions, as big as anything else – is coping with the media, its sheer scale, weight and constant hyperactivity', said Tony Blair in 2006, as he departed the office of the British prime ministership.

'At points, it literally overwhelms … people don't speak about it because, in the main, they are afraid to. But it is true, nonetheless, and those who have been around long enough will also say that it has changed significantly in the past years. The danger is, however, that we then commit the same mistake as the media do with us; it's the fault of bad people. My point is; it is not the people who have changed; it is the context within which they work. We devote reams of space to debating why there is so much cynicism about politics and public life. In this, the politicians are obliged to go into self-flagellation, admitting it is all our fault. Actually, not to have a proper press operation nowadays is like asking a batsman to face bodyline bowling without pads or headgear.'

Blair, in his speech, was not so disingenuous as to suggest that his own, famously robust approach to media management had not contributed in some way to the phenomenon he bemoans in his speech. After all, a man who once entered Northern Ireland peace talks with the comment 'A day like today is not a day for soundbites, really. But I feel the hand of history upon our shoulders' can hardly complain about a media operation which rewards glibness. But his expressed concerns are more than fair. And we should all be grateful for politicians who are still game to say interesting, controversial or even obvious things in the knowledge that to do so will bring them grief in the short term.

To take a minor example from this year: remember, during the post-Grech leadership rumblings that began to run through the Coalition several months ago, a radio interview in which Joe Hockey was asked if he had been asked by colleagues to consider contesting the leadership? Hockey acknowledged that he had received phone calls. Of course he had. Everyone knew he had. If he denied it, he would have been lying. But Hockey's admission bought him a starring role in what our prime minister would call a 'shitfight', in which his motives for saying what he did were sliced and diced, and whizzed under the microscope to be examined for traces of organised insurrection.

This is the real corruption of contemporary politics; truthful answers are so unexpected in the realm of parliamentary and related discourse that when they appear, they are immediately assumed to be either a colossal gaffe or the tip of a Machiavellian strategic iceberg.

Some days, it's hard to understand why any person would be part of this system. Not for the money, which for the good ones would be much, much better elsewhere. And it's what makes me like the ones that stick around anyway.

Obviously, there is a degree of self-interest here. I like the ones that are worth writing about – the ones who give truthful answers even when doing so earns them the contempt of commentators or peers. Partly, this is because I like having a job. But mostly, it's because these are the politicians who make you think, and who continue to make democracy worth it. Even if you don't agree with what they actually say – after all, isn't that supposed to be the point of the democratic process?

I do not argue that Australian politicians are without fault. Like fish, or house guests, they go off after a bit. They are at their best when they've been in politics for long enough to have the confidence to take risks and speak frankly about their own views, but not so long that they have become so impervious to public criticism that they fail to notice when it's accurate.

It is popular to think that all politicians are ego-maniacs. And it's certainly true that in order to survive in politics, you do need a fairly robust sense of self-belief. How, otherwise, would you get out of bed every day? But after a long while, this protective mechanism can evolve into arrogance; the political brain can become so encrusted with scar tissue that it can no longer recognise fair criticism when they hear it.

Every government is different, but when they are past their use-by date, they tend to become horribly similar. Which brings us, briefly, to the state of New South Wales. One of the reasons that New South Wales is chafing under the raddled rule of its ageing Labor government is that the state introduced fixed four-year terms in 1995. The reform, driven by independent MPs on whom the Greiner Liberal government relied at the time, was intended to stop beady-eyed, cynical and otherwise unelectable state governments from calling elections at their own whim in order to maximise their chances of hanging on to power. Fourteen years later, the four-year fixed term rule is driving NSW voters crazy, as they realise that the very same reform is now serving to protect a beady-eyed, cynical and otherwise unelectable state government.

As I said, New South Wales isn't a good place to talk about liking politicians. But it would be a pity to tar all politicians with the sins of the worn-out incumbents. Keep them, value them, and change them when necessary: it's a good formula.

24 December 2009